LITERARY CHARLESTON
& THE LOWCOUNTRY

LITERARY CHARLESTON & THE LOWCOUNTRY

edited by

CURTIS WORTHINGTON

foreword by

LOUIS D. RUBIN, JR.

TRINITY UNIVERSITY PRESS
SAN ANTONIO

Published by Trinity University Press
San Antonio, Texas 78212
Copyright © 2011 by Trinity University Press

Design by Anne Richmond Boston

Trinity University Press strives to produce its books using methods and materials in an environmentally sensitive manner. We favor working with manufacturers that practice sustainable management of all natural resources, produce paper using recycled stock, and manage forests with the best possible practices for people, biodiversity, and sustainability. The press is a member of the Green Press Initiative, a nonprofit program dedicated to supporting publishers in their efforts to reduce their impacts on endangered forests, climate change, and forest dependent communities.

The paper used in this publication meets the minimum requirements of the American National Standard for Information Sciences—Permanence of Paper for Printed Library Materials, ANSI Z39.48-1992.

Library of Congress Cataloging-in-Publication Data

Literary Charleston and the lowcountry / edited by Curtis Worthington ; foreword by Louis D. Rubin, Jr.
    p. cm.
  Summary: "Fiction, nonfiction, and poetry selections by local and internationally acclaimed authors provide a rich tapestry of one of the most popular tourist destinations worldwide. The often mysterious and much-loved Colonial city of Charleston is revealed through the eyes of writers who lived there or visited over the centuries"—Provided by publisher.
    ISBN 978-1-59534-079-5 (pbk. : alk. paper)
    1. Charleston (S.C.)—Literary collections. 2. Charleston Region (S.C.)—Literary collections. I. Worthington, Curtis, 1951–
  PS559.C5L59 2011
  810.8'032757915—dc23   2011040832

15   14   13   12   11   5   4   3   2   1

Cover illustration: Courtesy of Maritime Heritage Prints by arrangement with Curtis Worthington

This time for Jane and the Celtic brothers,
Ian and Aidan

Contents

CONTENTS

Foreword

What is there to the city of Charleston, South Carolina, that makes so many people write about it? By any ratio of population to total number of words on the printed page, Charleston must surely be among the more intensely chronicled cities in the United States.

To attempt to collect everything that has been written about Charleston, or even merely those writings of a literary nature, as distinct from journalism, sociology, political analysis, or whatever, would be a formidable assignment. For better or for worse, prose and poetry that takes Charleston for its inspiration has been produced with the regularity of those Clyde-Mallory liners that for generations provided thrice-weekly service between the city and other Atlantic seaboard ports. The coastal passenger ships have long since disappeared, but the application of literary craft to the city not only continues but has gained both in quantity and—with the advent of Josephine Humphreys on the local literary scene—in excellence as well.

Curtis Worthington set out in this book to assemble, from among the formidable trove of eligible literary work, representative writings that importantly involve Charleston and the Carolina Lowcountry. Dating from the late eighteenth century to the early years of the twenty-first, the selections are essentially of two kinds: those written by noted visitors to the city, and those by resident authors.

The former, whose ranks include Edgar Allan Poe, Henry James, Amy Lowell, Owen Wister, John Galsworthy, and Walker Percy, were sufficiently impressed with the locale itself to wish to recreate it in its own right. Charleston, Amy Lowell declared, "has more poetic appeal than almost any city in America"—this from a resident of Boston! Even Poe, who habitually set his fiction in imaginary places "out of SPACE—out of TIME," was so taken with the tangible reality of harbor and land that the onetime U.S. Army sergeant, stationed for a time at Fort Moultrie, did what otherwise he almost never did: he set "The Gold Bug" specifically and identifiably in a known American place. So much so, indeed, that it is quite possible, from the description of the treasure hunters' route, to trace their approximate path across the harbor to Sullivan's Island, through the marsh and up the creek, and onto the mainland to the east of Mount Pleasant.

As for the numerous local authors, Charlestonians whether by birth or by adoption, their topography is not only geographical but of the spirit as well. From William Gilmore Simms and Henry Timrod of antebellum and Confederate days, to DuBose Heyward and Beatrice Witte Ravenel in the 1920s, and nowadays Josephine Humphreys, the urge to write has involved the need to explore one's identity in and through the relationship to the community. Heyward even went so far as to declare lyrically that "these my songs, my all, belong to" his native city. For Simms and Humphreys (and very likely for Heyward as well) the motivation would appear to be rather more complicated. But whoever the Charleston writer may be and whatever the nature of his or her formal linkage to the city, the literary evocation of the place is almost taken for granted, never a mere convenience of plausible setting. Inevitably it is made to matter profoundly.

I do not envy Curtis Worthington the task of selecting which writings, from among so many possible choices, should be contained in this book. There was so much there, with strong claims for inclusion. One's own choices might in some instances have been different. But beyond doubt he has assembled a remarkably interesting book, offering a Lowcountry literary harvest of generous and striking dimensions. There can be no question about it: the place has a way of seizing the imagination, compelling a response to its pervasive immanence. It can be loved, it can be hated; there can be some of both in one's reaction; but it cannot be ignored.

Visitors to Charleston—and nowadays they arrive in throngs not only during the garden season but all year around—will enjoy matching up what others have made of the place with their own responses. Residents and ex-residents will experience the thrill of watching what is local and familiar take on the intensity and strangeness of the artistic image. An intelligent, informative preface by the editor sets the stage historically for this fascinating literary visit to a unique American city.

Louis D. Rubin, Jr.

Preface

Consider the relationship between a real place and the representation of that place in fiction. Fiction, indeed all creative writing, subverts geographic realities to its own purpose, creating a particular relationship between the literal place of experience and the experience of that place through imaginative language. The literal place, present in the created world of the imaginative work, is a place transfigured: the mundane face of reality transposed to another plane.

How does one transpose the reality of Charleston and the Lowcountry—of the unique place that has served as a source of inspiration to the generations of writers and artists who have experienced it?

One describes the smell of the salt air and the pluff mud, the wisteria and Confederate jasmine; the languorous atmosphere of sea breeze and humidity; the landscape of moss-covered oaks, magnolia, palmetto, oleander, and cypress.

One draws a picture of a school of bottlenose dolphins playing alongside the departing shrimp boat, or the deep-sea fishing boat returning with its catch of king mackerel, tuna, and wahoo; the appearance at dawn of an alligator, a snowy egret, or a great blue heron in a tidal creek; the creekman in his johnboat seeking shrimp, crabs, and oysters.

One records the voice of the "crabman" (sadly, now silent) pulling his cart through narrow streets past single houses south of Broad; the song of musicians (happily, still here) practicing or performing in the same streets during the Spoleto Festival; the night music of the cicadas and whippoorwills; the Gullah language and the quaint mispronunciations of French Huguenot names.

One captures the beauty of St. Michael's spire, the formal gardens and piazzas, the sailing regattas in the harbor, the dark swamps of Berkeley County, and the white sand of the barrier island beaches.

All play a part in the imagery, in a geography that is lush, sensuous, and tropical—full of brooding mystery and inescapable romance.

The literary heritage of Charleston and the South Carolina Lowcountry was born in the earliest days of the city. Founded in 1670, Charleston quickly became the leading center of politics, commerce, and culture in the colonial South. From its inception, the city was marked by a great cultural diversity that included Europeans of Spanish, French, and English descent, native Americans indigenous to the region, and black Africans imported as slaves. Diverse religious traditions further colored the colony: Anglican, Huguenot, Jewish, Baptist, Presbyterian, Catholic. Merchants, planters, and pirates all had a hand in shaping society as it evolved through the eighteenth and nineteenth centuries. Charleston became a city which, as Alexandra Ripley has said, "was civilized and hedonistic in a balance that created a culture of exquisitely refined grace in which incomparable luxury was tempered by a demanding discipline of intellect and education."

The attentive and successful preservation of gardens, homes, and historic places in modern Charleston provides a physical setting that enhances an appreciation for early cultural influences. The society that produced such elegant architecture and landscaping was also concerned with other forms of aesthetic pursuit.

Perhaps the earliest literary genre in which Charleston established its reputation was drama. One of the first theaters in North America opened at the corner of Church and Dock (now Queen) streets on February 12, 1736, with a production of George Farquhar's *The Recruiting Officer*. The present Dock Street Theater, built in the early part of the nineteenth century as the Planters' Hotel, was renovated in 1937 on the design of an eighteenth-century theater, and each spring provides a performance site for Spoleto Festival USA. Thus, as in many other unique elements of Charleston, an important manifestation of contemporary artistic and literary achievement remains connected to the earliest cultural pursuits of the city. The longstanding municipal appreciation for creativity and the ambience of this "sea-drinking city" (Josephine Pinckney's phrase) has for centuries attracted an ever-growing artistic community.

Blessed with ground fertile for agriculture, forests abundant with game, and waters rich with the fruits of the sea, the Lowcountry harbored the development of a social system—plantation society—that exerted a wide-ranging influence on local culture. As the plantations thrived, an aristocratic class grew that, as Boyd Saunders and Ann McAden have noted, "built Barbadian-influenced single houses, Georgian mansions with walled gardens and piazzas, stately public buildings and dignified churches." As trading and shipping developed, luxuries were imported, and the sons of planters were sent to Europe for their education. The society flourished and, with it, music, dance, and literary pursuits.

The plantation system, with its attendant slavery, also yielded the rich folklore and musical traditions of Africa. As Harlan Greene said, "The delicate interplay of black and white that would write Charleston's history began quite early. Their overlapping chronicles are as connected and fretted as the coils in the sweetgrass Gullah baskets sold in the city market."

The cultural mélange that is Charleston has evolved and developed from colonial times through the Revolutionary, antebellum, Confederate War, and Reconstruction eras into the twenty-first century. Through these changing times, Charleston has nurtured a generous share of literary activity—a share not obvious on cursory consideration.

The present collection of fiction, poetry, and essays attempts to reflect something of the spirit of Charleston and its environs through imaginative language. It includes the writings of local residents, as well as those of well-known literary visitors. It runs a historical and philosophical gamut from William Bartram's *Travels*, which presents Charleston as a well-ordered haven, a symbol of mankind's innocence at the beginning of life before the fall, to the ironic reversal of such an image in Andy Warhol's story of the Charleston debutante whose life of debauchery among the demimonde of New York violates the sense of an ordered world.

Writers from Charleston's two literary "schools" are presented in this collection. Included are the antebellum men of letters, Paul Hamilton Hayne, William Gilmore Simms, and Henry Timrod, whose work in support of the southern cause appeared in *Russell's Magazine*, a well-known literary review of the day named for the King Street bookstore that was the group's chief venue and meeting place. These writers created a mythos to complement the emerging southern philosophy that ultimately resulted in secession and the formation of the Confederate States of America, a mythos that was founded on an agrarian economy, chattel slavery, and a sense of aristocratic entitlement, enlightened benevolence, and chivalry. That these writers are rarely read today may have a great deal to do with the fact that writing in this philosophical milieu, as Louis D. Rubin, Jr. has pointed out, may have barred any kind of searching inquiry into the tension between man in nature and in society; or perhaps they are not read because of the subversion of an imaginative vision to a social or political goal.

Similarly, a literary "movement" emerged in the 1920s and '30s in Charleston, the focal point of which became the Poetry Society of South Carolina, founded by DuBose Heyward, John Bennett, Hervey Allen, Beatrice Witte Ravenel, and others. Writers hosted and published by the Poetry Society of South Carolina included Carl Sandburg, Robert Frost, Gertrude Stein, Ford Maddox Ford, John Crowe Ransom, and Allen Tate. Harriet Monroe, the editor of *Poetry Magazine* in the 1920s, published an entire issue devoted to the Poetry Society of South Carolina writers.

One sees in the themes of so many of these writers certain tense relationships that are common and recurrent: North versus South, black versus white, innocence versus experience, urban sophistication versus rural wholesomeness, rigid social standards versus energetic, life-affirming exuberance. DuBose Heyward's long-standing interest in the way of life of the local African-American population clearly reflects many of these dichotomies and is seen particularly in his novels *Porgy* and *Mamba's Daughters*. Heyward was no social reformer, but he was able to observe and render black culture in a way never before achieved or even attempted, depicting it with objectivity and affection, without the pity or cant of the time. He was fascinated by the juxtaposition of the two cultures existing in Charleston and the Lowcountry, and saw each, it can be argued, especially after reading *Mamba's Daughters*, as an ironic reflection of the other—*Upstairs, Downstairs* in a Charleston setting.

Indeed, the social fabric of Charleston figures prominently in local literature. White society, governed by rigid standards in a long tradition, appears to hold sway—the upper consciousness. It is constantly impinged upon by forces from below or within: a dark side, the underconsciousness, a central core of unbridled creative energy and will, primitive and unrelenting. These two positions are paradoxically ever-present in the social framework of Charleston, and in the writing not only of Heyward, but of many of the writers represented in this collection.

The relationship between Charleston writers and Charleston society has been considered by Michael O'Brien in his 1993 essay "'The South Considers Her Most Peculiar': Charleston and Modern Southern Thought." He alludes to Nashville's "Fugitive/Agrarian" school and Allen Tate's theory regarding the best southern literature, a theory that calls for a balance between the dictates of a set of standards—social, cultural, and artistic—and alienation from such standards. Charleston writers, according to Tate's scheme, have adhered too much to social convention. Indeed, Heyward's novel *Peter Ashley* "is a meditation on alienation and belonging," in which the protagonist, a scion of the pre-war South, comes down squarely in the camp of belonging. But as O'Brien points out:

> [T]he critical standards that have marginalized Charleston are not immortal. It is becoming fair to hazard that the neo-agrarian interpretation of southern literature is in decline, perhaps moribund. The canon of southern literature begins to change, to take previously marginal voices more seriously, most obviously the female and the black. To put it politely, the relevance of Nashville to these themes is modest. But the relevance of Charleston in the 1920s

and 1930s, oddly enough for so elite a white culture, is much greater. For one thing, its interest in landscape and preservation is likely to seem less quaint to a younger generation reared on the environmental movement. For another, an unusual number of Charleston writers were women, and one of the great ventures of the city's literature was representing black culture.

While the two "schools" of Charleston literature represent the periods of greatest intensity in the literary life of Charleston, each was considered eccentric when judged by the critical standards of its own day. They fare little better when judged by most modern literary standards, and the writers in each have achieved little in the way of status in the larger context of literature as a whole. In the latter half of the twentieth century, however, Charleston has progressively attained greater attention and influence in the artistic and literary worlds. Writers of national prominence have become interested in the city. At the same time, the Lowcountry has recently inspired writers from the region who have attained distinguished reputations on a national scale.

Many readers will be disappointed by certain omissions in this anthology. Limitations of time and space dictated selectivity, but the works that were finally chosen attempt to reflect the totality of the imaginative Charleston in all its facets. Many outstanding writers, some internationally recognized, some only known to local audiences, have lived in, written about, performed, directed, and otherwise been associated with Charleston and the Lowcountry: Benjamin Brawley, Clyde Bresee, Mary Boykin Chesnut, Donald Davidson, Ralph Waldo Emerson, Dorothea Benton Frank, Robert Frost, Edward King, Susan Petigru King, Allen Ginsberg, Francis Griswold, Hugh Swinton Legare, James Matthewes Legare, Robert Molloy, Carson McCullers, Isaac Jenkins Mikell, Edna St. Vincent Millay (who is said to have scandalized the servants at Magnolia Gardens by wandering through the grounds naked), Arthur Miller, Chalmers Murray, Julia Peterkin, Elizabeth Allston Pringle, Patricia Robinson, Theodore Rosengarten, George Herbert Sass, Valerie Sayers, Gertrude Stein, Samuel Gaillard Stoney, William Styron, William Makepeace Thackeray, John Townsend Trowbridge,

Oscar Wilde, and Tennessee Williams. Unfortunately, their contributions could not be included.

The Charleston of the imagination has appealed to many more writers than may be evident at first glance. Sinclair Lewis has Carol Kennicott in *Main Street* stay in the Villa Margherita, "by the palms of the Charleston battery and the metallic harbor." Likewise, Vladimir Nabokov's protagonist travels to Magnolia Gardens to entertain "grim" Lolita, in the novel of the same name. What is it about Charleston and the Lowcountry that appeals specifically to writers? For John James Audubon, it was the lifestyle enjoyed by his host, the Rev. John Bachman: "out shooting every Day—Skinning, Drawing, Talking Ornithology, the Whole Evening, Noon and Morning—in a word. . . , I certainly would be as happy a mortal as Mr. Bachman himself is at this present moment, when he has returned from his congregation—congratulated me on my day's work and now sets amid his family in a room above me enjoying the results. . . ."

Carl Sandburg admired the city's physical proportions: "the skylines, gables, porches, harbor lights and silhouettes, streets full of life, grace of speech and custom, in Charleston, a wide range of tangible and intangible presences, pull at one's heart and memory after having been in that town and felt its heartbeats." Thomas Wolfe allowed a character to explain some of the more basic attractions of the area: "'You can still git beer in Charleston,'" he wrote in the 1929 *Look Homeward, Angel*. "'You can go swimmin' in the ocean at the Isle of Palms,' . . . then, reverent, he added, 'you can go the Navy Yard and see the ships.'"

The abiding sense of the past interests V. S. Naipaul: "Charleston was claimed by the large events of a continental history, and its small time beginnings are now indescribably romantic, when it was on a par with slave colonies like Antigua or Barbados or Jamaica, and looked to them for trade and support."

Charlestonians themselves constitute one of Harlan Greene's main sources of inspiration: "Charleston residents still eat rice and she-crab soup and hoppin' john on New Year's. They sit on piazzas and paint their shutters 'Charleston green.' They dislike difference and encourage eccentricity. They go to oyster roasts at

Rockville and to St. Cecilia balls where the guest list is determined by inheritance and geography. They live in a city that demands good manners, yet smiles tolerantly on many things as anyone must who has seen for so long the vanity and nobility of the human species. She just may be that combination of Mediterranean manners and Caribbean ways suggested by John Bennett."

It is perhaps because of all these things that writers are attracted to Charleston and the Lowcountry: the architecture, the pleasure-seeking style, the vegetation, the decadence, the climate, the sense of history, the tradition. The writer's Charleston possesses an honorable heritage. May it continue to shine as a literary gem of the new South.

Curtis Worthington
Editor

A Note on the Second Edition

In 1996 the first edition of this volume, then titled *Literary Charleston: A Lowcountry Reader*, was published by Wyrick and Company and had a highly successful print run in hardcover. When Tom Payton at Trinity University Press suggested a new edition of *Literary Charleston* as part of its Literary Cities series (*Literary New Orleans, Literary Savannah, Literary Nashville*), it seemed the perfect opportunity to review once again the endeavors and accomplishments of the many writers who have used Charleston and the surrounding Lowcountry environs as setting and subject matter for their work.

In order to be consistent with the format of the other books in the series, it was necessary to reformat the new edition, though all of the writers from the first edition are represented in the second. Very few of the original selections have been eliminated or excerpted slightly. Since more than a decade has passed, it also seemed a good opportunity to help round out this imaginative vision of Charleston by including a few works by writers not previously represented, including the most recent writer on the Charleston literary scene to achieve national acclaim, Sue Monk Kidd. Louis D. Rubin, Jr.'s foreword seems as relevant today as it did in 1996 and is included with his generous approval. The order of the works in the present volume follows a more or less chronological "imaginative history in words" that begins in the colonial period and moves forward through the Revolutionary War era, the early nineteenth century, the War Between the States, Reconstruction, the early nineteenth century, the Charleston Renaissance, and on to more contemporary work.

Here is a Lowcountry literary cornucopia, rich in variety, served up for your reading delectation. It is a pleasure once again to present some of the very best of Charleston's literati. Enjoy.

Curtis Worthington
Editor

from *Travels through North and South Carolina, Georgia, East and West Florida*

WILLIAM BARTRAM (1739–1823)

William Bartram, son of the naturalist John Bartram, attended the Academy of Philadelphia, which later became the University of Pennsylvania. Though he failed in his early career as a planter in the Caribbean, he had from a young age shown talent in drawing and painting, and in later life he distinguished himself as a botanist, explorer, and writer. With Charleston as his base he spent four years, beginning in March 1773, exploring the coastline of South Carolina, Georgia, and Florida. The descriptions of flora and fauna in his *Travels through North & South Carolina, Georgia, East & West Florida, the Cherokee Country, the Extensive Territories of the Muscogulges, or Creek Confederacy, and the Country of the Chactaws* (1791) provided source material for a number of English romantic poets, including Samuel Taylor Coleridge and William Wordsworth. In the excerpt below, Bartram describes a voyage on the open sea on which he encountered a terrible storm. He presents nature's fury unleashed and the chaos of a disordered universe, but also the primordial sea, the wellspring of life. From chaos, Bartram sails into Charleston harbor, likening what he sees to earthly paradise at the beginning of time.

At the request of Dr. Fothergill, of London, to search the Floridas, and the western parts of Carolina and Georgia, for the discovery of rare and useful productions of nature, chiefly in the vegetable kingdom; in April, 1773, I embarked for Charleston, South-Carolina, on board the brigantine *Charleston Packet*, Captain Wright, the brig __, Captain Mason, being in company with us, and bound to the same port. We had a pleasant run down the Delaware, 150 miles to Cape Henlopen, the two vessels entering the Atlantic together. For the first twenty-four hours, we had a prosperous gale, and were cheerful and happy in the prospect of a quick and pleasant voyage; but, alas! how vain and uncertain are human expectations! how quickly is the flattering scene changed! The powerful winds, now rushing forth from their secret abodes, suddenly spread terror and devastation; and the wide ocean, which, a few moments past, was gentle and placid, is now thrown into disorder, and heaped into mountains, whose white curling crests seem to sweep the skies!

This furious gale continued near two days and nights, and not a little damaged our sails, cabin furniture, and state-rooms, besides retarding our passage. The storm having abated, a lively gale from N.W. continued four or five days, when shifting to N. and lastly to N.E. on the tenth of our departure from Cape Henlopen, early in the morning, we descried a sail astern, and in a short time discovered it to be Capt. Mason, who soon came up with us. We hailed each other, being joyful to meet again, after so many dangers. He suffered greatly by the gale, but providentially made a good harbour within Cape Hatteras. As he ran by us, he threw on board ten or a dozen bass, a large and delicious fish, having caught a great number of them whilst he was detained in harbour. He got into Charleston that evening, and we the next morning, about eleven o'clock.

There are few objects out at sea to attract the notice of the traveller, but what are sublime, awful, and majestic: the seas themselves, in a tempest, exhibit a tremendous scene, where the winds assert their power, and, in furious conflict, seem to set the ocean on fire. On the other hand, nothing can be more sublime than the view of the encircling horizon, after the turbulent winds have taken their flight, and the lately agitated bosom of the deep has again become calm and pacific; the gentle moon rising in dignity from the east, attended by millions of glittering orbs; the luminous appearance of the seas at night, when all the waters seem transmuted into liquid silver; the prodigious bands of porpoises foreboding tempest, that appear to cover the ocean; the mighty whale, sovereign of the watery realms, who cleaves the seas in his course; the sudden appearance of land from the sea, the strand stretching each way, beyond the utmost reach of sight; the alternate appearance and recess of the coast, whilst the far distant blue hills slowly retreat and disappear; or, as we approach the coast, the capes and promontories first strike our sight, emerging from the watery expanse, and, like mighty giants, elevating their crests towards the skies; the water suddenly alive with its scaly inhabitants; squadrons of sea-fowl sweeping through the air, impregnated with the breath of fragrant aromatic trees and flowers; the amplitude and magnificence of these scenes are great indeed, and may present to the imagination, an idea of the first appearance of the earth to man at the creation.

On my arrival at Charleston, I waited on Doctor Chalmer[s], a gentleman of eminence in his profession and public employments, to whom I was recommended by my worthy patron, and to whom I was to apply for counsel and assistance, for carrying into effect my intended travels: the Doctor received me with perfect politeness, and, on every occasion, treated me with friendship; and by means of the countenance which he gave me, and the marks of esteem with which he honoured me, I became acquainted with many of the worthy families. . . .

Indians and Pirates

BEATRICE WITTE RAVENEL (1870–1956)

Beatrice Witte, the third daughter of a well-to-do Charleston banker, lived for many years in her family's house at 172 Rutledge Avenue, now Ashley Hall School. After graduating from Miss Kelly's Female Seminary, she moved to Cambridge, Massachusetts, and attended Radcliffe College, studying philosophy, literature, and foreign languages with William James, George Santayana, and George Kitteridge. Witte began her writing career in college, publishing short stories in the *Harvard Monthly* and eventually serving as one of its editors. Returning to Charleston in 1900, she married Francis Ravenel, son of Harriott Horry Ravenel, who had written the social history *Charleston: The Place and the People* (1906) and biographies of Eliza Lucas Pinckney and U.S. Congressman William Lowndes. When her husband died unexpectedly in 1920, Ravenel began writing in earnest to support herself. Her fiction appeared in the *Saturday Evening Post* and *Harper's* and editorials in *The State* newspaper in Columbia, South Carolina. Her poetry was published in the *Atlantic Monthly, Sewanee Review*, and numerous other publications. In 1925 her poems were gathered in *The Arrow of Lightning*.

Instrumental in the early activities of the Poetry Society of South Carolina, Beatrice Ravenel befriended Amy Lowell during the Massachusetts poet's visit to Charleston on behalf of the society. The two carried on an active correspondence, and Lowell's progressive ideas on poetry and poetics influenced Ravenel. Increasingly, her poetry is regarded as the very best of the Charleston Renaissance. In 1969 Louis D. Rubin, Jr. republished some of her poems under the title *The Yemassee Land*. She was inducted into the South Carolina Academy of Authors in 1995.

In the two poems below, Ravenel considers two groups of outsiders who figured prominently in the early days of colonial Charleston: Indians and pirates. She mentions Chief Justice Nicholas Trott in "The Pirates"; as an admiralty judge he presided over the trial of the pirate Stede Bonnet in 1718. Bonnet was convicted and hanged at the Battery.

The Yemassee Lands

I.
In the Yemassee Lands
Peace-belts unwind in the Spring on the banks of Savannah;
Flowers like wampum weave in the grass
Reiterate beads of pink-orange, of clouded white, of
        pale, shimmerless ochre,
Mile after mile.

II.
Round the curve of the river,
Meshed by conniving impatient shoots of the gum tree,
Streamers of silver dart, muffled lapping of paddles.
Always, just round the turning, the stealthy canoe
        with its naked upstanding warrior
Comes . . . for the wild-fowl rise in a hurtling of
        startled feathers;
Never comes into sight.

III.
In the Yemassee Lands
Cypress roots, at the edge of the swamp, roughly
        fluted, age-wrinkled,
Have budded their rufous knobs like dim and reptilian eyes,
That watch.
Orchids, liquid gold, bend from cylindrical sheaths
Under a phantom moccasined tread.
Gossamer webs, barring the overgrown way through
        the woods,
Shudder but do not break, betraying the passage
Of footsteps gone by.

IV.

In the undulant mist of the sunsets of summer
Slim pines stand with scarlet and quivering outlines—
Initiate boys whose whipped young blood leaps up
Now, the first time, to the war-path.
Shadows of red, shadows of bronze and of copper
Disengage from the wood-growth;
Cowering, melting, lost, reappearing,
One after one, the long, lithe, menacing war-line
Loops through the stems.
Light cups the crouching knees,
Splinters on polished shoulders,
Ravels in towering head-plumes.

V.

In the Yemassee Lands
When with blowing of wood-smoke and throbbing
        of hidden drums
Indian Summer fashions its spell,
Trembling falls on the air.
Wild things flatten themselves in the jeopardy of the
        shade.
Out of the snarling keen-toothed vines
Berries wink with the cunning obsidian gleam
Of the arrow-head, and deep in the shuddering fern
The rattlesnake coils his pattern of war.
Silence, inimical, lurks in the dark:
Softly on buckskinned soles, halting a step behind,
Something follows and waits . . .
And will not be appeased.

VI.

But when Autumn unleashes the winds
And storm treads the lowlands,
Trees, like a panic of horses galloping over the sky-line,
(Charging of chesnut and roan and bay,
Tossing their frantic forelocks)
Flee from the rush
Of invisible hunters.

VII.

Stars in the coppery afterglow of the sundown
Hang like strings of teeth on the savage breast of a warrior;
Water-willows trail in the shadowy depths of Savannah,
Draggle like scalps from the war-belt;
And the night-wind sings overhead
Like arrows on deadly sendings,
In the Yemassee Lands.

VIII.

Gray through young leaves blows the smoke from the
        ancient fires;
The thud of the young men's dances troubles the earth.
Shadows from ambushed boughs
Reach with a plucking hand for the hair.
The lightning-set pine far away blazes with
        hideous cracklings,
Remembering the long black tresses of captive squaws
Tied to the death-pyre.

IX.

After two hundred years
Has the forest forgotten?
Always the trees are aware
(Significant, perilous, shaken with whispers of dread
        and of welcome)
Of the passage of urgent feet.
Violent shoots strain up to the air and the sunshine
Of cut-over land;
Leaves crowd over the barrows of last year's skeleton leaves.
Ever and ever again
The Red Man comes back to his own
In the Yemassee Lands.

The Pirates

The garden of Garret Vanselvin
Swam in the golden spray of October.
The Mexican rose, like a sun-dial,
In tremulous upstaring blossoms
Told off the day:—
Gemmules, white for the dawn; flushing with desperate
        hope in the noon;
And drawn into cowering balls of disastrous red—
Thrown-away red—with the sundown.
Into the wide-set windows
Catspaws of south-flavored wind laughed from the harbor,
Where the town, like a giant child, sat on the knees of the
        islands
And played with a lapful
Of silvery ships.

Did they watch it, day after day—
The pirates—
The doomed gold arcs of their hours slip through the
        sun-dial tree?

In the house-place of Garret Vanselvin—
Charles Town, in the province of South Carolina,
Seventeen-hundred-eighteen—
They were trying the pirates;
Men of Stede Bonnet's, shipmates of Vaughn and of
        Blackbeard;
Noisome things of the sea, vicious with spines,
        smeared with abhorrent blood.
They had scooped them a netful and flung it into a
        corner.
This vile *frutto di mare*.
The pearly swell and color of coral and amber drained
        out of them,
Flaccid and lax they lay,

Hardly with wills to answer, only waiting the outcome,
The gasp in this cursed, foreign air,
The last alien strangle . . .

What did they dream of day after day, the trammeled
    sea creatures?
It all must have tasted of dreams.
Dry waves and billows of sound, climbing, discharging
    above them;
Voices of lawyers, sleek, desiccate, deadly.
All of eleven judges.
Chief Justice, black-robed, wigged and appurtenanced,
    just as in England.
Goose-Creek gentry the rest, well-born planters come
    from Barbadoes;
Gentlemen laced and red-coated, men of the crack
    troop of horse
Coloneled by Logan.
A shifting of juries.
And all of them, gentle and simple, cut to the quick of
    their pride and their pockets
When the seemly and gravid rice-ships, matronly
    moving out of the harbor,
Plumped in the arms of fell and insolent sea-thieves
Skulking outside.
Wait!
Chief Justice Nicholas Trott, Judge of the Court of
    Vice-Admiralty,
He it is, speaking.
Will he remember?—

Governor once of Providence in the Bahamas,
Not unreputed as over-friendly to rovers,
Not unrebuked for their fellowship.
For the sake of old days, will he . . .
Wait!

His voice! Those are the melting, significant accents
That won on their lordships in London, that pull at the
    eyelids
Of lattice-bred women. (Their women live here behind
    windows and iron-tusked walls.
You passed them—the narrow, still streets, ambushed with
    eyes—you two who bore Blackbeard's message,
Laying their high-stomached Province under his
    contribution.—
Ay, but that flicked them!)
Hearken!

And first he lifts from your shoulder the cover of
    common humanity.
Men? You are not men. You are *hostes humani generis.*
Enemies of all mankind. Neither faith, nay, nor oath
    need be kept with you.
You were formerly ousted of clergy.
Now the law grants you this comfort; and, with a
    smooth lovingkindness
Equal to that of the law, he trusts you will profit.
But—he may allow you no counsel.

He is telling you further
That the God of the land made the ocean,
(He swivels the Scriptures about like a gun, texts
    spitting for grapeshot);
That he parceled it out and placed it under the thumbs of
    Kings and lawyers.
(O ye fowls of the air, ye wild winds, ye waterspouts,
Praise ye the Lord!)
And against all these three, God, King, and lawyers,
have you offended.

And the witnesses now.
Will they humor the gentry, tickle their notion of
        pirates' ways,
Got from old chap-books, old songs of the Barbary Coast?
Pshaw! This is tame, this has no tang!
No decks swashing in blood? No one walking the plank?
You, James Killing, mate of the ravished sloop, *Francis*,
Did they not cut you down?—Nay, and their captain,
        he that's escaped, Major Bonnet,
Was civil, uncommon civil.—Cutlasses drawn?—Why,
        yes . . .
To cut down the pineapple-nets over the captain's lockers.
Asked me to join in a health in rum punch to the King—
        over the water;
Asked why I looked so melancholy. Told them I looked
        as well as I could.
Sang two-three glees . . . asked me to join 'em a-pirating.
And now they are questioning you.
How came you such monsters, outlaws?
Not by your wills? Forced to that way of life? Why did
        you join then?
How should one tell this Judge, in his awful and
        spiteful majesty,
His sinister magpie dress,—
"Man—or, my lord—or your honor—had you been left
        on a Maroon shore,
With the sea in front and behind you a present death—
        Indians howling at night,
Or worser than Indians, made out of night, broke loose
        from hell—
Just for the smell of a ship and the jog of a shipmate's
        elbow
You'd have turned pirate too!"
God! How mouth it
To his honor, a Lord Chief Justice?

What does it profit to listen
To the long, long, day-long drone,
While the sun spills gold through the Mexican rose-tree?
Better to listen instead
To the winding importunate wind, blowing up from
    palm-tasseled Barbadoes;
Wind that damasks the water, silky wind in the sails
When, like an overripe fruit, rolled in the quickening wash,
The ship is tugging at anchor.
Wind like the hair of girls, so soft, so perfumed and
    resilient,
Tangling the memory now . . .

But here, swelled with importance,
Assistant-Judge Thomas Hepworth, dangerous, droll as
    a pincushion-fish, altercative,
Turns to the jury.
Shall the Carolinas be ruined as one hears that Jamaica
    is ruined?
Are not our rice-ships seized at our very gates?
Is not the incredible true? In our own walled town
    what disturbance, what rioting,
What threatenings to burn it—burn Charles Town—
    burn it about our ears!
And all with design
To rescue these pestilent pirates.
Only too well have arts and practice effected
The flight of Stede Bonnet. Certain are favorable
    toward him,
Citing his gentle blood, his fortune, his education—
Enhancements these of his crimes.
An example then, gentlemen all, a substantial and
    speedy example:
The times demand it!

And the trial clicks to the verdict.

No record remains
In the ancient records of Charles Town,
No scribble, no note—
Only the outraged, discretionless speech of his judgeship,
Forwarded straight to London, from his Majesty's
        Court of Vice-Admiralty,
Witnesses yet
To the people's love for the pirates.

They threw doubloons on the counters
Of honest taverns fringing the wharves.
It was Fair-day in Charles Town harbor,
Silks to be brought good cheap, spices and loaves of
        blue-coated sugar,
When the sunburned traffickers landed.
Trinkets they fetched and wines . . .
Ah, but richer and fiercer,
Surely they brought Romance!
(Do you notice that burly man, his scared eyes
        watching the captives
As men watch plague-struck comrades?
Do you mark that girl, twisting, with hunted glances,
Her apron-tail in her teeth?)
They brought in their stained red scarves aromas of
        dangerous rapture
That comfort men who live by the sea and resist its
        challenge,—
Romance that lifted the blurred, resentful drab of their
        days
As sunrise opals the sea-mist.

As the shop of a Greek near the wharves
Where the quick white sailors cluster like sea-gulls
Over his tubs of grapes, his ropy netting of melons,
I shall stop, I shall buy a pineapple,
Heavy with tropic flavors.
I shall go to the White Point gardens, as near as may be
To the place where we hanged the pirates—
We Carolinians—
Where the gun from Granville Bastion
Ripped the sky with the sunrise;
And the merciful quicksand took them,—
Twisted, discolored sea-things.

I shall study my pineapple,
Its desperate-clinging points . . .
As a man might cling to life with his finger-nails and
        his toe-nails
When the breath is squeezed in his throat!
As one lays flowers on a grave
I shall toss it over the sea-wall.

Because you laughed when you ravished the *Francis*;
Because you drank to your fallen King—over the water;
But most because they once loved you,
The humble, whose very life is in some sort a piracy,
Marauding the sun and air from the well-found and
        solid citizen;
Because they fought for your lives—
May your quicksand, O pirates,
Be soft as the arms of a girl,
May your sleep be forever
And pleasant with dreams of sea-changes,

Interpreters of the sea!

Prologue to *The Orphan*

ANONYMOUS

Charleston's literary and artistic tradition began with drama. The British actor Antony Aston arrived in South Carolina about 1730 and as a strolling player gave colonial audiences some of the first dramatic performances in British North America. The theatre in Dock Street (now Queen Street) opened in 1736 with performances of *The Recruiting Officer* by George Farquhar, but theatrical seasons began in Charleston as early as 1734. Prologues and epilogues that were created to accompany the dramatic offerings constitute the first material ever written for the American stage, and there is none older than the following item, printed in the *South-Carolina Gazette*, the contemporary Charleston paper, in the edition that was dated February 1 to February 8, 1734/5. *The Orphan: or The Unhappy Marriage* was performed first on January 24, 1735, and was repeated several times in the next decades. (A year after its first appearance it was already called "this old favorite.") The anonymous local author, as Eola Willis has pointed out in *The Charleston Stage in the XVIII Century*, "did not sign his Prologues. He did not know that he was to be acclaimed one of the earliest American poets, and he could not foresee that these productions of his would be hailed with delight by eager historical students, almost two centuries later, as the 'First American Prologues.'"

When first Columbus touch'd this distant Shore,
And vainly hop'd his Fears and Dangers o'er,
One boundless Wilderness in View appear'd!
No Champain Plains or rising Cities chear'd
His wearied Eye.—
Monsters unknown travers'd the hideous Waste,
And Men more Savage than the Beasts they chac'd.
But mark! How soon these gloomy Prospects clear,
And the new World's late horrors disappear.

The soil obedient to the industrious Swains,
What happy Harvests crowns their honest Pains,
And Peace and Plenty triumph o'er the Plains.
What various Products float on every Tide?
What numerous Navys in our Harbors ride?
Tillage and Trade conjoin their Friendly Aid,
T'enrich, the thriving Boy and Lovely Maid,
Hispania, it's true, her precious Mines engross'd,
And bore her shining Entrails to its Coast.
Britannia more humane supplys her wants,
The British sense and British Beauty plants.
The Aged Sire beholds with sweet Surprize
In foreign Climes a numerous Offspring rize,
Sense, Virtue, Worth and Honour stand confest,
In each brave Male, his prosp'rous hands have blest,
While the admiring Eye improv'd may trace,
The Mother's charms in each chast Virgin's Face.
Hence we presume to usher in those Arts
Which oft have warm'd the best and bravest Hearts.
Faints our endeavours, rude are our Essays,
We strive to please but can't pretend at praise;
Forgiving Smiles o'erpay the grateful Task,
They're all we hope and all we humbly ask.

Yankee Doodle

JOSIAH QUINCY JR. (1744–1775)

Josiah Quincy Jr. traveled from his native Boston to the South in 1773 in hopes of restoring his health. A Harvard-educated lawyer, he had written several powerful essays critical of the British and defending American rights. He called upon his countrymen "to break off all social intercourse with those whose commerce contaminates, whose luxuries poison, whose avarice is insatiable, and whose unnatural oppressions are not to be borne." No doubt he sought to spread his views to the colonists he met in the South on his travels, but he also had a sharp eye for the people he met, including the two "Macaronis," just arrived from London. A Macaroni was an individual who dressed—or ate or gambled—extravagantly. Their wigs were often gargantuan. This account first appeared in the *Massachusetts Historical Society Proceedings* in 1915–16.

February 28.

We now were off Charlestown Bar, and the wind being right in our teeth we were the whole day beating up. Just before sunset we passed the fort. Charleston appeared situated between two large spacious rivers (the one on the right called Cooper River and the other on the left, Ashley River), which here empty themselves into the sea. The number of shipping far surpassed all I had ever seen in Boston. I was told there were then not so many as common at this season, tho' about 350 sail lay off the town. The town struck me very agreeably; but the New Exchange which fronted the place of my landing made a most noble appearance. On landing, Sunday evening just before dark, the numbers of inhabitants and appearance of the buildings far exceeded my expectation. I proceeded to the Coffee-house, where was a great resort of company as busy and noisy as was decent. . . .

March 2.

This day I was waited upon by several gentlemen to whom yesterday I had delivered letters. Those who came in my absence left
cards with their names. Received a ticket from David Deis, Esquire,
for the St. Cecilia Concert, and now quit my journal to go.

March 3.

The Concert-house is a large inelegant building situated down a
yard at the entrance of which I was met by a Constable with his
staff. I offered him my ticket, which was subscribed by the name
of the person giving it, and directing admission of me by name,
the officer told me to proceed. I did and was next met by a white
waiter, who directs me to a third to whom I delivered my ticket
and was conducted in. The Hall is preposterously and out of all
proportion large, no orchestra for the performers, though a kind
of loft for fiddlers at the Assembly. The performers were all at
one end of the hall and the company in front and on each side.
The musick was good. The two bass-viols and French horns were
grand. One Abbercrombie, a Frenchman just arrived, played a
first fiddle and solo incomparably, better than any I ever had
heard: I have several times heard John Turner and Morgan play
a solo. Abbercrombie can't speak a word of English and has a
salary of 500 guineas a year from the St. Cecilia Society. Hartley
was here, and played as I thought badly on the harpsichord. The
capital defect of this concert was want of an organ.

Here was upwards of two hundred fifty ladies, and it was
called no great show. I took a view of them, but I saw no E_____.
However I saw
    Beauty in a Brow of Egypt.
    To be sure not a Helen's.
In loftiness of head-dress these ladies stoop to the daughters of
the North: in richness of dress surpass them: in health and flo-
ridity of countenance veil to them: in taciturnity during the performances greatly before our ladies: in noise and flirtations after

the music is over pretty much on a par. If our women have any advantage, it is in white and red, vivacity and fire.

The gentlemen many of them dressed with richness and elegance uncommon with us—many with swords on. We had two Macaronis present—just arrived from London. This character I found real, and not fictitious. "See the Macaroni," was a common phrase in the hall. One may well be stiled the bag—and the other the Cue-Macaroni.

from *The Carolinian*

RAFAEL SABATINI (1875–1950)

Rafael Sabatini, born in Italy to an English mother and Italian father, learned English as a second language, yet he wrote exclusively in it. Closely associated with Joseph Conrad, Sabatini wrote several historical romances, including *Scaramouche* (1921), about the French revolution, and the pirate tale *Captain Blood* (1922), which served as the source for the 1935 motion picture of the same name, starring Errol Flynn. He was a prolific author, producing a new volume almost every year. His novel of the American Revolution set in Charleston, *The Carolinian* (1924), reflects Sabatini's extensive research into local history and geography, as he never visited the area.

Everything concerned with Myrtle's marriage fell out precisely as her ladyship promised and subsequently planned, which was the way of things of which her ladyship had the planning.

To quiet Myrtle's grievous misgivings on the score of her father, her ladyship undertook that after the departure of the bridal couple she would, herself, not merely inform Sir Andrew of what had been done, but compel him to see reason and obtain his pardon for the runagates.

"And never doubt that I shall," said Lady William [Campbell] with convincing emphasis. "What men can't alter they soon condone."

Thus, out of her own splendid confidence, she allayed at last Myrtle's lingering fears and only abiding regrets.

So much accomplished, her ladyship unfolded the further details of her plan for getting the couple safely away. The Brewtons' ball that same Thursday night, being of an almost official character, Lady William's viceregal position demanded that she should go attended by two ladies of honour. From the position of one of these she would depose her Cousin Jane in favour of Myrtle. As a result, Myrtle would be expected to attend her throughout, and to facilitate this, Lady William would arrange with Sir Andrew that Myrtle be allowed to spend the night at the Governor's residence. Thus the bridal couple would be ensured a clear and unhampered start whilst all Charles Town was still entirely unsuspicious. For the rest, the real arrangement was that Harry Latimer should be at hand with a travelling-carriage, and that, as soon as Myrtle could conveniently leave the ball without being missed, she should join him, and they should immediately start for his plantation at Santee Broads, a drive of fifty miles, which would consume the whole of the night. Thence, after resting, they were to push on to a distant estate of Mr. Latimer's in the hills above Salisbury, where for the present they were to abide. There, in the cotton-fields of North Carolina, their honeymoon might peacefully be spent without fear of pursuit from any save Sir Andrew, who would in any case be powerless to untie the knot which the law of England was so securely to tie aboard the *Tamar*.

And so, soon after breakfast on Thursday morning, Myrtle departed from Tradd Street, on the pretext that her ladyship had bidden her come early. There would be a deal to do in preparation for the ball, she casually announced in explanation.

"Not a doubt," said her father. And when he beheld the dimensions of the clothes-box that was being borne after her, he raised eyes and hands to heaven. "Lord! The vanity of woman!"

But Myrtle was already down the steps and into her sedan chair, lest he should detect the tears that had suddenly come to fill her eyes at the thought that she was definitely leaving her father's home, and leaving it under cover of a deceit.

It needed all Lady William's stout cheeriness and confidence to dispel the black clouds that were gathering about Myrtle's soul when presently she came into her ladyship's radiant presence. Nor was she given much time for further brooding. Within a half-hour of reaching the Governor's residence, she was taking boat at the Exchange Wharf with her ladyship, a boat manned by four British tars and commanded by a pert boy-officer.

Out in the bay, as they drew near the *Tamar*, with her black-and-white hull, the snowy sails furled along her yards and the gleam of brass from her deck, they were joined by another boat, rowed by blacks in linsey-woolsey jackets, and carrying Harry Latimer and Tom Izard.

In the waist of the warship they found a guard of honour drawn up, whilst Captain Thornborough, the handsome sunburnt officer in command of the sloop, came forward to receive them.

All was ready, as her ladyship had predisposed. But to satisfy the pretext on which they came, there was first a tour of inspection of the ship. When this was over, the Captain invited the guests to a glass of Madeira in his cabin before leaving. He contrived unostentatiously to include in the invitation the chaplain, who had, somehow, got in the way at the last moment.

In the cabin no time was wasted. No sooner had the steward retired after pouring for them than with naval despatch Captain Thornborough made them come to business. The chaplain was brisk, and confined himself to the essentials of the ceremony. Within a few minutes all was accomplished, and the Captain of the *Tamar* was raising his glass to toast Mrs. Henry Latimer.

"I'd fire a salute in your honour, ma'am, but it would occasion questions we may not be prepared to answer."

In the vessel's waist, where they had met scarcely an hour ago, husband and wife parted again for the present, and Myrtle and Lady William went down the steps to the waiting cockboat.

Myrtle bore now on her finger the ring that had belonged to Harry's mother, the very ring that once, and not so long ago, she had returned to him. In her heart she bore perhaps the oddest conflict of emotions that has ever been a bride's. There was happiness in the thought that Harry now belonged to her, and that nothing could ever again come between them; there was happiness, too, in the reflection that thus she had conquered Harry's obstinacy and jealous doubts and prevailed upon him to save his life by leaving Charles Town. But there were regrets at the manner of her marriage, and infinitely more poignant regrets at the thought of what her father must suffer in his affection and his pride when he learnt of these hole-and-corner nuptials between herself and a man against whom he bore a prejudice that was amounting almost to hatred.

There were tears blurring her vision as she looked back over the waves on which the sunlight was dancing to that other boat at the foot of the ship's ladder into which her husband and his friend were stepping. And the boy-officer, chatting briskly with Lady William, gave her ladyship no opportunity to offer Myrtle any of the comfort of which she perceived the poor child to stand in need.

They reached at last the Exchange Wharf, and, whilst a sailor held the boat firmly alongside by means of a boathook, the gallant stripling of an officer, standing on the wet slippery steps, handed the ladies ashore, to set them face to face with Captain Mandeville.

Delayed until then by official duties, the Captain was on his way to Fort Johnson to inform Major Sykes that his services that night would no longer be required. He was looking about for a wherry to convey him at the very moment that the cockboat from the *Tamar* containing her ladyship and Myrtle drew alongside the wharf.

Lady William, conscious as she was of being engaged upon a deed of secrecy, paused to stare at him, suspecting an excess of coincidence in his presence. Nor did his air of surprise allay her suspicions, as it should have done, for Captain Mandeville was not the man to show surprise when he actually felt it.

He doffed his black three-cornered hat and bowed.

"I did not know your ladyship addicted to water-jaunts."

Myrtle, esteeming him, persuaded of his sincere and selfless friendship, and detesting fraud beyond what was absolutely necessary to her safety and Harry's, would there and then have given him the real reason for her journeyings by water, had not her ladyship forestalled her.

"I am not," she told the equerry. "But Captain Thornborough offered to show his ship to Myrtle, and the child had never been aboard a man-of-war. But we detain you, Captain," she added, bethinking her of the second boat that followed, and preferring that he should not stay to meet its occupants.

"No, no," he answered. "I am not pressed. I am only going to Fort Johnson. I was looking for a boat. I trust you found the man-of-war all that you expected it, Myrtle?"

"Why, yes," she said, and lowered her lids under his sharp gaze lest he should perceive the signs of tears about her eyes.

"But we have no enthusiasm," he faintly rallied her, smiling.

Her ladyship promptly rescued her.

"Come, Myrtle. The man will keep us talking here all day."

"Nay, a moment of your mercy. This may be my only chance before the ball to-night."

"Your chance of what?"

"To ensure myself the dance I covet. The first minuet, Myrtle, if you will honour me so far?"

"But, of course, Robert." And impulsively she held out her hand.

He took it, and, bareheaded as he had remained, bowed low over it. For an instant, as he did so, his eyes dilated; but his bowed head screened this from both the ladies. And then her ladyship whirled Myrtle away without further ceremony.

He stood watching them until they were lost in the bustling crowd about the New Exchange. Then, slowly resuming his hat, a deep line of thought between his fine brows, he turned his attention once more to that other craft which had already caught his eye.

He signaled to a wherry to stand by, but made no move to enter it until the boat he watched was alongside, and out of it sprang Latimer and Tom Izard. They exchanged bows formally, and without words, despite the fact that the equerry was—or had been—on easy terms with her ladyship's brother. Then Captain Mandeville stepped into the boat he had summoned, and sat down in the sternsheets.

"Push off!" he curtly bade the negroes.

The four men bent to their oars, and the boat shot away from the wharf.

"Where does yo' honour want fer to go?" the nearest negro asked him.

Captain Mandeville considered a long moment. Then he stretched out a hand to grasp the tiller.

"To the sloop *Tamar*," he answered.

When he reached her decks, her captain was below, but he came instantly upon being informed that the Governor's equerry had come aboard.

"Ah, Mandeville! Good-day to you," he greeted him.

Mandeville gave him a short good-day in return. "I want a word with you in private, Thornborough."

The sailor looked at him, mildly surprised by his tone.

"Come aft to my cabin," he invited, and led the way.

Mandeville sat down upon a locker with his back to the square windows that opened upon the stern gallery. On the table before him he observed a book, a decanter at a low ebb, and six glasses, in two of which a little wine remained. He could account for five of the glasses and assumed the sixth to have been for some other officer of the *Tamar*.

Thornborough, standing straight and tall in his blue uniform with white facings, looked at him questioningly across the table.

"Well?" he asked. "What brings you?"

"Mr. Harry Latimer has been aboard your ship this morning."

He had deliberately placed himself so that the light was on Thornborough's face, and his own in shadow. Watching the sailor now, he fancied that his eyes shifted a little to avoid his own. Also there was a perceptible pause before Thornborough answered him.

"That is so. What, then?"

"What do you know of him?"

"I? What should I know? He is a wealthy colonial gentleman. But you should know more about him, yourself."

"I do. That is why I am questioning you. What was he doing aboard your ship?"

Thornborough stiffened. "Sink me, Mandeville! What's the reason for this catechism?"

"This fellow Latimer is a rebel, a dangerous spreader of sedition, and a daring spy. That is the reason. That is why I ask you what he came to do aboard your ship."

Thornborough laughed. "It had nothing to do with spying. Of that I can assure you. What should he have spied here that could profit him?"

"You are not forgetting that you have Kirkland on board?" Mandeville asked him.

"All Charles Town knows that. What should Mr. Latimer discover by spying on Kirkland?"

"Possibly he came to ascertain whether he is still here. But if you were to tell me on what pretext he did come, I might be able to obtain a glimpse of his real reason."

It happened, however, that Thornborough's instructions from Lady William were quite explicit; and in nothing that Mandeville had said could he see any reason for departing from them.

"Mandeville, you're hunting a mare's nest. Mr. Latimer came aboard with Lady William Campbell and one or two others so as to view a British man-of-war. To suppose that he could discover here anything of possible advantage to his party or of detriment to ours is ridiculous."

"You may find that you take too much for granted, Thornborough." Mandeville spoke mysteriously. As he spoke, he rose, and proceeded to relate to the sailor how Latimer had visited the Governor only yesterday in disguise and pumped him dry on more than one subject. "If I had not subsequently discovered this, and ascertained the extent of the information he drew from us, I might have remained as unsuspecting as yourself."

Whilst speaking, he had idly picked up the book from the table, to make the surprising discovery that it was a book of Common-Prayer. A bookmark of embroidered silk hung from its pages, and the book opened naturally in Mandeville's hands at the Marriage Service, which was the place marked. Idly he continued to turn its leaves. He even looked at the name on the flyleaf, which was "Robert Faversham." It was odd to find such a volume on the Captain's table. He set it down again, and assuming at last that Thornborough really had nothing to tell him beyond the fact which he had desired to ascertain—namely that Latimer actually had been on board the ship in Myrtle's company—he took his leave.

With a final admonition to Thornborough to be careful of whom he admitted to his sloop, the equerry went down the entrance ladder to his waiting boat, with intent to resume his voyage to the fort. But within a dozen cables' length of the *Tamar*, he abruptly changed his mind.

"Put about," he ordered, and added curtly: "Back to Charles Town."

He was obeyed without question, and the clumsy boat swung round to pull against the tide, which was beginning to ebb.

Ahead of them, drenched in brilliant sunshine, and looking dazzlingly white, the low-lying town appeared to float like another Venice upon the sea, the water-front dominated by the classical pile of the Custom-House with its Ionic pillars and imposing entablature, whilst above the red roofs towered the spires of Saint Philip's and Saint Michael's, the latter so lofty that it served as a landmark for ships far out at sea.

Captain Mandeville, however, beheld nothing but a slender woman's hand, with white tapering fingers protruding from mittens of white silk, and round one of these fingers a circlet of gold, gleaming through the strained silken meshes.

That in some mysterious way Myrtle and Harry had become reconciled was clear from their joint presence aboard the *Tamar*, whilst the discovery of that restored ring betrayed the fact that the reconciliation had gone the extent of renewing their betrothal.

That was reason enough to restrain him from going to Fort Johnson to bid Sykes hold his hand. At all costs, and whatever the consequence with which the Governor might afterwards visit him, Mandeville must allow the plan laid with Sykes to be carried out. He was in a difficult position. But he must deal with one difficulty at a time, and in dealing first with Harry Latimer he dealt with the more imminent danger to himself and all his hopes.

He sat there, elbow on knee and chin in hand, absorbed in thought, piecing together little tenuous scraps of evidence, and plagued to irritation the while by the obstinate association in his mind of the ring he had seen on her finger and the book he had found on Captain Thornborough's table. Those things and that visit of theirs to the sloop that morning forced a dreadful suspicion on his mind, a suspicion too dreadful to be entertained. He rejected it, as wildly fantastic; and yet the thought of the ring and the book persisted until he was landing on the wharf at Charles Town. Finally he shook it off. "What can it matter, after all?" he asked himself. "Sykes will make it all of no account tonight. I rid the State of a dangerous enemy and myself of a dangerous rival at one stroke. And I shall be treading a minuet while it is done."

. . .

The Executive of the General Assembly, which had by now replaced the old Provincial Congress, was in the hands of a legislative and privy council. John Rutledge had been elected President and invested with all the powers of Governor.

Despite a temperamental antipathy, which he believed mutual, and some lingering remains of that rancor provoked by Rutledge's hard, unsentimental criticisms of his conduct in the Featherstone affair, Harry Latimer could not withhold his admiration of the sagacity, energy, and strength with which the new President went to work to establish and maintain order, to levy troops, and to advance the fortification of the town materially and morally against all emergencies.

In those first days of June there arrived in Charles Town that English soldier of fortune Major-General Charles Lee, sent by Washington to command the troops engaged in the defence of the Southern seaboard. He was a man of great experience and skill, who had spent his life campaigning wherever campaigns

were being conducted; and Moultrie tells us that his presence in
Charles Town was equivalent to a reinforcement of a thousand
men. But his manners, Moultrie adds, were rough and harsh.

The unfinished state in which he found the great fort of palmetto logs seems to have fretted him considerably. His correspondence with Moultrie in these days bears abundant witness
to that, and we have a glimpse of the irritation caused him by the
calm, unexcited manner in which the stout-hearted Moultrie
continued the works as if he still had months in which to complete them. Two things Lee was frenziedly demanding: the com-
pletion of the fort, and the building of a bridge to secure the
retreat to the mainland of the force on Sullivan's Island.

If Moultrie was leisurely in the matter of the former, he was
entirely negligent on the subject of the latter. He had not, he
said, come there to retreat, and there was no need to be wasting
time, energy, and material in providing the means for it.

Lee's great experience of war had taught him to leave nothing
to chance. Moreover, in this instance he was fully persuaded that
the fort could not be held—particularly in its unfinished state—
against the powerful fleet under Sir Peter Parker standing off the
bar. He reckoned without two factors: the calm, cool courage of
its defender and the peculiar resisting quality of palmetto wood,
experience of which was not included in all his campaignings,
extensive and varied though they had been.

Action by the fleet was delayed until the end of June, in order
that with it might be combined the operation of a land force under
Sir Henry Clinton. This had been put ashore on Long Island with
the same object of reducing the fort, which was the key to the
harbour. To this end Clinton erected a battery which should cover
the transport and fording of troops across the narrow neck of
shallow water dividing the two islands. But to defend the passage
there was a battery on the east end of Sullivan's Island commanded by Colonel Thomson with a picked body of riflemen.

The defence of Fort Sullivan is one of the great epics of the
war, and few of its battles were of more far-reaching effect than

this, coming as it did in a time of some uncertainty in the affairs of the Americans.

At half-past ten o'clock on the morning of the 28th of June, Sir Peter Parker on board the flagship *Bristol* gave the signal for action, and the fleet of ten vessels, carrying two hundred and eighty-four guns, advanced to anchor before the fort, confidently to undertake the work of pounding it into dust.

At eleven o'clock that night, nine shattered ships dropped down to Five Fathom Hole, out of range, leaving the tenth—the frigate *Actæon*—crippled and aground to westward of the fort, there to be destroyed by fire the next morning.

Throughout the action, Moultrie's supplies of powder had been inadequate. Hence the need, not only for economy of fire, but for greater marksmanship, so that as few shots as possible should be wasted. And whilst the careful, steady fire from the fort battered the ships and made frightful carnage on their decks, the British shot sank more or less harmlessly into the soft, spongy palmetto logs or fell into the large moat in the middle of the fort where the fuses were extinguished before the shells could explode. It is said that of over fifty shots thrown by the *Thunder-Bomb* alone into the fort, not a single one exploded.

But if these did not, there were others that did, and although the casualties of the garrison were surprisingly small, yet throughout that terrible day of overpowering heat the Carolinians in Fort Sullivan may well have deemed themselves in hell. Toiling there, naked to the waist for the most part, under a pall of acrid smoke that hung low and heavy upon them and at times went near to choking them, and amid an incessant roar of guns, with shells bursting overhead, they fought on desperately and indomitably against a force they knew greatly superior to their own. And amongst them, ever where the need was greatest, hobbling hither and thither—for he was sorely harassed by gout at the time—was Moultrie in his blue coat and three-cornered hat, his rugged face calm, smoking his pipe as composedly as if he had been at his own fireside.

Only once did he and his officers, who in this matter emulated their leader, lay aside their pipes; and that was out of respect for General Lee, when in the course of the action he came down to see how things were with them, and to realize for himself that it was possible that with all his great experience of war he had been wrong in his assumption that the place could not be held.

The thing he chiefly dreaded had by then been averted. He had perceived that the fort's alarming weakness lay in the unfinished western side—the side that faced the main. Thence it might easily be enfiladed by any ship that ran past and took up a position in the channel. This vulnerable point had not been overlooked by Sir Peter Parker, and comparatively early in the battle he had ordered forward the *Sphynx*, the *Actœon*, and the *Syren* to attack it. But here Fortune helped the garrison that was so stoutly helping itself. In the haste of their advance the three ships fouled one another's rigging, became entangled, and drifted thus on to the shoal known as the "Middle Ground." Before they could clear themselves, the guns of the fort had been concentrated upon them, and poured into them a fire as destructive as it was accurate. The *Sphynx* and the *Syren* eventually got off in a mangled condition, one of them trailing her broken bowsprit. The *Actœon* remained to be destroyed at leisure.

And all this while, Myrtle, in apprehension which was increased to anguish when she remembered the manner of her parting with Harry, lay on the roof of the house on the Bay endeavouring thence by the aid of a telescope to follow the action that was being fought ten miles away, whilst the windows below rattled and the very world seemed to shake with the incessant thunder of the British guns and the slow, deliberate replies from the fort.

Once she saw that the flag—the first American flag displayed in the South; a blue flag with a white crescent in the dexter corner—was gone from the fort. And her dismay in that moment made her realize, as once before she had realized, the true feelings that underlay the crust of vain prejudice upon her soul. There followed a pause of dreadful uncertainty as to whether this meant surrender—the pause during which the heroic Sergeant Jasper leapt down from one of the embrasures in the face of a withering fire to rescue the flag which had been carried away by a chance shot. Attaching it to a sponge staff, he hoisted it once more upon the ramparts, and when she saw it fluttering there again, a faint cheer broke from her trembling lips and was taken up by the negro servant who shared her eyrie and some of her anxiety for the garrison among which was the master they all loved.

There she remained until after darkness had fallen, a darkness still rent and stabbed by the flashes from the guns, and until a terrific thunderstorm broke overhead and the artillery of heaven came to mingle with the artillery of man.

Then at last, unable to follow the combat with her eyes, and already drenched by the downpour which descended almost without warning, she allowed the slaves to lead her down from the rook, and went within to spend a sleepless night of anguish.

In the morning the news of victory filled Charles Town with joy and thanksgiving. It was a victory less complete than it might have been if Moultrie had not been starved of powder. With adequate ammunition, every ship of the British fleet would have been sunk or forced to surrender. But it was complete enough. The battered and defeated vessels were beaten off, and Charles Town was safe for the present.

Whole-heartedly Myrtle shared the general joy and thanksgiving. She knew herself now, she thought, beyond possibility of ever again being mistaken in her feelings. She had been through an experience of anguish, which had sharpened the sight of her soul so that she had come to see her own fault in the discords that had poisoned her married life. It should never, never be so again, she vowed, if only Harry were now safely restored to her. That was the abiding anxiety. Was he safe?

But amid the general rejoicing how could she doubt it? It was known that the casualties had been few in the fort, only some ten killed and twice that number wounded. Surely Heaven would not be so cruel as to include her husband among these.

She went actively about the house during that endless morning, stimulating all into preparations for welcoming Harry home, confident that he would come to her soon in the course of the day.

And come to her he did somewhere about noon, inanimate upon a stretcher borne by two of his men. The click of the garden-gate and the sound of steps on the gravel brought her, swift-footed, eager, to the porch, to swoon there under the shock of what she beheld, believing that it was a dead body those men bore.

When, restored to her senses, she was told that he still lived, though sorely wounded, she would have gone to him at once. But they restrained her—old Julius, Mauma Dido, and Dr. Parker, the latter having flown instantly to Harry's side in response to the news borne him by Hannibal of his master's homecoming.

The doctor, elderly and benevolent, and an old friend of Harry's, very gently broke to her the news that, although her husband's life was not to be despaired of, yet it hung by the most tenuous of threads, and that only the utmost care and vigilance could avoid the severing of this. He had been shot through the body in two places. One of these was a slight wound; but the other was grave, and Dr. Parker had only just extracted the bullet. He was easier now; but it would be better if she did not see him yet.

"But who is to tend and nurse him?" she inquired.

"We must provide for that."

"Who better than myself?"

"But you have not the strength, my dear," he demurred. "The very sight of him wounded has so affected you that . . ."

She interrupted him. "That shall not happen again," she promised firmly, and rose commanding her still trembling limbs. Although very white, she was so calm and so resolved, that presently Dr. Parker gave way, and permitted her at once to take up her duties by Harry's side.

He was delirious and fever-tossed, so that there was no danger of any excitement to him from her presence. She received the doctor's instructions attentively, displaying now the calm of an intrepid combatant, preparing for battle. And save for one concession to her emotions, when she knelt by his bedside and offered up a prayer that he might be spared to her, she did not again depart from that stern role.

Down in her heart there was an instinctive knowledge that she, herself, was in part responsible for his condition, even before Moultrie came, as he did later that day, to leave her, by the admissions she drew from him, no doubt upon that score.

It was like the kindly, easy-going soldier to find time amid the many preoccupations of the moment to seek her, all battle-stained as he was, to offer comfort and obtain news of Harry's condition.

"It is precarious," she answered him. "But Dr. Parker assures me that he is to be saved by care and vigilance, and these I can provide. Be sure that Harry shall get well again."

He marveled at her calm confidence; marveled, admired, and was reassured. Here was the spirit in which the battle of Fort Sullivan had been won by his gallant lads, the spirit which conquers all material things.

He spoke of the fight yesterday and of Harry's conduct in it, conduct of valour amounting to recklessness.

"If I had not known him for a man with every inducement to live, with everything to make life dear for him, I might almost have suspected him of courting death. Twice I had to order him down from the parapet, where he was needlessly exposing himself in his zeal to stimulate the men. And when the flag was carried away a second time by a shot from the *Bristol*, before I could stop him he had done what Jasper did on the first occasion of that happening. He was over the parapet and out on the sand under fire to rescue and bring back our standard. He was standing on the ramparts waving it to the men when he was shot. I caught him in my arms, and, desperately wounded as he was, at the moment I really think my chief emotion was anger with him that he should so recklessly have exposed himself."

When presently he left her, and she went back to Harry's bedside, where her place had been filled in her absence by Mauma

Dido, she took back with her the burning memory of Moultrie's words.

"If I had not known him for a man with every inducement to live, with everything to make life dear for him . . ."

And the truth, she told herself, was that, through her, he was become a man with every inducement to die. Deliberately he had sought death, that he might deliver her from a bond which had been forged by charity instead of love. For this was the lie she had led him to believe; this was the lie which, for a time, she had almost believed herself. Because he imagined that bond grown odious to her—and she had given him all cause so to imagine it—he had sought to snap it, that he might set her free.

How like him was that! How like the high-spirited selfless Harry she had always known! Impetuous and impulsive always, but always upon impulses to serve others. It was the service of others had made him a patriot, where a self-seeker of his wealth and prosperity under the Royal Government would have striven to avoid all change. Whether his political views were right or wrong, noble and altruistic they certainly were. For that she must honour him, and for that, too, since she was his wife, she must make his faith her own.

Never again, if it should please God in His infinite mercy to spare him, would she give him occasion to doubt her, or to suppose that anything but love had brought about that precipitate marriage of theirs. And if he should not be spared, why, then she would spend the wealth that she would inherit to the last penny in forwarding the cause he had espoused.

In such a spirit did she address herself to wrestle with the Angel of Death.

"The Edge of the Swamp"

WILLIAM GILMORE SIMMS (1806–1870)

William Gilmore Simms, today the best-known writer of the antebellum Charleston School, is principally remembered for his prose and for the volume of his work, which far exceeds that of his compatriots. As a young adult, Simms spent a lengthy period with his father in Mississippi. Their frequent travels by horseback through what was then the western frontier gave Simms the source material for his "border romances." After his return to Charleston, Simms married Chevilette Roche, heiress to Woodlands Plantation near Orangeburg.

Simms wrote both fiction and nonfiction, including essays and treatises. His novels are often divided into the categories of "border romances," including *The Yemassee* (1835), the fictional treatment of Indians in 1715 South Carolina, and the "Revolutionary War romances," such as *The Partisan* (1835), in which he creates a Falstaff-like character named Captain Porgy, and his last and possibly best known novel, *The Cassique of Kiawah* (1859). The "border romances" have been compared to the work of James Fenimore Cooper and Sir Walter Scott.

Simms also wrote a number of noteworthy poems; "The Edge of the Swamp" was taken by Louis D. Rubin, Jr. as the title for his collection of essays on the "literature and society of the old South."

In the two decades preceding the Civil War, Simms served in the South Carolina legislature. He contributed to numerous literary journals, including *Russell's Magazine*, and edited for a time the *Southern Quarterly Review*. He also carried on a then little-noticed feud with another major southern writer with Charleston connections, Edgar Allan Poe. At the time, Simms was the better known of the two. During the war, Simms's home at Woodlands was burned, and shortly thereafter his wife and four of his children died. He continued to make a living through his writing until his own death.

Simms was inducted into the South Carolina Academy of Authors in 1986.

'Tis a wild spot, and even in summer hours,
With wondrous wealth of beauty and a charm
For the sad fancy, hath the gloomiest look,
That awes with strange repulsion. There, the bird
Sings never merrily in the sombre trees,
That seem to have never known a term of youth,
Their young leaves all being blighted. A rank growth
Spreads venomously round, with power to taint;
And blistering dews await the thoughtless hand
That rudely parts the thicket. Cypresses,
Each a great ghastly giant, eld and gray,
Stride o'er the dusk, dank tract,—with buttresses
Spread round, apart, not seeming to sustain,
Yet link'd by secret twines, that underneath,
Blend with each arching trunk. Fantastic vines,
That swing like monstrous serpents in the sun,
Bind top to top, until the encircling trees
Group all in close embrace. Vast skeletons
Of forests, that have perish'd ages gone,
Moulder, in mighty masses, on the plain;
Now buried in some dark and mystic tarn,
Or sprawl'd above it, resting on great arms,
And making, for the opossum and the fox,
Bridges, that help them as they roam by night.
Alternate stream and lake, between the banks,
Glimmer in doubtful light: smooth, silent, dark,
They tell not what they harbor; but, beware!
Lest, rising to the tree on which you stand,
You sudden see the moccasin snake heave up
His yellow shining belly and flat head
Of burnish'd copper. Stretch'd at length, behold
Where yonder Cayman, in his natural home,
The mammoth lizard, all his armor on,
Slumbers half-buried in the sedgy grass,
Beside the green ooze where he shelters him.
The place, so like the gloomiest realm of death,

Is yet the abode of thousand forms of life,—
The terrible, the beautiful, the strange,—
Winged and creeping creatures, such as make
The instinctive flesh with apprehension crawl,
When sudden we behold. Hark! at our voice
The whooping crane, gaunt fisher in these realms,
Erects his skeleton form and shrieks in flight,
On great white wings. A pair of summer ducks,
Most princely in their plumage, as they hear
His cry, with senses quickening all to fear,
Dash up from the lagoon with marvelous haste,
Following his guidance. See! aroused by these,
And startled by our progress o'er the stream,
The steel-jaw'd Cayman, from his grassy slope,
Slides silent to the slimy green abode,
Which is his province. You behold him now,
His bristling back uprising as he speeds
To safety, in the center of the lake,
Whence his head peers alone,—a shapeless knot,
That shows no sign of life; the hooded eye,
Nathless, being ever vigilant and sharp,
Measuring the victim. See! a butterfly,
That, traveling all the day, has counted climes
Only by flowers, to rest himself a while,
And, as a wanderer in a foreign land,
To pause and look around him ere he goes,
Lights on the monster's brow. The surly mute
Straightway goes down; so suddenly, that he,
The dandy of the summer flowers and woods,
Dips his light wings, and soils his golden coat,
With the rank waters of the turbid lake.
Wondering and vex'd, the plumed citizen
Flies with an eager terror to the banks,
Seeking more genial natures,—but in vain.
Here are no gardens such as he desires,
No innocent flowers of beauty, no delights

Of sweetness free from taint. The genial growth
He loves, finds here no harbor. Fetid shrubs,
That scent the gloomy atmosphere, offend
His pure patrician fancies. On the trees,
That look like felon spectres, he beholds
No blossoming beauties; and for smiling heavens,
That flutter his wings with breezes of pure balm,
He nothing sees but sadness—aspects dread,
That gather frowning, cloud and fiend in one,
As if in combat, fiercely to defend
Their empire from the intrusive wing and beam.
The example of the butterfly be ours.
He spreads his lacquer'd wings above the trees,
And speeds with free flight, warning us to seek
For a more genial home, and couch more sweet
Than these drear borders offer us to-night.

"A Day at Chee-ha"

WILLIAM ELLIOTT (1788–1863)

William Elliott was descended from a Beaufort County, South Carolina, family of social distinction. Following his education at Harvard University, Elliott returned home in 1808 to take over the administration of the family plantation after the death of his father. He served in the South Carolina legislature, but in 1832 he stood down from his seat because of his opposition to nullification. From that time until the outbreak of the Civil War, his writing career developed. He also traveled extensively and lectured frequently on agricultural topics, representing South Carolina in the 1855 Paris Exposition. Elliott vehemently opposed secession but sided with the Confederacy once the war began. Like so many planters, he lost virtually everything when the Confederacy crumbled. He died before the war ended.

The tale included below comes from his best-known volume, *Carolina Sports by Land and Water; Including Incidents of Devilfishing, Wildcat, Deer, and Bear Hunting, Etc.* (1846), a collection of hunting and fishing tales that gives an excellent picture of country life in the Lowcountry in the early part of the nineteenth century. Derived from the style of James Boswell's eighteenth-century English essays, these pieces offer an approach to hunting not dissimilar to that of sportsmen today. Today a historical marker on Highway 17 commemorates the "Temple of Sport" described by Elliott.

The traveler in South Carolina, who passes along the road between the Ashepoo and Combahee rivers will be struck by the appearance of two lofty white columns, rising among the pines that skirt the road. They are the only survivors of eight, which supported, in times anterior to our revolutionary war, a sylvan temple, erected by a gentleman, who, to the higher qualities of a devoted patriot, united the taste and liberality of the sportsman. The spot was admirably chosen, being on the brow of a piney ridge, which slopes away at a long gun-shot's length into a thick swamp; and many a deer has, we doubt not, in times past, been shot from the temple when it stood in its pride—as we ourselves have struck them from its ruins. From this ruin, stretching east-wardly some twelve to fourteen miles, is a neck of land, known from the Indian name of the small river that waters and almost bisects it, as Chee-ha—or, as it is incorrectly written, Chy-haw! It is now the best hunting-ground in Carolina—for which the following reasons may be given. The lands are distributed in large tracts; there are therefore few proprietors. The rich land is confined to the belt of the rivers, and there remains a wide expanse of barrens, traversed by deep swamps, always difficult and sometimes impassable, in which the deer find a secure retreat.

At a small hunting-lodge located in this region, it has often been my good fortune to meet a select body of hunting friends, and enjoy in their company the pleasures of the chase.

I give you one of my "days"—not that the success was unusual, it was by no means so; but that it was somewhat more marked by incident than most of its fellows. We turned out, *after breakfast*, on a fine day in February, with a pack of twelve hounds, and two whippers in, or drivers, as we call them. The field consisted of one old shot besides myself, and two sports-men who had not "fleshed their maiden swords." When we reached the ground, we had to experience the fate which all tardy sportsmen deserve, and must often undergo: the fresh print of dogs' feet, and the deep impression of horses' hoofs, showed us that another party had anticipated us in the drive, and that the game had been started and was off. Two expedients suggested themselves—we must either leave our ground, and in that case incur the risk of sharing the same fate in our next drive; or, we must beat up the ground now before us in a way which our predecessors in the field had probably neglected to do. We chose the latter part: and finding that the drive embraced two descriptions of ground— first, the main wood, which we inferred had already been taken, and next, the briery thickets that skirted a contiguous old field—into these thickets we pushed. Nor had we entered far, before the long, deep, querulous note of "Ruler," as he challenged on a trail, told us to expect the game. A few minutes later, and the whole pack announced the still more exciting fact—"the game is up." The first move of the deer was into a back-water, which he crossed, while the pack, half swimming, half wading, came yelping at his heels. He next dashed across an old field and made for a thicket, which he entered; it was a piece of briery and tangled ground, which the dogs could not traverse without infinite toil. By these two moves, he gained a great start of the hounds: if he kept on, we were thrown out, and our dogs lost for the day—if he doubled, and the nature of the ground favored that supposition, there were two points whereat he would be most likely to be intercepted. I consulted the wind, and made my choice. I was wrong. It proved to be a young deer, who did not need the wind, and he made for the pass I had *not selected*. The pack now turned; we found from their cry, that the deer had doubled, and our hearts beat high with expectation, as mounted on our respective hunters, we stretched ourselves across the old field which he must necessarily traverse, before he could regain the shelter of the wood. And now I saw my veteran comrade stretch his neck as if he spied something in the thicket; then with a sudden fling he brought his double barrel to his shoulder and fired. His horse, admonished by the spur, then fetched a caracole; from the new position, a new glimpse of the deer is gained—and crack! goes the second barrel. In a few moments, I saw one of our recruits dismount and fire. Soon after, the deer made his appearance and approached the second, who descended from his horse and fired. The deer kept on seemingly untouched, and had gained the crown of the hill when his second barrel brought him to the ground in sight of the whole field. We all rode to the spot, to congratulate our novice on his first exploit in sylvan warfare—when, as he stooped to examine the direction of his shot, our friend Loveleap slipped his knife into the throat of the deer, and before his purpose could be guessed at, bathed his face with the blood of his victim. (This, you must know, is *hunter's law* with us, on killing a first deer.)

As our young sportsman started up from the ablution—his face glaring like an Indian chief's in all the splendor of war-paint—Robin the hunter touched his cap and thus accosted him:

"Maussa Tickle, if you wash off dat blood dis day—you neber hab luck again so long as you hunt."

"Wash it off!" cried we all, with one accord; "who ever heard of such a folly. He can be no true sportsman, who is ashamed of such a livery."

Thus beset, and moved thereunto, by other sage advices showered upon him by his companions in sport, he wore his bloody mask to the close of that long day's sport, and sooth to say, returned to receive the congratulations of his young and lovely wife, his face still adorned with the stains of victory. Whether he was received, as victors are wont to be, returning from other fields of blood, is a point whereon I shall refuse to satisfy the impertinent curiosity of my reader; but I am bound, in deference to historic truth, to add—that the claims of our novice, to the merit and penalties of this day's hunt, were equally incomplete, for it appeared on after inspection, that Loveleap had given the mortal wound, and that Tickle had merely given the "coup de grâce" to a deer, that, if unfired on, would have fallen of itself, in a run of a hundred yards. It must be believed, however, that we were quite too generous to divulge this unpleasant discovery to our novice, in the first pride of his triumph!

And now we tried other grounds, which our precursors in the field had already beaten; so that the prime of the day was wasted before we made another start. At last, in the afternoon, a splendid burst from the whole pack made us aware that a second deer had suddenly been roused. I was riding to reach a pass (or *stand* as we term it), when I saw a buck dashing along before the hounds at the top of his speed; the distance was seventy-five yards—but I reined in my horse and let slip at him. To my surprise, he fell; but before I could reach the spot, from which I was separated by a thick underwood, he had shuffled off and disappeared. The hounds came roaring on, and showed me by their course that he had made for a marsh that lay hard by. For that we all pushed in hopes of anticipating him. He was before us, we saw him plunge into the canal, and mount the opposite bank, though evidently in distress and crippled in one of his hind legs. The dogs rush furiously on (the scent of blood in their nostrils), plunge into the canal, sweep over the bank, and soon pursuers and pursued are shut out from sight, as they wind among the thick covers that lie scattered over the face of the marsh.

"What use of horse now!" said Robin, as (sliding from his saddle where his horse instinctively made a dead halt at the edge of the impracticable Serbonian bog that lay before him) he began to climb a tree that overlooked the field of action—"what use of horse now?"

From this "vantage ground," however, he looked in vain to catch a glimpse of the deer. The eye of a lynx could not penetrate the thick mass of grass, that stretched upward six feet from the surface of the marsh. The cry of the hounds now grew faint from distance, and now again came swelling on the breeze; when suddenly our ears were saluted by a full burst from the whole pack, in that loud, open note, which tells a practised ear that the cry comes from the water.

"Zounds, Robin!" cried I, in the excitement of the moment, "they have him at bay there—there in the canal. Down from your perch, my lad, or they'll eat him, horns and all, before you reach him."

Robin apparently did not partake of this enthusiasm, for he maintained his perch on the tree, and coolly observed—"What use, maussa? fore I git dere, dem dog polish ebery bone."

"You are afraid, you rascal! you have only to swim the canal and then—"

"Got maussa," said Robin, as he looked ruefully over the field of his proposed missionary labors; "if he be water, I swim 'um— if he be bog, I bog 'um—if he be brier, I kratch tru 'um—but who de debble, but otter, no so alligator, go tru all tree one time!"

The thought was just stealing its way into my mind, that under the excitement of my feelings, I was giving an order that I might have hesitated personally to execute, when the cry of the hounds, lately so clamorous, totally ceased. "There," cried I, in the disappointed tone of a sportsman who had lost a fine buck, "save your skin, you loitering rascal! You may sleep where you sit, for by this time they have eaten him sure enough." This conclusion was soon overset by the solitary cry of Ruler, which was now heard, half a mile to the left of the scene of the late uproar.

"Again! What is this? *It is* the cry of Ruler! ho! I understand it—the deer is not eaten, but has taken the canal—and the nose of that prince of hounds, has scented him down the running stream.—Aye, aye, he makes for the wood—and now to cut him off." No sooner said than done. I gave the spur to my horse, and shot off accordingly; but not in time to prevent the success of the masterly manœuver by which the buck, baffling his pursuers, was now seen straining every nerve to regain the shelter of the wood. I made a desperate effort to cut him off, but reached the wood only in time to note the direction he had taken. It was now sunset, and the white, outspread tail of the deer was my only guide in the pursuit, as he glided among the trees. "Now for it, Boxer—show your speed, my gallant nag." The horse, as if he entered fully into the purpose of his rider, stretched himself to the utmost, obedient to the slightest touch of the reins, as he threaded the intricacies of the forest; and was gaining rapidly on the deer, when plash! he came to a dead halt—his fore legs plunged in a quagmire, over which the buck with his split hoofs had bounded in security. What a baulk! "but here goes"—and the gun was brought instantly to the shoulder, and the left-hand barrel fired. The distance was eighty yards, and the shot ineffectual. Making a slight circuit to avoid the bog, I again push at the deer and again approach. "Ah, if I had but reserved the charge, I had so idly wasted!" But no matter, I must run him down—and gaining a position on his flank, I spurred my horse full upon his broad-side, to bear him to the ground. The noble animal (he *was* a noble animal, for he traced, with some baser admixture indeed, through Boxer, Medley, Gimcrack, to the Godolphin Arabian) refused to trample on his fellow quadruped; and, in spite of the goading spur, ranged up close along side of the buck, as if his only pride lay in surpassing him in speed. This brought me in close contact with the buck. Detaching my right foot from the stirrup, I struck the armed heel of my boot full against his head; he reeled from the blow and plunged into a neighboring thicket—too close for horse to enter. I fling myself from my horse, and pursue on foot—he gains on me: I dash down my now useless gun, and, freed from all encumbrance, press after the panting animal. A large, fallen oak lies across his path; he gathers himself up for the leap, and falls exhausted directly across it. Before he could recover his legs, and while he lay thus poised on the tree, I fling myself at full length upon the body of the struggling deer—my left hand clasps his neck, while my right detaches the knife; whose fatal blade, in another moment, is buried in his throat. There he lay in his blood, and I remained sole occupant of the field. I seize my horn, but am utterly breathless, and incapable of sounding it: I strive to shout, but my voice is extinct from fatigue and exhaustion. I retrace my steps, while the waning light yet sufficed to show me the track of the deer—recover my horse and gun, and return to the tree where my victim lay. But how apprise my comrades of my position? My last shot, however, had not been unnoted—and soon their voices are heard cheering on "Ruler," while far in advance of the yet baffled pack, he follows unerringly on the tracks of the deer. They came at last: but found me still so exhausted from fatigue, that to wave my blood knife, and point to the victim where he lay at my feet, were all the history I could then give of the spirit-stirring incidents I have just recorded. Other hunting matches have I been engaged in, wherein double the number of deer have been killed; but never have I engaged in one of deeper and more absorbing interest, than that which marked this "day at Chee-ha."

from "The Gold Bug"

EDGAR ALLAN POE (1809–1849)

Edgar Allan Poe surely had no recollection of his first visit to Charleston as the infant child of traveling actors. It is uncertain what became of Poe's father, but upon his mother's death in 1811 the three-year-old Poe was adopted (though not legally) by John Allan, a merchant of Scottish birth. Poe attended schools in England and Richmond and later entered the University of Virginia at Charlottesville for a short sojourn. Although he performed well academically, especially in English and foreign languages, Poe apparently spent a good deal of his time engaged in hard drinking and gambling. His vices yielded enormous debts, which his foster father refused to cover.

In May 1827, Poe enlisted in the U.S. Army under the name Edgar Perry. The regiment to which he belonged was dispatched to Fort Moultrie on Sullivan's Island, from which Gen. William Moultrie had repulsed the British attack on Charleston harbor in 1776. During the time that Poe was billeted to the fort, he wrote the poems "Al Aaraaf" and "To Science." Clearly, his year and a half on Sullivan's Island provided images that remained with him throughout his life, as is evident in "The Oblong Box" (1844), "The Balloon Hoax" (1850), and "The Gold Bug" (1843), excerpted below, in which the romantic landscape of the Lowcountry serves as a setting. The end of "The Gold Bug," a detailed explanation of cryptograms, is not included here.

What ho! what ho! this fellow is dancing mad!
He hath been bitten by the Tarantula.
All in the Wrong.

Many years ago, I contracted an intimacy with a Mr. William Legrand. He was of an ancient Huguenot family, and had once been wealthy; but a series of misfortunes had reduced him to want. To avoid the mortification consequent upon his disasters, he left New Orleans, the city of his forefathers, and took up his residence at Sullivan's Island, near Charleston, South Carolina.

This Island is a very singular one. It consists of little else than the sea sand, and is about three miles long. Its breadth at no point exceeds a quarter of a mile. It is separated from the main land by a scarcely perceptible creek, oozing its way through a wilderness of reeds and slime, a favorite resort of the marsh hen. The vegetation, as might be supposed, is scant, or at least dwarfish. No trees of any magnitude are to be seen. Near the western extremity, where Fort Moultrie stands, and where are some miserable frame buildings, tenanted, during summer, by the fugitives from Charleston dust and fever, may be found, indeed, the bristly palmetto; but the whole island, with the exception of this western point, and a line of hard, white beach on the seacoast, is covered with a dense undergrowth of the sweet myrtle, so much prized by the horticulturists of England. The shrub here often attains the height of fifteen or twenty feet, and forms an almost impenetrable coppice, burthening the air with its fragrance.

In the inmost recesses of this coppice, not far from the eastern or more remote end of the island, Legrand had built himself a small hut, which he occupied when I first, by mere accident, made his acquaintance. This soon ripened into friendship—for there was much in the recluse to excite interest and esteem. I found him well educated, with unusual powers of mind, but infected with misanthropy, and subject to perverse moods of alternate enthusiasm and melancholy. He had with him many books, but rarely employed them. His chief amusements were gunning and fishing, or sauntering along the bank and through the myrtles, in quest of shells or entomological specimens;—his collection of the latter might have been envied by a Swammerdamm. In these excursions he was usually accompanied by an old negro, called Jupiter, who had been manumitted before the reverses of the family, but who could not be induced, neither by threats nor by promises, to abandon what he considered his right of attendance upon the footsteps of his young

"Massa Will." It is not improbable that the relatives of Legrand, conceiving him to be somewhat unsettled in intellect, had contrived to instill this obstinacy into Jupiter, with a view to the supervision and guardianship of the wanderer.

The winters in the latitude of Sullivan's Island are seldom very severe, and in the fall of the year it is a rare event indeed when a fire is considered necessary. About the middle of October, 18—, there occurred, however, a day of remarkable chilliness. Just before sunset I scrambled my way through the evergreens to the hut of my friend, whom I had not visited for several weeks—my residence being, at that time, in Charleston, a distance of nine miles from the island, while the facilities of passage and re-passage were very far behind those of the present day. Upon reaching the hut I rapped, as was my custom, and getting no reply, sought for the key where I knew it was secreted, unlocked the door and went in. A fine fire was blazing upon the hearth. It was a novelty, and by no means an unwelcome one. I threw off an overcoat, took an armchair by the crackling logs, and awaited patiently the arrival of my hosts.

Soon after dark they arrived, and gave me a most cordial welcome. Jupiter, grinning from ear to ear, bustled about to prepare some marsh-hens for supper. Legrand was in one of his fits— how else shall I term them?—of enthusiasm. He had found an unknown bivalve, forming a new genus, and, more than this, he had hunted down and secured, with Jupiter's assistance, a *scarabæus* which he believed to be totally new, but in respect to which he wished to have my opinion on the morrow.

"And why not to-night?" I asked, rubbing my hands over the blaze, and wishing the whole tribe of *scarabæi* at the devil.

"Ah, if I had only known you were here!" said Legrand, "but it's so long since I saw you; and how could I foresee that you would pay me a visit this very night of all others? As I was coming home I met Lieutenant G—, from the fort, and, very foolishly, I lent him the bug; so it will be impossible for you to see it until the morning. Stay here to-night, and I will send Jup down for it at sunrise. It is the loveliest thing in creation!"

"What?—sunrise?"

"Nonsense! no!—the bug. It is of a brilliant gold color—about the size of a large hickory-nut—with two jet black spots near one extremity of the back, and another, somewhat longer, at the other. The *antennæ* are—"

"Dey aint *no* tin in him, Massa Will, I keep a tellin on you," here interrupted Jupiter; "de bug is a goole bug, solid, ebery bit of him, inside and all, sep him wing—neber feel half so hebby a bug in my life."

"Well, suppose it is, Jup," replied Legrand, somewhat more earnestly, it seemed to me, than the occasion demanded, "is that any reason for your letting the birds burn? The color"—here he turned to me—"is really almost enough to warrant Jupiter's idea. You never saw a more brilliant metallic lustre than the scales emit—but of this you cannot judge till to-morrow. In the mean time I can give you some idea of the shape." Saying this, he seated himself at a small table, on which were a pen and ink, but no paper. He looked for some in a drawer, but found none.

"Never mind," said he at length, "this will answer"; and he drew from his waistcoat pocket a scrap of what I took to be very dirty foolscap, and made upon it a rough drawing with the pen. While he did this, I retained my seat by the fire, for I was still chilly. When the design was complete, he handed it to me without rising. As I received it, a loud growl was heard, succeeded by a scratching at the door. Jupiter opened it, and a large Newfoundland, belonging to Legrand, rushed in, leaped upon my shoulders, and loaded me with caresses; for I had shown him much attention during previous visits. When his gambols were over, I looked at the paper, and, to speak the truth, found myself not a little puzzled at what my friend had depicted.

"Well!" I said, after contemplating it for some minutes, "this is a strange *scarabæus*, I must confess: new to me: never saw anything like it before—unless it was a skull, or a death's-head—which it more nearly resembles than anything else that has come under *my* observation."

"A death's-head!" echoed Legrand, "Oh—yes—well, it has something of that appearance upon paper, no doubt. The two upper black spots look like eyes, eh? and the longer one at the bottom like a mouth—and then the shape of the whole is oval."

"Perhaps so," said I; "but, Legrand, I fear you are no artist. I must wait until I see the beetle itself, if I am to form any idea of its personal appearance."

"Well, I don't know," said he, a little nettled, "I draw tolerably—*should* do it at least—have had good masters, and flatter myself that I am not quite a blockhead."

"But, my dear fellow, you are joking then," said I, "this is a very passable *skull*—indeed, I may say that it is a very *excellent* skull, according to the vulgar notions about such specimens of physiology—and your *scarabæus* must be the queerest *scarabæus* in the world if it resembles it. Why, we may get up a very thrilling bit of superstition upon this hint. I presume you will call the bug *scarabæus caput hominis*, or something of that kind—there are many similar titles in the Natural Histories. But where are the *antennæ* you spoke of?"

"The *antennæ*!" said Legrand, who seemed to be getting unaccountably warm upon the subject; "I am sure you must see the *antennæ*. I made them as distinct as they are in the original insect, and I presume that is sufficient."

"Well, well," I said, "perhaps you have—still I don't see them"; and I handed him the paper without additional remark, not wishing to ruffle his temper; but I was much surprised at the turn affairs had taken; his ill humor puzzled me—and, as for the drawing of the beetle, there were positively *no antennæ* visible, and the whole *did* bear a very close resemblance to the ordinary cut of a death's-head.

He received the paper very peevishly, and was about to crumple it, apparently to throw it in the fire, when a casual glance at the design seemed suddenly to rivet his attention. In an instant his face grew violently red—in another as excessively pale. For some minutes he continued to scrutinize the drawing minutely where he sat. At length he arose, took a candle from the table, and proceeded to seat himself upon a sea-chest in the farthest corner of the room. Here again he made an anxious examination of the paper; turning it in all directions. He said nothing, however, and his conduct greatly astonished me; yet I thought it prudent not to exacerbate the growing moodiness of his temper by any comment. Presently he took from his coat pocket a wallet, placed the paper carefully in it, and deposited both in a writing-desk, which he locked. He now grew more composed in his demeanor; but his original air of enthusiasm had quite disappeared. Yet he seemed not so much sulky as abstracted. As the evening wore away he became more and more absorbed in reverie, from which no sallies of mine could arouse him. It had been my intention to pass the night at the hut, as I had frequently done before, but, seeing my host in this mood, I deemed it proper to take leave. He did not press me to remain, but, as I departed, he shook my hand with even more than his usual cordiality.

It was about a month after this (and during the interval I had seen nothing of Legrand) when I received a visit, at Charleston, from his man, Jupiter. I had never seen the good old negro look so dispirited, and I feared that some serious disaster had befallen my friend.

"Well, Jup," said I, "what is the matter now?—how is your master?"

"Why, to speak de troof, massa, him not so berry well as mought be."

"Not well! I am truly sorry to hear it. What does he complain of?"

"Dar! dat's it!—him neber plain ob notin—but him berry sick for all dat."

"*Very* sick, Jupiter!—why didn't you say so at once? Is he confined to bed?"

"No, dat he aint!—he aint find nowhar—dat's just whar de shoe pinch—my mind is got to be berry hebby bout poor Massa Will."

"Jupiter, I should like to understand what it is you are talking about. You say your master is sick. Hasn't he told you what ails him?"

"Why, massa, taint worf while for to git mad about de matter—Massa Will say noffin at all aint de matter wid him—but den what make him go about looking dis here way, wid he head down and he soldiers up, and as white as a gose? And den he keep a syphon all de time—"

"Keeps a what, Jupiter?"

"Keeps a syphon wid de figgurs on de slate—de queerest figgurs I ebber did see. Ise gittin to be skeered, I tell you. Hab for to keep mighty tight eye pon him noovers. Todder day he gib me slip fore de sun up and was gone de whole ob de blessed day. I had a big stick ready cut for to gib him d—n good beatin when he did come—but Ise sich a fool dat I hadn't de heart arter all—he look so berry poorly."

"Eh?—what?—ah yes!—upon the whole I think you had better not be too severe with the poor fellow—don't flog him, Jupiter—he can't very well stand it—but can you form no idea of what has occasioned this illness, or rather this change of conduct? Has anything unpleasant happened since I saw you?"

"No, massa, dey aint bin noffin onpleasant *since* den— 'twas *fore* den I'm feared—'twas de berry day you was dare."

"How? what do you mean?"

"Why, massa, I mean de bug—dare now."

"The what?"

"De bug—I'm berry sartain dat Massa Will bin bit somewhere bout de head by dat d—n goole-bug."

"And what cause have you, Jupiter, for such a supposition?"

"Claws enuff, massa, and mouff too. I nebber did see sich a d—n bug—he kick and he bite ebery ting what cum near him. Massa Will cotch him fuss, but had for to let him go gin mighty quick, I tell you—den was de time he must ha got de bite. I didn't like de look oh de bug mouff, myself, no how, so I wouldn't take hold ob him wid my finger, but cotch him wid a piece ob paper dat I found. I rap him up in de paper and stuff piece ob it in he mouff—dat was de way."

"And you think, then, that your master was really bitten by the beetle, and that the bite made him sick?"

"I don't tink noffin about it—I nose it. What make him dream bout de goole so much, if taint cause he bit by de goole-bug? Ise heerd bout dem goole-bugs fore dis."

"But how do you know he dreams about gold?"

"How I know? why cause he talk about it in he sleep—dat's how I nose."

"Well, Jup, perhaps you are right; but to what fortunate circumstance am I to attribute the honor of a visit from you today?"

"What de matter, massa?"

"Did you bring any message from Mr. Legrand?"

"No, massa, I bring dis here pissel"; and here Jupiter handed me a note which ran thus:

My Dear—

Why have I not seen you for so long a time? I hope you have not been so foolish as to take offence at any little brusquerie of mine; but no, that is improbable.

Since I saw you I have had great cause for anxiety. I have something to tell you, yet scarcely know how to tell it, or whether I should tell it at all.

I have not been quite well for some days past, and poor old Jup annoys me, almost beyond endurance, by his well-meant attentions. Would you believe it?—he had prepared a huge stick, the other day, with which to chastise me for giving him the slip, and spending the day, solus, among the hills on the main land. I verily believe that my ill looks alone saved me a flogging.

I have made no addition to my cabinet since we met.

If you can, in any way, make it convenient, come over with Jupiter. Do come. I wish to see you to-night, upon business of importance.. I assure you that it is of the highest importance.

Ever yours,

William Legrand

There was something in the tone of this note which gave me great uneasiness. Its whole style differed materially from that of Legrand. What could he be dreaming of? What new crotchet possessed his excitable brain? What "business of the highest importance" could *he* possibly have to transact? Jupiter's account of him boded no good. I dreaded lest the continued pressure of misfortune had, at length, fairly unsettled the reason of my friend. Without a moment's hesitation, therefore, I prepared to accompany the negro.

Upon reaching the wharf, I noticed a scythe and three spades, all apparently new, lying in the bottom of the boat in which we were to embark.

"What is the meaning of all this, Jup?" I inquired.

"Him syfe, massa, and spade."

"Very true; but what are they doing here?"

"Him de syfe and de spade what Massa Will sis pon my buying for him in de town, and de debbil's own lot of money I had to gib for em."

"But what, in the name of all that is mysterious, is your 'Massa Will' going to do with scythes and spades?"

"Dat's more dan *I* know, and debbil take me if I don't blieve 'tis more dan he know, too. But it's all cum ob de bug."

Finding that no satisfaction was to be obtained of Jupiter, whose whole intellect seemed to be absorbed by "de bug," I now stepped into the boat and made sail. With a fair and strong breeze we soon ran into the little cove to the northward of Fort Moultrie, and a walk of some two miles brought us to the hut. It was about three in the afternoon when we arrived. Legrand had been awaiting us in eager expectation. He grasped my hand with a nervous *empressement* which alarmed me and strengthened the suspicions already entertained. His countenance was pale even to ghastliness, and his deep-set eyes glared with unnatural lustre. After some inquiries respecting his health, I asked him, not knowing what better to say, if he had yet obtained the *scarabæus* from Lieutenant G—.

"Oh, yes," he replied, coloring violently, "I got it from him the next morning. Nothing should tempt me to part with that *scarabæus*. Do you know that Jupiter is quite right about it?"

"In what way?" I asked, with a sad foreboding at heart.

"In supposing it to be a bug of *real gold*." He said this with an air of profound seriousness, and I felt inexpressibly shocked.

"This bug is to make my fortune," he continued, with a triumphant smile, "to reinstate me in my family possessions. Is it any wonder, then, that I prize it? Since Fortune has thought fit to bestow it upon me, I have only to use it properly and I shall arrive at the gold of which it is the index. Jupiter; bring me that *scarabæus*!"

"What! de bug, massa? I'd rudder not go fer to trubble dat bug—you mus git him for your own self." Hereupon Legrand arose, with a grave and stately air, and brought me the beetle from a glass case in which it was enclosed. It was a beautiful *scarabæus*, and, at that time, unknown to naturalists—of course a great prize in a scientific point of view. There were two round, black spots near one extremity of the back, and a longer one near the other. The scales were exceedingly hard and glossy, with all the appearance of burnished gold. The weight of the insect was very remarkable, and, taking all things into consideration, I could hardly blame Jupiter for his opinion respecting it; but what to make of Legrand's concordance with that opinion, I could not, for the life of me, tell.

"I sent for you," said he, in a grandiloquent tone, when I had completed my examination of the beetle, "I sent for you, that I might have your counsel and assistance in furthering the views of Fate and of the bug—"

"My dear Legrand," I cried, interrupting him, "you are certainly unwell, and had better use some little precautions. You shall go to bed, and I will remain with you a few days, until you get over this. You are feverish and—"

"Feel my pulse," said he.

I felt it, and, to say the truth, found not the slightest indication of fever.

"But you may be ill and yet have no fever. Allow me this once to prescribe for you. In the first place, go to bed. In the next—"

"You are mistaken," he interposed, "I am as well as I can expect to be under the excitement which I suffer. If you really wish me well, you will relieve this excitement."

"And how is this to be done?"

"Very easily. Jupiter and myself are going upon an expedition into the hills, upon the main land, and, in this expedition, we shall need the aid of some person in whom we can confide. You are the only one we can trust. Whether we succeed or fail, the excitement which you now perceive in me will be equally allayed."

"I am anxious to oblige you in any way," I replied; "but do you mean to say that this infernal beetle has any connection with your expedition into the hills?"

"It has."

"Then, Legrand, I can become a party to no such absurd proceeding."

"I am sorry—very sorry—for we shall have to try it by ourselves."

"Try it by yourselves! The man is surely mad!—but stay!—how long do you propose to be absent?"

"Probably all night. We shall start immediately, and be back, at all events, by sunrise."

"And will you promise me, upon your honor, that when this freak of yours is over, and the bug business (good God!) settled to your satisfaction, you will then return home and follow my advice implicitly, as that of your physician?"

"Yes; I promise; and now let us be off, for we have no time to lose."

With a heavy heart I accompanied my friend. We started about four o'clock—Legrand, Jupiter, the dog, and myself. Jupiter had with him the scythe and spades—the whole of which he insisted upon carrying—more through fear, it seemed to me, of trusting either of the implements within reach of his master, than from any excess of industry or complaisance. His demeanor was dogged in the extreme, and "dat d—n bug" were the sole words which escaped his lips during the journey. For my own part, I had charge of a couple of dark lanterns, while Legrand contented himself with the *scarabæus*, which he carried attached to the end of a bit of whip-cord; twirling it to and fro, with the air of a conjuror, as he went. When I observed this last, plain evidence of my friend's aberration of mind, I could scarcely refrain from tears. I thought it best, however, to humor his fancy, at least for the present, or until I could adopt some more energetic measures with a chance of success. In the meantime I endeavored, but all in vain, to sound him in regard to the object of the expedition. Having succeeded in inducing me to accompany him, he seemed unwilling to hold conversation upon any topic of minor importance, and to all my questions vouchsafed no other reply than "we shall see!"

We crossed the creek at the head of the island by means of a skiff; and, ascending the high grounds on the shore of the main land, proceeded in a northwesterly direction, through a tract of country excessively wild and desolate, where no trace of a human footstep was to be seen. Legrand led the way with decision; pausing only for an instant, here and there, to consult what appeared to be certain landmarks of his own contrivance upon a former occasion.

In this manner we journeyed for about two hours, and the sun was just setting when we entered a region infinitely more dreary than any yet seen. It was a species of table land, near the summit of an almost inaccessible hill, densely wooded from base to pinnacle, and interspersed with huge crags that appeared to lie loosely upon the soil, and in many cases were prevented from precipitating themselves into the valleys below, merely by the support of the trees against which they reclined. Deep ravines, in various directions, gave an air of still sterner solemnity to the scene.

The natural platform to which we had clambered was thickly overgrown with brambles, through which we soon discovered that it would have been impossible to force our way but for the scythe; and Jupiter, by direction of his master, proceeded to clear for us a path to the foot of an enormously tall tulip-tree, which stood, with some eight or ten oaks, upon the level, and far surpassed them all, and all other trees which I had then ever seen, in the beauty of its foliage and form, in the wide spread of its branches, and in the general majesty of its appearance. When we reached this tree, Legrand turned to Jupiter, and asked him if he thought he could climb it. The old man seemed a little staggered by the question, and for some moments made no reply. At length he approached the huge trunk, walked slowly around it, and examined it with minute attention. When he had completed his scrutiny, he merely said, "Yes, massa, Jup climb any tree he ebber see in he life."

"Then up with you as soon as possible, for it will soon be too dark to see what we are about."

"How far mus go up, massa?" inquired Jupiter.

"Get up the main trunk first, and then I will tell you which way to go—and here—stop! take this beetle with you."

"De bug, Massa Will!—de goole bug!" cried the negro, drawing back in dismay—"what for mus tote de bug way up de tree?—d—n if I do!"

"If you are afraid, Jup, a great big negro like you, to take hold of a harmless little dead beetle, why you can carry it up by this string—but, if you do not take it up with you in some way, I shall be under the necessity of breaking your head with this shovel."

"What de matter now, massa?" said Jup, evidently shamed into compliance; "always want for to raise fuss wid old nigger. Was only funnin any how. Me feered de bug! what I keer for de bug?" Here he took cautiously hold of the extreme end of the string, and, maintaining the insect as far from his person as circumstances would permit, prepared to ascend the tree.

In youth, the tulip-tree, or *Liriodendron tulipferum*, the most magnificent of American foresters, has a trunk peculiarly smooth, and often rises to a great height without lateral branches; but, in its riper age, the bark becomes gnarled and uneven, while many short limbs make their appearance on the stem. Thus the difficulty of ascension, in the present case, lay more in semblance than in reality. Embracing the huge cylinder, as closely as possible, with his arms and knees, seizing with his hands some projections, and resting his naked toes upon others, Jupiter, after one or two narrow escapes from falling, at length wriggled himself into the first great fork, and seemed to consider the whole business as virtually accomplished. The *risk* of the achievement was, in fact, now over, although the climber was some sixty or seventy feet from the ground.

"Which way mus go now, Massa Will?" he asked.

"Keep up the largest branch—the one on this side," said Legrand. The negro obeyed him promptly, and apparently with but little trouble; ascending higher and higher, until no glimpse of his squat figure could be obtained through the dense foliage which enveloped it. Presently his voice was heard in a sort of halloo.

"How much fudder is got for go?"

"How high up are you?" asked Legrand.

"Ebber so fur," replied the negro; "can see de sky fru de top ob de tree."

"Never mind the sky, but attend to what I say. Look down the trunk and count the limbs below you on this side. How many limbs have you passed?"

"One, two, tree, four, fibe—I done pass fibe big limb, massa, pon dis side."

"Then go one limb higher."

In a few minutes the voice was heard again, announcing that the seventh limb was attained.

"Now, Jup," cried Legrand, evidently much excited, "I want you to work your way out upon that limb as far as you can. If you see anything strange, let me know."

By this time what little doubt I might have entertained of my poor friend's insanity, was put finally at rest. I had no alternative but to conclude him stricken with lunacy, and I became seriously anxious about getting him home. While I was pondering upon what was best to be done, Jupiter's voice was again heard.

"Mos feerd for to ventur pon dis limb berry far—'tis dead limb putty much all de way."

"Did you say it was a *dead* limb, Jupiter?" cried Legrand in a quavering voice.

"Yes, massa, him dead as de door-nail—done up for sartain—done departed dis here life."

"What in the name of heaven shall I do?" asked Legrand, seemingly in the greatest distress.

"Do!" said I, glad of an opportunity to interpose a word, "why come home and go to bed. Come now!—that's a fine fellow. It's getting late, and, besides, you remember your promise."

"Jupiter," cried he, without heeding me in the least, "do you hear me?"

"Yes, Massa Will, hear you ebber so plain."

"Try the wood well, then, with your knife, and see if you think it *very* rotten."

"Him rotten, massa, sure nuff," replied the negro in a few moments, "but not so berry rotten as mought be. Mought ventur out leetle way pon de limb by myself, dat's true."

"By yourself!—what do you mean?"

"Why I mean de bug. 'Tis *berry* hebby bug. Spose I drop him down fuss, and den de limb won't break wid just de weight ob one nigger."

"You infernal scoundrel!" cried Legrand, apparently much relieved, "what do you mean by telling me such nonsense as that? As sure as you drop that beetle I'll break your neck. Look here, Jupiter, do you hear me?"

"Yes, massa, needn't hollo at poor nigger dat style."

"Well! now listen!—if you will venture out on the limb as far as you think safe, and not let go the beetle, I'll make you a present of a silver dollar as soon as you get down."

"I'm gwine, Massa Will—deed I is," replied the negro very promptly—"mos out to the end now."

"*Out to the end!*" here fairly screamed Legrand, "do you say you are out to the end of that limb?"

"Soon be to de eend, massa,—o-o-o-o-oh! Lor-gol-amarcy! what *is* dis here pon de tree?"

"Well!" cried Legrand, highly delighted, "what is it?"

"Why taint noffin but a skull—somebody bin lef him head up de tree, and de crows done gobble ebery bit ob de meat off."

"A skull, you say!—very well!—how is it fastened to the limb?—what holds it on?"

"Sure nuff, massa; mus look. Why dis berry curous sarcumstance, pon my word—dare's a great big nail in de skull, what fastens ob it on to de tree."

"Well now, Jupiter, do exactly as I tell you—do you hear?"

"Yes, massa."

"Pay attention, then!—find the left eye of the skull."

"Hum! hoo! dat's good! why dare aint no eye lef at all."

"Curse your stupidity! do you know your right hand from your left?"

"Yes, I nose dat—nose all bout dat—'tis my lef hand what I chops de wood wid."

"To be sure! you are left-handed; and your left eye is on the same side as your left hand. Now, I suppose, you can find the left eye of the skull, or the place where the left eye has been. Have you found it?"

Here was a long pause. At length the negro asked, "Is de lef eye of de skull pon de same side as de lef hand of de skull, too?—cause de skull aint got not a bit ob a hand at all—nebber mind! I got de lef eye now—here de lef eye! what mus do wid it?"

"Let the beetle drop through it, as far as the string will reach—but be careful and not let go your hold of the string."

"All dat done, Massa Will; mighty easy ting for to put de bug fru de hole—look out for him dare below!"

"Very well!—now just keep as you are for a few minutes."

During this colloquy no portion of Jupiter's person could be seen; but the beetle, which he had suffered to descend, was now visible at the end of the string, and glistened, like a globe of burnished gold, in the last rays of the setting sun, some of which still faintly illumined the eminence upon which we stood. The *scarabæus* hung quite clear of any branches, and, if allowed to fall, would have fallen at our feet. Legrand immediately took the scythe, and cleared with it a circular space, three or four yards in diameter, just beneath the insect, and, having accomplished this, ordered Jupiter to let go the string and come down from the tree.

Driving a peg, with great nicety, into the ground, at the precise spot where the beetle fell, my friend now produced from his pocket a tape measure. Fastening one end of this at that point of the trunk of the tree which was nearest the peg, he unrolled it till it reached the peg, and thence farther unrolled it, in the direction already established by the two points of the tree and the peg, for the distance of fifty feet—Jupiter clearing away the brambles with the scythe. At the spot thus attained a second peg was driven, and about this, as a centre, a rude circle, about four feet in diameter, described. Taking now a spade himself, and giving one to Jupiter and one to me, Legrand begged us to set about digging as quickly as possible. . . .

The lanterns having been lit, we all fell to work with a zeal worthy of a more rational cause; and, as the glare fell upon our persons and implements, I could not help thinking how picturesque a group we composed, and how strange and suspicious our labors must have appeared to any interloper who, by chance, might have stumbled upon our whereabouts.

We dug very steadily for two hours. Little was said; and our chief embarrassment lay in the yelpings of the dog, who took exceeding interest in our proceedings. He, at length, became so obstreperous that we grew fearful of his giving the alarm to some stragglers in the vicinity;—or, rather, this was the apprehension of Legrand;—for myself, I should have rejoiced at any interruption which might have enabled me to get the wanderer home. The noise was, at length, very effectually silenced by Jupiter, who, getting out of the hole with a dogged air of deliberation, tied the brute's mouth up with one of his suspenders, and then returned, with a grave chuckle, to his task.

When the time mentioned had expired, we had reached a depth of five feet, and yet no signs of any treasure became manifest. A general pause ensued, and I began to hope that the farce was at an end. Legrand, however, although evidently much disconcerted, wiped his brow thoughtfully and recommenced. We had excavated the entire circle of four feet diameter, and now we slightly enlarged the limit, and went to the farther depth of two feet. Still nothing appeared. The gold-seeker, whom I sincerely pitied, at length clambered from the pit, with the bitterest disappointment imprinted upon every feature, and proceeded, slowly and reluctantly, to put on his coat, which he had thrown off at the beginning of his labor. In the mean time I made no remark. Jupiter, at a signal from his master, began to gather up his tools. This done, and the dog having been unmuzzled, we turned in a profound silence towards home.

We had taken, perhaps, a dozen steps in this direction, when, with a loud oath, Legrand strode up to Jupiter, and seized him by the collar. The astonished negro opened his eyes and mouth to the fullest extent, let fall the spades, and fell upon his knees.

"You scoundrel," said Legrand, hissing out the syllables from between his clenched teeth—"you infernal black villain!— speak, I tell you!—answer me this instant, without prevarication!—which—which is your left eye?"

"Oh, my golly, Massa Will! aint dis here my lef eye for sartain?" roared the terrified Jupiter, placing his hand upon his *right* organ of vision, and holding it there with a desperate pertinacity, as if in immediate dread of his master's attempt at a gouge.

"I thought so!—I knew it! hurrah!" vociferated Legrand, letting the negro go, and executing a series of curvets and caracols, much to the astonishment of his valet, who, arising from his knees, looked, mutely, from his master to myself, and then from myself to his master.

"Come! we must go back," said the latter, "the game's not up yet"; and he again led the way to the tulip-tree.

"Jupiter," said he, when we reached its foot, "come here! was the skull nailed to the limb with the face outwards, or with the face to the limb?"

"De face was out, massa, so dat de crows could get at de eyes good, widout any trouble."

Well, then, was it this eye or that through which you dropped the beetle?"—here Legrand touched each of Jupiter's eyes.

"Twas dis eye, massa—de lef eye—jis as you tell me," and here it was his right eye that the negro indicated.

"That will do—we must try it again."

Here my friend, about whose madness I now saw, or fancied that I saw, certain indications of method, removed the peg which marked the spot where the beetle fell, to a spot about three inches to the westward of its former position. Taking, now, the tape measure from the nearest point of the trunk to the peg, as before, and continuing the extension in a straight line to the distance of fifty feet, a spot was indicated, removed, by several yards, from the point at which we had been digging.

Around the new position a circle, somewhat larger than in the former instance, was now described, and we again set to work with the spades. I was dreadfully weary, but, scarcely understanding what had occasioned the change in my thoughts, I felt no longer any great aversion from the labor imposed. I had become most unaccountably interested—nay, even excited. Perhaps there was something, amid all the extravagant demeanor of Legrand—some air of forethought, or of deliberation, which impressed me. I dug eagerly, and now and then caught myself actually looking, with something that very much resembled expectation, for the fancied treasure, the vision of which had demented my unfortunate companion. At a period when such vagaries of thought most fully possessed me, and when we had been at work perhaps an hour and a half, we were again interrupted by the violent howlings of the dog. His uneasiness, in the first instance, had been, evidently, but the result of playfulness or caprice, but he now assumed a bitter and serious tone. Upon Jupiter's again attempting to muzzle him, he made furious resistance, and, leaping into the hole, tore up the mould frantically with his claws. In a few seconds he had uncovered a mass of human bones, forming two complete skeletons, and intermingled with several buttons of metal, and what appeared to be the dust of decayed woollen. One or two strokes of a spade upturned the blade of a large Spanish knife, and, as we dug farther, three or four loose pieces of gold and silver coin came to light.

At sight of these the joy of Jupiter could scarcely be restrained, but the countenance of his master wore an air of extreme disappointment. He urged us, however, to continue our exertions, and the words were hardly uttered when I stumbled and fell forward, having caught the toe of my boot in a large ring of iron that lay half buried in the loose earth.

We now worked in earnest, and never did I pass ten minutes of more intense excitement. During this interval we had fairly unearthed an oblong chest of wood, which, from its perfect preservation and wonderful hardness, had plainly been subjected to some mineralizing process—perhaps that of the Bi-chloride of Mercury. This box was three feet and a half long, three feet broad, and two and a half feet deep. It was firmly secured by bands of wrought iron, riveted, and forming a kind of open trellis-work over the whole. On each side of the chest, near the top, were three rings of iron—six in all—by means of which a firm hold could be obtained by six persons. Our utmost united endeavors served only to disturb the coffer very slightly in its bed. We at once saw the impossibility of removing so great a weight. Luckily, the sole fastenings of the lid consisted of two sliding bolts. These we drew back—trembling and panting with anxiety. In an instant, a treasure of incalculable value lay gleaming before us. As the rays of the lanterns fell within the pit, there flashed upwards a glow and a glare, from a confused heap of gold and of jewels, that absolutely dazzled our eyes.

I shall not pretend to describe the feelings with which I gazed. Amazement was, of course, predominant. Legrand appeared exhausted with excitement, and spoke very few words. Jupiter's countenance wore, for some minutes, as deadly a pallor as it is possible, in nature of things, for any negro's visage to assume. He seemed stupified—thunderstricken. Presently he fell upon his knees in the pit, and, burying his naked arms up to the elbows in gold, let them there remain, as if enjoying the luxury of a bath. At length, with a deep sigh, he exclaimed, as if in a soliloquy,

"And dis all cum ob de goole-bug! de putty goole bug! de poor little goole-bug, what I boosed in dat sabage kind ob style! Aint you shamed ob yourself, nigger?—answer me dat!"

It became necessary, at last, that I should arouse both master and valet to the expediency of removing the treasure. It was growing late, and it behooved us to make exertion, that we might get every thing housed before daylight. It was difficult to say what should be done, and much time was spent in deliberation—so confused were the ideas of all. We, finally, lightened the box by removing two thirds of its contents, when we were enabled, with some trouble, to raise it from the hole. The articles taken out were deposited among the brambles, and the dog left to guard them, with strict orders from Jupiter neither, upon any pretence, to stir from the spot, nor to open his mouth until our return. We then hurriedly made for home with the chest; reaching the hut in safety, but after excessive toil, at one o'clock in the morning. Worn out as we were, it was not in human nature to do more immediately. We rested until two, and had supper; starting for the hills immediately afterwards, armed with three stout sacks, which, by good luck, were upon the premises. A little before four we arrived at the pit, divided the remainder of the booty, as equally as might be, among us, and, leaving the holes unfilled, again set out for the hut, at which, for the second time, we deposited our golden burthens, just as the first faint streaks of the dawn gleamed from over the tree-tops in the East.

We were now thoroughly broken down; but the intense excitement of the time denied us repose. After an unquiet slumber of some three or four hours' duration, we arose, as if by preconcert, to make examination of our treasure.

The chest had been full to the brim, and we spent the whole day, and the greater part of the next night, in a scrutiny of its contents. There had been nothing like order or arrangement. Every thing had been heaped in promiscuously. Having assorted all with care, we found ourselves possessed of even vaster wealth than we had at first supposed. In coin there was rather more than four hundred and fifty thousand dollars—estimating the value of the pieces, as accurately as we could, by the tables of the period. There was not a particle of silver. All was gold of antique date and of great variety—French, Spanish, and German money, with a few English guineas, and some counters, of which we had never seen specimens before. There were several very large and heavy coins, so worn that we could make nothing of their inscriptions. There was no American money. The value of the jewels we found more difficulty in estimating. There were dia- monds—some of them exceedingly large and fine—a hundred and ten in all, and not one of them small; eighteen rubies of remarkable brilliancy; three hundred and ten emeralds, all very beautiful; and twenty-one sapphires, with an opal. These stones had all been broken from their settings and thrown loose in the chest. The settings themselves, which we picked out from among the other gold, appeared to have been beaten up with hammers as if to prevent identification. Besides all this, there was a vast quantity of solid gold ornaments;—nearly two hundred massive finger and earrings;—rich chains—thirty of these, if I remem- ber;—eighty-three very large and heavy crucifixes;—five gold censers of great value;—a prodigious golden punch bowl, orna- mented with richly chased vine-leaves and Bacchanalian figures, with two sword-handles exquisitely embossed; and many other smaller articles which I cannot recollect. The weight of these valuables exceeded three hundred and fifty pounds avoirdupois; and in this estimate I have not included one hundred and ninety- seven superb gold watches; three of the number being worth each five hundred dollars, if one. Many of them were very old, and as time keepers valueless; the works having suffered, more or less, from corrosion—but all were richly jewelled and in cases of great worth. We estimated the entire contents of the chest, that night, at a million and a half of dollars; and upon the sub- sequent disposal of the trinkets and jewels (a few being retained for our own use), it was found that we had greatly undervalued the treasure. . . .

"Alchemy"

HERVEY ALLEN (1889–1949)

When Hervey Allen, a native of Philadelphia, first visited Charleston in 1918 he had already been injured in World War I, requiring braces, and his writings had been included in the Yale Series of Younger Poets. Upon settling in Charleston he taught English at the Porter Military Academy and befriended both DuBose Heyward and John Bennett. The three authors played crucial roles in the founding of the Poetry Society of South Carolina. With Heyward, Allen published a collection of poems, *Carolina Chansons* (1924). He went on to become an authority on Edgar Allan Poe, editing an anthology of Poe's writings and penning a biography entitled *Israfel* (1934) after Poe's poem of that name. His fascination with Poe and his interest in Poe's connection to Charleston are reflected in the poem "Alchemy," with its central concept of Poe's sojourn on Sullivan's Island. Though he only lived in Charleston until 1924, he went on to have a major literary career. He published more than a dozen volumes, including at least three novels that were part of a series about colonial America. His novel *Anthony Adverse* (1933) was one of the best-selling books of its day.

Some souls are strangers in this bourne;
   Beauty is born from such men's discontent;
   Earth's grass and stones,
  Her seas, her forests, and her air
Are seas and forests till they mirror on some pool
   Unusually reflecting in an exile's mind,
   Who tarries here protesting and alone;
And then they get strange shapes from memories of
    other stars
  The banished knew, or spheres he dreams will be.
  Thus is the fivefold vision of the earth recast
    By ghostly alchemy.

But there are favored spots
Where all earth's moods conspire to make a show
Of things to be transmuted into beauty
By alchemic minds.
Such is this island beach where Poe once walked,
And heard the melic throbbing of the sea,
With muffled sound of harbor bells—
Bells—he loved bells!
And here are drifting ghosts of city chimes
Come over water through the evening mist,
Like knells from death-ships off the coasts of spectral
lands.

I think some dusk their metal voices
Yet will call him back
To walk upon this magic beach again,
While Grief holds carnival upon the harbor bar.
Heralded by ravens from another air,
The master will pass, pacing here,
Wrapped in a cape dark as the unborn moon.
There will be lightning underneath a star;
And he will speak to me
Of archipelagoes forgot,
Atolls in sailless seas, where dreams have married
thought.

"Madame Margot"

If anyone can be said to be the father of the Charleston Renaissance of the 1920s, it is John Bennett. Born in Chillicothe, Ohio, in 1865, Bennett came to Charleston from New York in 1898 and married Susan Adger Smythe in 1902. He remained in the Lowcountry for the rest of his life. Bennett's Shakespearean novel *Master Skylark* (1897) is still considered a classic of children's literature, while *The Treasure of Peyre Gaillard* (1906), set in the Lowcountry, was his first attempt at writing fiction for adults. He contributed frequently to *Harper's Magazine* and the *Atlantic Monthly* and to the children's periodical *St. Nicholas Magazine*, which also published his imaginative silhouettes.

Bennett served as DuBose Heyward's confidante and confessor in the creation of the character Porgy, throughout his appearances in novel, play, and opera. When the first director of the opera *Porgy and Bess*, Rouben Mamoulian, visited Charleston and the sea islands to get an impression of the local scene, John Bennett introduced him to the city.

In 1907 Bennett presented a lecture to the Federation of Charleston Women's Clubs on "Grotesque Legends of Charleston," including accounts of a "Doctor to the Dead" and "Madame Margot," a retelling of Faust. The local audience found the stories "revolting," as a newspaper reporter wrote, but over the years Bennett continued to work on the folk tales and eventually published them. Bennett's version of "Madame Margot" includes some of the frequently examined themes in local literature, including an interest in the occult and supernatural, the connection between Lowcountry and Caribbean cultures, and the complex relationships between black and white societies in Charleston. The version below appeared as a short story in his collection *Doctor to the Dead*. He later expanded it to a novella.

John Bennett was inducted into the South Carolina Academy of Authors in 1998.

A Legend of Old Charleston

In an age so glorious, rich and fine, and so be-starred with splendor that one almost forgets the bottomless abyss into which it plunged at last, there lived a woman in Charleston of whom a very odd story is told.

Among the fugitives from massacre in San Domingo was a young girl of mixed blood, named Marguerite Lagoux. By her intimates called Rita, by familiar acquaintances, Morgoton, by those who envied her beauty, in disparagement, Margot, she was, after all was done, known merely as Old Mother Go-go.

But, among the golden-skinned San Domingans, loveliest of all, admittedly, was Marguerite Lagoux.

Marguerite was beautiful, as is the case with many of her kind. She was almost white, and the lines of her loveliness were something to look on and desire.

Men, seeing her for the first time, stopped to look, catching their breaths. There was something about her more than beauty which took men like a spell. Her body was cast in a gloriously perfect mold; she was tall, and full of tigerlike grace, the envy of other women. She walked as an empress might, if God gave her grace, with perfect and exquisite motion, effortlessly, not striding, but seeming to glide like a swan on untroubled waters.

Dressed in bright merino, crimson, orange and blue, with a blood-colored silken kerchief bound round her head in Oriental fashion, beads of amber around her neck, and in each ear a hoop of gold, she looked like a great golden tiger lily dusted with *sang-dieu*.

Ducie Poincignon was lovely; so was Rose Lemesurier; but there was only one Margot Lagoux.

She was a milliner and mantuamaker, her shop in King Street, on the western side, beyond Mignot's Garden, a little above the bend. Its location is now altogether uncertain, for all that part of King Street was destroyed by fire.

Her home was a small house in a court long since forgotten, to which led a narrow alley, known as Lilac Lane, from two large *melia azederach* trees, Indian lilacs, which arched its entrance.

Lilac Lane entered the block now bounded by King, Calhoun, St. Philip and George Streets, from George Street, just behind the old Hummel apothecary shop. The apothecary shop also is long since forgotten, and the lane exists no more. All that survives of that inner court and its flowery small cottages is a narrow, pinched and abbreviated exit in St. Philip Street, two doors above Greene.

Her shop was the most popular in Charleston; for of all milliners of her day, Margot was foremost . . . first beyond compare. Her taste was beyond criticism; her instinct for color faultless; her choice of fabrics perfect; her knowledge of women complete; her dexterity infinite.

Her lady patrons were patrician. Those who desired perfect taste and material loveliness combined with exquisite charm found what they sought at Margot Lagoux's. She was employed by the very best people of Charleston; she had no successful competitor; beside her work Eloise Couesnon's was but maladroit.

Lilac Lane was but a narrow entry between two estates, and rambled into that interspace like a brook into a wood, growing narrower as it went, until the high hedges which bordered it met and knit themselves together into what seemed a cul-de-sac, or dead-end passage. The footpath ran on a little yet, until it disappeared in green uncertainty. The unfamiliar traveler, bewildered, here turned back to find a bolder thoroughfare, leaving within that entangled green a little tranquil space withdrawn from curious eyes and from the brawling town, as peaceful as a convent close, a sanctuary from the rude intrusions of a troubling world. Where the strait path vanished into the green Margot's cottage stood snug as the stone in a plum.

It was inevitable that when Margot Lagoux came to the full loveliness of her womanhood she should be pursued by men; and that, sooner or later, and rather soon than late, she should become the indulged mistress of a wealthy man, after the habit of the time, by whom she had a daughter of loveliness even more exquisite than her mother's, and of complexion fairer still, so fair, indeed, that none save those who knew the fact could say whether she were white or black.

As this daughter, whom Margot named Gabrielle, grew from infancy to childhood, from childhood to maidenhood, and approached the perilous age of wakening to the heart's desire, fear laid hold of her mother's heart lest Gabrielle should be what she herself was, and nothing more. Such perfect loveliness asked far more, and bespoke a better fate than that of milliner and mistress, forever doomed from birth until death to be only "a free person of color." Gabrielle, as Margot knew but too well, was possessed of perilous loveliness.

Of Gabrielle's parentage further one can only shrug one's shoulders . . . no one can say more certainly . . . aristocratic beyond a doubt . . . else where had she her radiant, fair beauty, her exquisite, slender body, her arched insteps like a Spanish girl's, and her lovely, aristocratic face? God alone knows.

Margot was lovely; but Gabrielle was lovelier, as brier rose is lovelier than pompadour pink. Gabrielle's was an exquisite ivory loveliness; her ankles were the loveliest things that ever a sandal ribbon bound; she was everywhere known as the loveliest girl in all old St. Finbar's parish. Margot was a pottery figurine molded with marvelous skill; Gabrielle was a statuette of exquisite porcelain. She walked like the wind of April through meadows after rain. Her face with its delicate high cheekbones was like the flowers of Normandy; but her lovely color was Eastern, not Western, Persian, like the roses which bloomed in the forgotten gardens of Istakhr, yesterday's flowers, full of yesterday's loveliness, yesterday's happiness, yesterday's tragedy, sweet with passionate, heart-breaking perfume and the pathos of swift-passing beauty. Her cheeks were the hue of peach flowers at dusk, more delicate than japonica color. God who gave them knew whence came both peach-flower color and dusk. Under her transparent skin a shadowy crimson flowed with the beat of her heart like a twilit tide . . . San Domingo's *sang de crépuscule*. She might have been a sister to Scheherazade.

This loveliness made Margot tremble. It is a perilous privilege for a girl to possess beauty rising above her station in life; there is always a price to be paid for it; sorrow the common fee. There was a thought from which Margot shrank as from a draught of poison: Gabrielle degraded and desolate. Such a heritage of beauty too often proves but a legacy of tragedy and shame.

There was nothing on earth so precious to Margot as her daughter's happiness and security, nothing so important; to Margot even more to be desired than her own eternal peace.

She perceived the ominous shadow which overhung her child from her cradle to her grave. She looked from side to side like a deer hard pressed by the dogs . . . can one escape destiny?

Where were the lovely and the fair she had known in her own youth? The graveyard sand lay cold on their lips; their sweetness and their passion were forgotten long ago. Margot knew that youth and summer nights were made for ecstasy. She knew also that in forgotten graveyards are many unmarked graves of hapless innocence and beauty. Life was stripped of all illusions for Margot Lagoux; the truth stood stark and bare before her in all its unmitigated ugliness. Every look into the future was filled with apprehension. She awoke at night, crying out, "No . . . no . . . no . . . it must not . . . cannot . . . shall not be!"

At adolescence Gabrielle Lagoux was a vision of delight. She was in temperament as ardent as a summer shower, which gives, when it gives, all that it has to give, in a rush of wind and rain. Unspoiled by knowledge, unruined by folly, too innocent still to be perplexed by life's anxieties, her soul mistook Earth for the pathway to Paradise, and nothing as yet had discovered her error. Her light feet stood at the smiling gate of the Primrose Way.

But Margot's days and nights were filled with increasing anxiety, as with increasing doubt she confronted destiny.

The inner door of Margot's cottage gave upon a small paved court, where two old fig trees grew. Here, remote from the curious observation of the world, preserved by cloistral hedges from prying indiscretion, flowed Gabrielle's untroubled existence.

Few ever saw her. Such as saw her by chance through some green interstice, dazzled by her loveliness, spread the tale of a princess in an enchanted wood; but few had ever seen her twice. Margot had kept the court a solitude lest Gabrielle suffer corruption, and maintained around her a very nunnery of care, hovering over her, and kept her as withdrawn from the world as a novice in a convent garth.

But beauty cannot be safely sequestered always anywhere. The less seen, the more thought of. Cloistral existence is all very well for souls of the convent sort; but youth and spring hate convents, and will have life's novitiate or none. There is a crevice in every hedge, no matter how tall or how thick it may be.

Spring came with its universal song; all living creatures voiced the universal theme: the blue dove moaned out his heart's desire; the copper beetle wooed and won his lady in the dust; butterflies and dragonflies glittered in the wind, happy in their airy ecstasy . . . all earth rejoiced in having its heart's desire.

Gabrielle was intoxicated by the unknown passion of her own heart; within her breast a questioning wonder grew.

"Mother," she said wistfully, "what is it fills the world with music day and night? What makes the world sing?"

"Happiness," said Margot, "and joy of the spring."

"If it be happiness," rejoined Gabrielle, "why does it make my heart ache?"

Margot, startled, stared, wrung with sudden fear.

"And what is this love of which everyone sings?"

"The source of all human wretchedness," cried Margot.

"But, mother, if love be the source of all wretchedness, why is its song so sweet?"

"Because fools have their folly," said Margot. "Worship God, and leave foolishness to the fool."

"Love . . . foolishness?" said Gabrielle. "You told me that God is love."

"What ails you?" demanded Margot.

"Nothing, mother"; but a flush crept up her cheeks. "How does a woman know that she loves, so that she may say surely, 'This is love'?"

"By the despair that tears her heart in two."

"But, mother," persisted Gabrielle, "they tell me that love is sweet."

"Sweet? As wormwood," said Margot hoarsely. "It is nothing but fever and fret."

"Many I see who have it; but none do I see that fret. I would I might know for myself this pretty play of lovers and beloved!"

"What man has snared your silly heart?" demanded Margot, seeing that shadow near, foreseeing the fate of loveliness, perceiving the lips of indiscretion already at the rim of the cup of danger.

"Why should any man snare my heart?" asked Gabrielle in pitiful wonder. "I have never harmed any man. And, mother, feel my heart! It beats as if it would burst. Am I dying? Must I die? My heart aches so that I would I might die. Was not man made by God? Is not what God made good? You told me that God is love . . . and is not love the world's delight?"

Margot's joy in Gabrielle's beauty was turned to bitterness. "I conjure you, by God's sorrow, close your heart against it."

"How can I close my heart against it when I hear it in my sleep?"

Margot recoiled as she faced the future. There is no woe so sickening as the shuddering, interior sense of impending disaster.

Day after day Gabrielle knelt in her garden and pleaded for her heart's desire. Night after night Margot crouched before her crucifix and prayed in agony that her desire might not be given her. Heaven's auditor mixed those prayers in fatal entanglement; one was answered, and one was not: he alone is responsible.

Sunset lay on Margot's garden. Gabrielle, puzzling upon life's unanswered riddle, stood listening to sounds beyond the hedge. Everywhere was the sound of running feet, and the whisper of wordless laughter mockingly borne on the evening wind. The world was full of the golden vision of light-footed maidens with fluttering garments flying through Lilac Lane pursued by breathless and ardent lovers eagerly following where they fled. The sound of laughter floated along the narrow way, and the little, faint echo of flying feet. It was the time of the year when all young maids are sweet as fresh-gathered flowers, and all men a little mad. Even the earth, drab clod, was astir with the ecstasy of approaching night with its quivering, sentient stars.

As she stood there Gabrielle was suddenly aware of a shadow on the grass. There was a face in the hedge, smiling . . . a lad's face, laughing and debonair. Over his head two butterflies hovered; his yellow hair curled round his face like crisp little golden flames; his eyes were bright and blue as the morning; there was confidence in his bearing, easy lordship and high pride. His eyes, incessantly roving, were audaciously bright as two wild stars.

Gabrielle's eyes were wide opened, round, unwinking, full of suddenly frightened tears. Her lips had fallen slightly apart to free her fluttering breath; she sighed, a little shuddering sigh, and crossed her hands upon her breast.

Her beauty startled him: delicate, frail, almost translucent in the golden sun; she seemed a being not of flesh, blood and gross mortality . . . saint, maid, dryad, nymph, or sprite . . . who could tell which? Silently drinking her loveliness he leaned through the hedge.

Again she sighed softly; stared at his face, and shivered a little. Was it a god or a man in the hedge? Had he sprouted from the boxwood or fallen from the sky? Into the crevice between her lips the sunshine had slipped; her lips were aglow, as if she were breathing ethereal flame.

He drew his breath with an audible sound; and, as he stared, longing seized his boy's heart and wrung it bitterly.

The flame which blazed in his bright eyes put an answering glow in hers. For the first time in her life she was awake to the sense of her own loveliness, wonderful and sweet. A throbbing, delicate fire came fluttering up through her breast. Her eyes met his: in his eyes were delight, surprise and longing. His eyes met hers: and all her doubts went out in wordless joy . . . like a wave which breaks along a beach her heart rushed out to greet him. The world seemed suddenly remote, withdrawn into the depths of incalculable space. There remained but two young love-stunned souls, groping to each other in the garden beneath the magnolia trees.

Night fell, and darkness voyaged the uncharted sky. Overhead the blue dome blazed with innumerable stars and golden planets heaving up heaven's arch; the tremulous green lamps of the fire-flies filled the earth with winking constellations around them. But the heavens and the earth were as nothing to them; love was there, and he, and she, and the forgotten starlight. And where youth and love are, life, death, good or ill, the bright stars over-head, or the dark mold below, for better or for worse, are noth-ing, and wisdom of little worth.

Into the house she came, one little slipper upon its foot, one slip-per gone . . . what became of that little lost slipper God only knows. Her stockinged foot was wet with the dew which had dripped from the leaves overhead. Her lips stung; her cheeks were on fire; all her soul was singing. She was so transfigured she seemed a winged creature. Her soft lips moved in inarticulate ecstasy. Hands, feet, neck, face, all told one story. Her eyes like blazing stars. Margot stared with narrowed eyes.

"Mother, I am happy . . . so happy that I want to live forever!"

Margot searched that radiant face, with a cold hand clutching at her heart.

"I was walking in the garden, mother, and the god of love was there. He kissed me on my mouth, mother; and, oh, mother, love is sweet!"

Margot's heart stopped. "Are you quite mad?" she asked. Then the truth dawned upon her. "Oh, my God!" she whispered. "I should have known! I should have known! Fool, fool, fool! Mother of Jesus! I should have known!" As if stunned, her head fell down upon her breast.

In the dark and breathless stillness of the night was a stern, strange loveliness; yet now something akin to wordless terror, the terror of a child that dreams, and, waking suddenly in the darkness, cries out in fear of unseen, unknown things.

An ill wind which had blown up since sunset with a far-off, moaning sound, had risen to a melancholy, screaming note. Clouds of soot and ashes blown from the fireplace whirled in drifts around the floor. A bird sped round the house with a shrill, terrified cry; the wind bellowed hoarsely in the chimney; the house shook; over the housetops could be heard the coming of the rain.

Before her crucifix Margot knelt, praying for her daughter as she never had prayed for herself:

"Mother of God, all merciful . . . spare my daughter!" But she heard nothing.

"St. Dominique, lover of souls, preserve my daughter from destruction!" Still she heard nothing.

"Mary, Mother, great in grace, defend and preserve my child! Mother of Sorrows, have mercy upon her!" Still she heard nothing.

"All ye Holy Virgins, intercede for her! Lord of Compassion, hear me! O Thou, Most Pitiful Lord of the Innocent, answer my prayer, and protect my child!"

Again she listened; yet she heard nothing but the whine and whistle of the wind.

"Lord, *Seigneur Dieu*, preserve and spare my daughter! Lord God, answer my prayer!"

But all was still.

It was taking too long for her anguish to reach the foot of God's throne. To her dismayed heart the night was appallingly still. The confident faithful may wait upon the leisure of Heaven; but the desperate have no time to wait. To hearts dismayed there is nothing so appallingly still as God.

She beat her breast; her garments were disarrayed; her voice grew shrill; by all vicars, saints and intercessors, by all interme- diaries, she pleaded with God to listen and reply. There was no answer. "Mary, Mother of Sorrows!" she gasped. "Does God not understand?"

Her appeal arose piercingly shrill: "*Dieu, Dieu, Eternal Dieu, écoute mes cris! Hatê-toi de ma secourir! Hatê-toi d'elle delivrer! O Toi, qui écoutes la prière, aie petié de nous! Ne tarde-pas! Écoute mes cris!*"

She waited; there was no sound; no answer; then her voice went up like the cry of delirium:

"*O Dieu, trés-haut, réveille-toi! Réveille-toi mon Dieu!*" Then in a tone of amazement and pathos, "Mary, Mother of Sorrows, do I have to explain to God?"

She paused a moment, while despair rose like a swelling flood; then through the night went up a bitter cry: "*Seigneur Dieu! Tout-puissant Dieu! sois attentif à ma prière* . . . *Gabrielle, ma fille, mon Dieu!* Forgive in her my transgressions; pardon in her my sins; deliver her from her inheritance . . . Oh, my God! . . . let her be white!"

The wind sucked through the chimney with a sound like awful laughter; but from Heaven there was no answer.

Then she cried out pitifully, the cry which through the unending ages stands archetype of despair: "*Mon Dieu, mon Dieu! pourquoi m'as-tu abandonné?*"

She crouched a moment, listening, her head on one side. There was no reply. She turned her back on the crucifix, saying bitterly, "I will call upon You no more!"

The candles sank to dull blue sparks. Over her shoulder a deep voice said, "Then why not try me awhile? I remember when God forgets."

It was Satan himself, outcast god of the discontented, who ever waits at the door of opportunity. "Why not try me awhile?" he said.

"You pray for loving-kindness," he continued sardonically. "If this be loving-kindness, why not try damnation awhile? You have seen all the piety under the sun, that its wages are vanity. God sends you grief. Has he sent you also a cure? or had compassion on you? If this be loving-kindness, why not try damnation instead? It can surely be no worse; and may be vastly better.

"My daughter, you have been cajoled. Come unto me, and I will give you your heart's desire."

"Master . . . Lord," whispered Margot, shivering as with cold, "give me my heart's desire!"

"What is your heart's desire?"

"That my daughter, Gabrielle, shall be white to all eternity. All that I have, all that I am, will I give . . . yea, for this will I give my soul!"

Satan smiled a saturnine smile: "Then lay down your burden at my feet, daughter. You shall have your heart's desire."

Forthwith she bargained with Satan that her daughter, Gabrielle, should be white to all eternity.

And by his eternal damnation Satan swore that she should have her heart's desire. Margot laid down her burden of fear at the feet of the Prince of the Powers of Darkness, and by her rejected hope of salvation swore to abide by their covenant.

She never knelt at a confessional again.

There is a convent school for orphaned girls kept by the nuns in New Orleans. The liveliest girl seen there in years was Gabrielle Lagoux, carried there between two nights, lest young love, like Death, insist. To that school, her origins unknown, went Gabrielle.

Her mother kissed her twice with feverish lips like dry leaves. The coach was at the gate. She said to the coach-boy who guarded her gown from the wheels, "Tell him that I love him." She paused again in the coach door, a dazed look on her face: "Tell him not to forget me. I love him."

She never came back. She never saw her golden lad again.

When she entered the coach young love was done for forever. The days became weeks, weeks months, months grew into years. She passed in through the convent's sheltering doors to a world of unfamiliar faces, and forgot.

God made memory cruel, that men might know remorse; but the Devil devised forgetfulness, anodyne of regret. She never returned to the place of her birth, nor saw her mother again.

Reputed heiress to great estates, provided with apparently boundless means, and gifted with rare loveliness, coming of age, Gabrielle was wedded to a substantial planter's son, whose love for her was very great.

She never knew want; her years were filled with happiness and peace; she had a thousand slaves to do her bidding; and bore her husband three children, fair as the morning and with hair like golden fire.

But she never returned to the place of her birth, nor saw her mother again.

The Devil in everything was as good as his promise. But, for favors granted, the Devil takes his pay in his own way.

That is why this story is singular.

Something inscrutable had come over Margot Lagoux.

Her work was oddly altered: it had more air, less ease; more spell; less charm; more force, and less dexterity. Her work retained distinction, but of a queer sort; reserve gave way to novelty; simple beauty was replaced by meretricious charm; her taste, which had been perfect, suffered gradual corruption; her exquisite craft was marked by crudity. She had style, to be sure; but it was style *malade du rouvieux*. Every line of her work was slurred by subtle default; always too much, or too little; never the happy mean. Everything she did was like sweet wine soured, the worse for having been so much better. A queerly degenerated taste marked everything she did. Her custom fell from *vendre cher* to *bon marché*. The air of distinction which had attracted gentility utterly faded away. Calls for her work became infrequent; more infrequent; came no more. One morning the milliner's shop was shut. It never was opened again. Cobwebs hung on the moldy walls; the trade which had known and frequented the place knew it no more.

Wealth was given to Margot Lagoux. Its source it is useless to question. She had money in quantity that made bankers bow. She had women to wait on her, deferential menservants, boys to run at her beck and call, maids to go before her, bond and free. Her cellar was famous for its wines; her dress for its wild extravagance; her riches increased beyond all bound of reason; she was spoken to with deference, referred to with finesse. She had her carriage, lined with yellow silk; her beauty laughed at sumptuary laws; despite all ordinance she rode the streets like a charioted queen, dressed in *outré*, unstudied colors, wild as Barbary, in amber gown and canary-colored turban fastened with a golden brooch; despite the law, she rode through the community like a lovely malady.

Time but increased the singularity of her beauty. It was gossiped about in the market stalls; it was babbled about in the streets. Her face was like beauty seen in dreams, incredible and untrue; even wise men's souls were disturbed; piety itself was troubled by her golden loveliness; though not notably altered, she was greatly changed; her beauty took a dull and leaden look. Her beautiful face had lost something, no one could say just what; had gained something, no one could exactly define. There was a foreignness in her features, and the look of alien things. She looked like a portrait of herself painted in irony.

On the day that her daughter was married in faraway New Orleans, Margot stood before her mirror, motionless, staring at her own reflection. Suddenly she burst into wild, shrill laughter, cheerless, tragic; with body shaking and hands wrung together she turned away with an epithet, reversed the glass, and never looked into a mirror again. Something had passed across her face like a strange, ambiguous stain; a shadow had fallen across her beauty like the dimness beneath a passing cloud.

Margot Lagoux was changing. Sultry beauty such as hers has always an earlier afternoon; but this was more than early afternoon; Margot Lagoux was changing; she was becoming tawny, *bisblanc*, as the Creoles say, as though a somber fountain was playing in her veins.

There were many women at that day on whom fate laid dreadful hands; Louise Briaud, who was blinded by the smallpox; Fanchette Bourie, whom God pitied with death; Hélène Richemont, the leper; Floride Biez, Doucie Baramont, Francesca Villeponteaux, wrecked by disfiguring maladies. God give them peace! But on none was laid so ruthless, unrelenting, deliberate a hand as fell upon Margot Lagoux. She had changed, like a portrait whose shadows, painted in bitumen, have stuck through and distempered the rest.

The Devil was as good as his promise; but he took his pay in his own way. The old enchantment was gone like a necromancer's spell. Like some strange, nocturnal creature Margot seemed to absorb the gloom. Her glorious eyes grew jaundiced; her rose-brown lips grew dun; the webs which joined her fingers grew yellow as baker's saffron.

Days turned to weeks, weeks to months, months to years. Margot grew swarthy; she put aside beauty like an outworn, bright castoff garment, and grew as grotesque as a teakwood carving.

As her daughter went to white, Margot went to black, by merciless shadowy, gathering degrees. She was paying the price of her daughter's deliverance by her own deterioration. With the passage of the years she grew darker; grew more and more dark; more and more sloven, dingy and daubed, until from the high place of her prosperity, from the riches and luxury in which her patron had installed her while her exotic loveliness was still his pleasure, she sank down, down, down into the slums of the town, as foul, ugly and unclean an old hag as ever haunted the lowest tenement. She became gross, misshapen and debased; of her once-unexampled beauty there was not even the remembrance left.

A young man, with the face of Adonai and hair like curling gold, came once to her door, asking for Marguerite Lagoux. "Is that Marguerite Lagoux?" he asked, shrinking away from the door . . . for her cheeks were blotched and flecked with brown like a decaying peach. "No," he said, "oh, no, no, no! That cannot be Marguerite Lagoux . . . Marguerite Lagoux was lovely . . . and had a beautiful daughter named Gabrielle!" And with that, shuddering, he went away wringing his hands.

She fell apart like an old house with nobody living in it; her sun of glory set. She went down, down, down to oblivion, down to the dusty corner of death . . . and one night died, during a great West Indian storm, in a dirty little hovel, in an unkempt alley, in the middle of a Negro quarter, foul, fallen, filthy, and filled with beggary.

All night long the thunder rolled; the storm was wild beyond comparison. Yet Margot's hovel was ablaze with light. The little tailor who dwelt next door said, "Aha! Old Mother Go-go has company!" But the only person seen to enter her house was a tall man, handsomely attired, but with a face like an unpleasant smell.

The thunder was terrific; the wind blew with a sound like mad, gigantic laughter; the gusts howled through the tailor's house; the wind sucked down the chimney with a sound like awful weeping; the little tailor's soul was filled with a sense of enormous terror.

All night the thunder rolled like the laughter of an angry god. Dislodged by the tremendous concussions, the cockroaches flew out of the walls; and in the morning all the parakeets in the alley were turned as gray as ashes.

The windows and doors of old Mother Go-go's house were standing open wide; it was plain that they had stood open all night, and that the rain had beaten into the house unopposed.

This, however, occasioned but brief surprise. When they peered in at the door the rats were playing about the floor with the scattered beads of a broken rosary.

The priest came early, hurrying in. He did not stay long; and when he came out his face was white as a sheet and his lips pinched and gray as lead. Then those who prepare the dead came.

All over the floor the soot which had fallen from the chimney and been blown around the room was trodden and trampled by great hoofprints, like those of the neighbor's goat.

And Madame Margot? Heh! God had perhaps designed her for tragedy; but here was gross comedy. Margot lay stretched out on the floor, dead, among the ashes and soot, charred like a fallen star, as black as ebony.

The coroner, douce man, found that the woman had died of a visitation of God; but the little tailor said simply, "Has God feet like a goat?"

That was why, everyone was sure, the bishop declined to have masses said for the repose of her soul, and why they would not permit her body to be buried in St. Sebastian's graveyard: her color was too peculiar. Too black to be buried among the white, too white to be buried among the black, too well-to-do to be buried in the Potter's Field, she was secretly buried in her own garden, under the magnolia trees.

And that was the end of Madame Margot.

Yet not even death could purge away the ambiguous spell which surrounded her and her possessions. Every place in which she had dwelt sank into irremediable decay, the swifter where it had seemed to be most permanent and secure. The great house in which she had spent the days of her beauty and power stood a ruin above a decaying court, a wreck of its former pride and splendor. Of Margot's cottage there was no trace, other than a heap of moldering brick, the rafters of a fallen roof, and one bleak, tumbling gable: of Gabrielle's garden nothing whatsoever remained. Even Lilac Lane was gone; there was no lane there any more.

Yet, strangely, about the forgotten lane there hung something obscure and malign. After a woman had hanged herself at the crook of the lane it was closed to public passage as an abandoned thoroughfare and its entries barred. Yet still for years about the forgotten thoroughfare hung a spell grotesque and anomalous: that every boy who dared to cross the former entry to the lane on his way to school was certain as the sun to shine to be thrashed at school that day, and thrashed most thoroughly.

Journey to Charleston

WILLIAM CULLEN BRYANT (1794–1878)

When William Cullen Bryant visited Charleston in March 1843, he was one of the leading poets in America and, as editor-in-chief of the *New-York Evening Post*, an influential political figure. His most famous poem, "Thanatopsis," appeared in the *North American Review* in 1817. Praised by Edgar Allan Poe, Bryant has been called the "first American writer of verse to win international acclaim." The following account of his trip was published in the first volume of his *Letters of a Traveler* (1850).

The next morning, at eight o'clock, we found ourselves entering Charleston harbor; Sullivan's Island, with Fort Moultrie, breathing recollections of the revolution, on our right; James Island on our left; in front, the stately dwellings of the town, and all around, on the land side, the horizon bounded by an apparent belt of evergreens—the live-oak, the water-oak, the palmetto, the pine, and, planted about the dwellings, the magnolia and the wild orange—giving to the scene a summer aspect. The city of Charleston strikes the visitor from the north most agreeably. He perceives at once that he is in a different climate. The spacious houses are surrounded with broad piazzas, often a piazza to each story, for the sake of shade and coolness, and each house generally stands by itself in a garden planted with trees and shrubs, many of which preserve their verdure through the winter. We saw early flowers already opening; the peach and plum-tree were in full bloom; and the wild orange, as they call the cherry-laurel, was just putting forth its blossoms. The buildings—some with stuccoed walls, some built of large dark-red bricks, and some of wood—are not kept fresh with paint like ours, but are allowed to become weather-stained by the humid climate, like those of the European towns. The streets are broad and quiet, unpaved in some parts, but in none, as with us, offensive both to sight and smell. The public buildings are numerous for the size of the city, and well-built in general, with sufficient space about them to give them a noble aspect, and all the advantage which they could derive from their architecture. The inhabitants, judging from what I have seen of them, which is not much, I confess, do not appear undeserving of the character which has been given them, of possessing the most polished and agreeable manners of all the American cities.

"Aspects of the Pines"

PAUL HAMILTON HAYNE (1830–1886)

Paul Hamilton Hayne, unique among the writers in the antebellum Charleston School, came from an aristocratic Charleston family of means. Following the death of his father, he was raised by his mother and uncle, Robert Y. Hayne, who served as U.S. senator from 1822 to 1834 and Charleston mayor from 1835 to 1837. Hayne and poet Henry Timrod became friends in childhood. Both were primarily interested in poetry and poetics, and were heavily influenced by English romantic poets of the day.

Hayne set out to read law, but his devotion to literature grew stronger. He contributed to the *Southern Literary Messenger*, served as editor of *Russell's Magazine*, and, along with his colleagues, became an apologist for the southern cause. When the war began, Hayne was unable to enlist in the Confederate army because of health problems. U.S. troops burned his family's home, and after the war the financially ruined Hayne settled in Augusta, Georgia. He lived modestly but was able to support his family through his writing. He remained devoted to Timrod and edited *The Poems of Henry Timrod* in 1873, after his friend's death.

Attention to Hayne's work has largely centered on his poetry of the war, including "The Battle of Charleston Harbor" and "Charleston," though much of the rest of his work, including the poem below, is at least as strong.

Tall, sombre, grim, against the morning sky
    They rise, scarce touched by melancholy airs,
Which stir the fadeless foliage dreamfully,
    As if from realms of mystical despairs.

Tall, sombre, grim, they stand with dusky gleams
    Brightening to gold within the woodland's core,

Beneath the gracious noontide's tranquil beams—
But the weird winds of morning sigh no more.

A stillness, strange, divine, ineffable,
Broods round and o'er them in the wind's surcease,
And on each tinted copse and shimmering dell
Rests the mute rapture of deep hearted peace.

Last, sunset comes—the solemn joy and might
Borne from the West when cloudless day declines—
Low, flutelike breezes sweep the waves of light,
And lifting dark green tresses of the pines,

Till every lock is luminous—gently float,
Fraught with hale odors up the heavens afar
To faint when twilight on her virginal throat
Wears for a gem the tremulous vesper star.

from *The Civil War: A Narrative*

SHELBY FOOTE (1916–2005)

> Shelby Foote, a native of Mississippi, was educated at the
> University of North Carolina at Chapel Hill. Recognized early
> by William Faulkner as a promising new southern writer,
> Foote wrote several novels that were both critical and compli-
> mentary of his native state. His career as novelist evolved into
> that of narrative historian. In 1952 he published *Shiloh*, a
> melodramatic account of the events surrounding the pivotal
> "western" battle in the War Between the States. Because of
> that volume, Foote was asked to write a short history of the
> war to be published for its centennial. Instead, from 1958 to
> 1972 he produced his magnum opus, the three-volume *The
> Civil War: A Narrative*, which combines historical accuracy
> with narrative power and from which the present excerpt is
> taken. Shelby Foote figured prominently in Ken Burns's PBS
> series *The Civil War*.

Pierre Gustave Toutant Beauregard was as flamboyant by nature
as by name, and over the course of the past two years this quality, coupled all too often with a readiness to lay down the sword
and take up the pen in defense of his reputation with the public,
had got him into considerable trouble with his superiors, who
sometimes found it difficult to abide his Creole touchiness off
the field of battle for the sake of his undoubted abilities on it.
Called "Old Bory" by his men, though he was not yet forty-five,
the Hero of Sumter had twice been relieved of important commands, first in the East, where he had routed McDowell's inva-
sion attempt at Manassas, then in the West, where he had saved
his badly outnumbered army by giving Halleck the slip at
Corinth, and now he was back on the scene of his first glory in
Charleston harbor. Here, as elsewhere, he saw his position as the
hub of the wheel of war. Defying Union sea power, Mobile on

the Gulf and Wilmington, Savannah, and Charleston on the
Atlantic remained in Confederate hands, and of these four it was
clear at least to Beauregard that the one the Federals coveted
most was the last, variously referred to in their journals as "the
hotbed of treachery," "the cradle of secession," and "the nurs-
ery of disunion." Industrious as always, the general was determined that this proud South Carolina city should not suffer the
fate of his native New Orleans, no matter what force the Yankees
brought against it. Conducting frequent tours of inspection and
keeping up as usual a voluminous correspondence—a steady
stream of requisitions for more guns and men, more warships
and munitions, nearly all of which were returned to him regret-
fully unfilled—he only relaxed from his duties when he slept,
and even then he kept a pencil and a note pad under his pillow,
ready to jot down any notion that came to him in the night.
"Carolinians and Georgians!" he exhorted by proclamation.
"The hour is at hand to prove your devotion to your country's
cause. Let all able-bodied men, from the seaboard to the mountains, rush to arms. Be not exacting in the choice of weapons;
pikes and scythes will do for exterminating our enemies, spades
and shovels for protecting your friends. To arms, fellow citizens!
Come share with us our dangers, our brilliant success, or our
glorious death."

. . .

Inside the harbor, Beauregard was about as deep in the doldrums
as were the blue-clad sailors beyond the bar. Disappointed that
he had not been ordered west to resume command of the army
Bragg had inherited from him, privately he was telling friends
that his usefulness in the war had ended, and he predicted defeat
for the Confederacy no later than spring or summer. He gave as
the cause for both of these disasters "the persistent inability and
obstinacy of our rulers." Primarily he meant Davis, of whom he
said: "The curse of God must have been on our people when we
chose him out of so many noble sons of the South, who would
have carried us safely through this Revolution."

In addition to the frustration proceeding from his belief that presidential animosity, as evidenced by slights and snubs, had cost him the western command he so much wanted, the Creole's gloom was also due to the apparent failure of a new weapon he had predicted would accomplish, unassisted, the lifting of the Union blockade by the simple process of sinking the blockaders. There had arrived by rail from Mobile in mid-August, disassembled and loaded on two flatcars, a cigar-shaped metal vessel about thirty feet in length and less than four feet wide and five feet deep. Put back together and launched in Charleston harbor, she resembled the little *David*-class torpedo boats whose low silhouette made them hard for enemy lookouts to detect. Actually, though she had been designed to carry this advantage a considerable step further, in that she was intended to travel under as well as on the water, and thus present no silhouette at all. She was, in short, the world's first submarine. Christened the *H. L. Hunley* for one of her builders, who had come from Alabama with her to instruct the Carolinians in her use, she was propeller-driven but had no engine, deriving her power from her eight-man crew, posted at cranks along her drive shaft, which they turned on orders from her coxswain-captain. Water was let into ballast tanks to lower her until she was nearly awash; then her two hatches were bolted tight from inside, and as she moved forward the skipper took her down by depressing a pair of horizontal fins, which were also used to level and raise her while in motion. To bring her all the way up, force pumps ejected the water from her tanks, decreasing her specific gravity; or in emergencies her iron keel could be jettisoned in sections by disengaging the bolts that held it on, thus causing her to bob corklike to the surface. A glass port in the forward hatch enabled the steersman to see where he was going while submerged, and interior light was supplied by candles, which also served to warn of the danger of asphyxiation by guttering when the oxygen ran low. Practice dives in Mobile Bay had demonstrated that the *Hunley* could stay down for two hours before coming up for air, and she had proved her effectiveness as an offensive weapon by torpedoing and sinking two flatboats there. Her method of attack was quite as novel as her design. Towing at the end of a 200-foot line a copper cylinder packed with ninety pounds of powder and equipped with a percussion fuze, she would dive as she approached her target, pass completely under it, then elevate a bit and drag the towline across the keel of the enemy ship until the torpedo made contact and exploded, well astern of the submarine, whose crew would be cranking hard for a getaway, still underwater, and a return to port for a new torpedo to use on the next victim. Beauregard looked the strange craft over, had her workings explained to him by Hunley, and predicted an end to the Yankee blockade as soon as her newly volunteered crew learned to handle her well enough to launch their one-boat offensive against the U.S. Navy.

Such high hopes were often modified by sudden disappointments, and the *Hunley* was no exception to the general application of the rule. Certain drawbacks were soon as evident here as they had been at Mobile earlier: one being that she was a good deal easier to take down than she was to bring back up, particularly if something went wrong with her machinery, and something often did. She was in fact—as might have been expected from her combination of primitive means and delicate functions—accident-prone. On August 29, two weeks after her arrival, she was moored to a steamer tied to the Fort Johnson dock, resting her "engine" between dives, when the steamer unexpectedly got underway and pulled her over on her side. Water poured in through the open hatches, front and rear, and she went down so fast that only her skipper and two nimble seamen managed to get out before she hit the bottom. This was a practical demonstration that none of the methods providing for her return to the surface by her own devices would work unless she retained enough air to lift the weight of her iron hull; a started seam or a puncture, inflicted by chance or by enemy action while she was submerged, would mean her end, or at any rate the end of the submariners locked inside her. If this had not been clear before, it certainly was now. Still, there was no difficulty in finding more volunteers to man her, and Hunley himself, as soon as she had been raised and cleared of muck and corpses, petitioned Beauregard to let him take command. He did so on September 22 and began at once a period of intensive training to familiarize his new crew with her quirks. This lasted just over three weeks. On October 15, after making a series of practice dives in the harbor, she "left the wharf at 9:25 a.m. and disappeared at 9:35. As soon as she sank," the official post-mortem continued, "air bubbles were seen to rise to the surface of the water, and from this fact it is supposed the hole at the top of the boat by which the men entered was not properly closed." That was the end of Hunley and all aboard, apparently because someone had been careless. It was also thought to be the end of the vessel that bore his name, for she was nine fathoms down. A diver found her a few days later, however, and she was hauled back up again. Beauregard was on hand when her hatch lids were removed. "The spectacle was indescribably ghastly," he later reported with a shudder of remembrance. "The unfortunate men were contorted into all sorts of horrible attitudes, some clutching candles . . . others lying in the bottom tightly grappled together, and the blackened faces of all presented the expression of their despair and agony."

Despite this evidence of the grisly consequences, a third crew promptly volunteered for service under George E. Dixon, an army lieutenant who transferred from an Alabama regiment to the *Hunley* and was also a native of Mobile. Trial runs were renewed in early November, but the method of attack was not the same. Horrified by what he had seen when the unlucky boat was raised the second time, Beauregard had ordered that she was never again to function underwater, and she was equipped accordingly with a spar torpedo like the one her rival *David* had used against the *Ironsides*, ten days before she herself went into her last intentional dive. A surface vessel now like all the rest, except that she was still propelled by muscle power, she continued for the next three months to operate out of her base on Sullivan's Island, sometimes by day, sometimes by night. But conditions were never right for an attack; tide and winds conspired against her, and at times the underpowered craft was in danger of being swept out to sea because of the exhaustion of the men along her crankshaft. Finally though, in the early dusk of February 17, with a near-full moon to steer her by, a low-lying fog to screen her, and a strong-running ebb tide to increase her normal four-knot speed, Dixon maneuvered the *Hunley* out of the harbor and set a course for the Federal fleet, which lay at anchor in the wintry darkness, seven miles away.

At 8:45 the acting master of the 1,200-ton screw sloop *Housatonic*—more than two hundred feet in length and mounting a total of nine guns, including an 11-inch rifle—saw what he thought at first was "a plank moving [towards us] in the water" about a hundred yards away. By the time he knew better and ordered "the chain slipped, engine backed, and all hands called to quarters" in an attempt to take evasive action and bring his guns to bear, it was too late; "The torpedo struck forward of the mizzen mast, on the starboard side, in line with the magazine." Still trembling from shock, the big warship heeled to port and went down stern first. Five of her crew were killed or drowned, but fortunately for the others the water was shallow enough for them to save themselves by climbing the rigging, from which they were plucked by rescuers before the stricken vessel went to pieces.

There were no Confederate witnesses, for there were no Confederate survivors; the *Hunley* had made her first and last attack and had gone down with her victim, either because her hull had been cracked by the force of the explosion, only twenty feet away, or else because she was drawn into the vortex of the sinking *Housatonic*. In any case, searchers found what was left of the sloop and the submarine years later, lying side by side on the sandy bottom, just beyond the bar.

Confederate War, Beginning and End

HENRY TIMROD (1828–1867)

Born in Charleston under relatively humble circumstances, Henry Timrod was raised by his mother after his father's death in 1838. Because Timrod lacked means and spent much of his life in ill health, his education was sporadic. He became friends with Paul Hamilton Hayne at an early age, and their friendship lasted his lifetime.

Timrod became known as "the poet laureate of the Confederacy" for his patriotic lyrics glorifying the southern cause in the War Between the States. "What makes Timrod's best war poetry superior in kind to the now forgotten verses of all his Southern contemporaries," points out Louis D. Rubin, Jr., "is [his] ability to go beyond the patriotic assertion of loyalty and defiance into a deeper evocation of the historical occasion." The public social and political concerns that served as the source material for Timrod's work are fully identified with the private vision of the poet. His literary colleagues were the English romantic poets of the nineteenth century, including George Gordon Byron, William Wordsworth, and Alfred Tennyson. His literary principles were recorded in the 1859 essay "Literature in the South," in which he argued that form and beauty constitute the true material of poetry, rather than philosophical truth.

Timrod contributed to *Russell's Magazine* and the *Southern Literary Messenger* before the war. After being discharged from the Confederate army in 1864, he settled in Columbia, where he died destitute, at just thirty-eight.

In 1992 Henry Timrod was inducted into the South Carolina Academy of Authors.

Charleston

Calm as that second summer which precedes
  The first fall of the snow,
In the broad sunlight of heroic deeds,
  The city bides the foe.

As yet, behind their ramparts stern and proud,
  Her bolted thunders sleep—
Dark Sumter, like a battlemented cloud,
  Looms o'er the solemn deep.

No Calpe frowns from lofty cliff or scar
  To guard the holy strand;
But Moultrie holds in leash her dogs of war
  Above the level sand.

And down the dunes a thousand guns lie couched,
  Unseen, beside the flood—
Like tigers in some Oriental jungle crouched
  That wait and watch for blood.

Meanwhile, through streets still echoing with trade,
  Walk grave and thoughtful men,
Whose hands may one day wield the patriot's blade
  As lightly as the pen.

And maidens, with such eyes as would grow dim
  Over a bleeding hound,
Seem each one to have caught the strength of him
  Whose sword she sadly bound.

Thus girt without and garrisoned at home,
  Day patient following day,
Old Charleston looks from roof, and spire, and dome,
  Across her tranquil bay.

Ships, through a hundred foes, from Saxon lands
   And spicy Indian ports,
Bring Saxon steel and iron to her hands,
   And summer to her courts.

But still, along yon dim Atlantic line,
   The only hostile smoke
Creeps like a harmless mist above the brine,
   From some frail, floating oak.

Shall the Spring dawn, and she still clad in smiles,
   And with an unscathed brow,
Rest in the strong arms of her palm-crowned isles,
   As fair and free as now?

We know not; in the temple of the Fates
   God has inscribed her doom;
And, all untroubled in her faith, she waits
   The triumph or the tomb.

Ode

Sung on the occasion of decorating the graves of the Confederate
Dead, at Magnolia Cemetery, Charleston, South Carolina, 1867

I.
Sleep sweetly in your humble graves,
   Sleep, martyrs of a fallen cause;
Though yet no marble column craves
   The pilgrim here to pause.

II.
In seeds of laurel in the earth
   The blossom of your fame is blown,

And somewhere, waiting for its birth,
The shaft is in the stone!

III.
Meanwhile, behalf the tardy years
Which keep in trust your storied tombs,
Behold! your sisters bring their tears,
And these memorial blooms.

IV.
Small tributes! but your shades will smile
More proudly on these wreaths to-day,
Than when some cannon-moulded pile
Shall overlook this bay.

V.
Stoop, angels, hither from the skies!
There is no holier spot of ground
Than where defeated valor lies,
By mourning beauty crowned!

from *The American Scene*

HENRY JAMES (1843–1916)

> Son and namesake of the noted theologian and brother to phi-
> losopher and psychologist William James, Henry James largely
> set the standard for literary tastes in the early part of the twen-
> tieth century. He is well known for his short stories and novels
> (*The Europeans* [1878], *Daisy Miller* [1878], *Washington Square*
> [1880], *Portrait of a Lady* [1881], *The Bostonians* [1886], *The
> Aspern Papers* [1888], *The Turn of the Screw* [1898], and *The
> Ambassadors* [1903]), as well as his essays. James, an expatriate
> for most of his life, came back to the United States in 1904 after
> a twenty-year sojourn in Europe, and traveled throughout the
> country, writing lengthy essays on his travels. The resulting *The
> American Scene* contains the essay "Charleston," from which
> the following excerpt is taken.

There was literally no single object that, from morn to nightfall,
it was not more possible to consider with tenderness, a rich consistency of tenderness, than to consider without it: *such* was the
subtle trick that Charleston could still play. There echoed for me
as I looked out from the Battery the recent speech of a friend
which had had at the time a depressing weight; the Battery of the
long, curved sea-front, of the waterside public garden furnished
with sad old historic guns, with live-oaks draped in trailing
moss, with palmettos that, as if still mindful of their State sym-
bolism, seem to try everywhere, though with a melancholy scep-
tical droop, to repeat the old escutcheon; with its large, thrilling
view in particular—thrilling to a Northerner who stands there
for the first time. "Filled as I am, in general, while there," my
friend had said, "with the sadness and sorrow of the South, I
never, at Charleston, look out to the old betrayed Forts without
feeling my heart harden again to steel." One remembered that,
on the spot, and one waited a little—to see what was happening

to one's heart. I found this to take time indeed; everything differed, somehow, from one's old conceived image—or if I had
anciently grasped the remoteness of Fort Sumter, near the mouth
of the Bay, and of its companion, at the point of the shore forming the other side of the passage, this lucidity had so left me, in
the course of the years, that the far-away dimness of the conse-
crated objects was almost a shock. It was a blow even to one's
faded vision of Charleston viciously firing on the Flag; the Flag
would have been, from the Battery, such a mere speck in space
that the vice of the act lost somehow, with the distance, to say
nothing of the forty years, a part of its grossness. The smitten
face, however flushed and scarred, was out of sight, though the
intention of smiting and the force of the insult were of course
still the same. This reflection one made, but the old fancied perspective and proportions were altered; and then the whole picture, at that hour, exhaled an innocence. It was as blank as the
face of a child under mention of his naughtiness and his punish-
ment of week before last. The Forts, faintly blue on the twin-
kling sea, looked like vague marine flowers; innocence,
pleasantness ruled the prospect: it was as if the compromised
slate, sponged clean of all the wicked words and hung up on the
wall for better use, dangled there so vacantly as almost to look
foolish. Ah, there again was the word: the air still just tasted of
the antique folly; so that in presence of a lesson so sharp and so
prolonged, of the general *sterilized* state, of the brightly-lighted,
delicate dreariness recording the folly, harshness was conjured
away. There was that in the impression which affected me after
a little as one of those refinements of irony that wait on deep
expiations: one could scarce conceive at this time of day that
such a place had ever been dangerously moved. It was the *bled*
condition, and mostly the depleted cerebral condition, that was
thus attested—as I had recognized it at Richmond; and I asked
myself, on the Battery, what more one's sternest justice could
have desired. If my heart wasn't to harden to steel, in short,
access to it by the right influence had found perhaps too many
other forms of sensibility in ambush.

To justify hardness, moreover, one would have had to meet something hard; and if my peregrination, after this, had been a search for such an element I should have to describe it as made all in vain. Up and down and in and out, with my companion, I strolled from hour to hour; but more and more under the impression of the consistency of softness. One could have expressed the softness in a word, and the picture so offered would be infinitely touching. It was a city of gardens and absolutely of no men—or of so few that, save for the general sweetness, the War might still have been raging and all the manhood at the front. The gardens were matter for the women; though even of the women there were few, and that small company—rare, discreet, flitting figures that brushed the garden walls with noiseless skirts in the little melancholy streets of interspaced, over-tangled abodes—were clad in a rigour of mourning that was like the garb of a conspiracy. The effect was superficially prim, but so far as it savoured of malice prepense, of the Southern, the sentimental *parti-pris*, it was delightful. What was it all most like, the incoherent jumble of suggestions?—the suggestion of a social shrinkage and an economic blight unrepaired, irreparable; the suggestion of byways of some odd far East infected with triumphant women's rights, some perspective of builded, plastered lanes over the enclosures of which the flowering almond drops its petals into sharp deep bands of shade or of sun. It is not the muffled ladies who walk about predominantly in the East; but that is a detail. The likeness was perhaps greater to some little old-world quarter of quiet convents where only priests and nuns steal forth— the priests mistakable at a distance, say, for the nuns. It was indeed thoroughly mystifying, the whole picture—since I was to get, in the freshness of that morning, from the very background of the scene, my quite triumphant little impression of the "old South." I remember feeling with intensity at two or three points in particular that I should never get a better one, that even this was precarious—might melt at any moment, by a wrong touch or a false note, in my grasp—and that I must therefore make the most of it. The rest of my time, I may profess, was spent in so doing. I made the most of it in several successive spots: under the south wall of St. Michael's Church, the sweetest corner of Charleston, and of which there is more to say; out in the old Cemetery on the edge of the lagoon, where the distillation of the past was perhaps clearest and the bribe to tenderness most effective; and even not a little on ground thereunto almost adjacent, that of a kindly Country-Club installed in a fine old semi-sinister mansion, and holding an afternoon revel at which I was privileged briefly to assist. The wrong touch and the false note were doubtless just sensible in this last connection, where the question, probed a little, would apparently have been of some new South that has not yet quite found the effective way romantically, or at least insidiously, to appeal. The South that is cultivating country-clubs is a South presumably, in many connections, quite in the right; whereas the one we were invidiously "after" was the one that had been so utterly in the wrong. Even there, none the less, in presence of more than a single marked sign of the rude Northern contagion, I disengaged, socially speaking, a faint residuum which I mention for proof of the intensity of my quest and of my appreciation.

There were two other places, I may add, where one could but work the impression for all it was, in the modern phrase, "worth," and where I had, I may venture to say, the sense of making as much of it as was likely ever to be made again. Meanings without end were to be read, under tuition, into one of these, which was neither more nor less than a slightly shy, yet after all quite serene place of refection, a luncheon-room or tea-house, denominated for quaint reasons an "Exchange"—*the very Exchange* in fact lately commemorated in a penetrating study, already much known to fame, of the little that is left of the local society. My tuition, at the hands of my ingenious comrade, was the very best it was possible to have. Nothing, usually, is more wonderful than the quantity of significant character that, with such an example set, the imagination may recognize in the scantest group of features, objects, persons. I fantastically feasted here, at my luncheon-table, not only, as the genius of the place demanded, on hot chocolate, sandwiches and "Lady Baltimore" cake (this last a most delectable compound), but on the exact *nuance* of oddity, of bravery, of reduced gentility, of irreducible superiority, to which the opening of such an establishment, without derogation, by the proud daughters of war-wasted families, could exquisitely testify. They hovered, the proud impoverished daughters, singly or in couples, behind the counter—a counter, again, delectably charged; they waited, inscrutably, irreproachably, yet with all that peculiarly chaste *bonhomie* of the Southern tone, on the customers' wants, even coming to ascertain these at the little thrifty tables; and if the drama and its adjusted theatre really contained all the elements of history, tragedy, comedy, irony, that a pair of expert romancers, closely associated for the hour, were eager to evoke, the scene would have been, I can only say, supreme of its kind. That desire of the artist to linger where the breath of a "subject," faintly stirring the air, reaches his vigilant sense, would here stay my steps—as this very influence was in fact, to his great good fortune, to stay those of my companion. The charm I speak of, the charm to cherish, however, was most exhaled for me in other conditions—conditions that scarce permit of any direct reference to their full suggestiveness. If I alluded above to the vivid Charleston background, where its "mystification" most scenically persists, the image is all rounded and complete, for memory, in this connection at which—as the case is of an admirably mature and preserved interior—I can only glance as I pass. The puzzlement elsewhere is in the sense that though the elements of earth and air, the colour, the tone, the light, the sweetness in fine, linger on, the "old South" could have had no such unmitigated mildness, could never have seen itself as subject to such strange feminization. The feminization is there just to promote for us some eloquent antithesis; just to make us say that whereas the ancient order was masculine, fierce and moustachioed, the present is at the most a sort of sick lioness who has so visibly parted with her teeth and claws that we may patronizingly walk all round her.

This image really gives us the best word for the general effect of Charleston—that of the practically vacant cage which used in the other time to emit sounds, even to those of the portentous shaking of bars, audible as far away as in the listening North. It is the vacancy that is a thing by itself, a thing that makes us endlessly wonder. How, in an at all complex, a "great political," society, can *everything* so have gone?—assuming indeed that, under this aegis, very much ever had come. How can everything so have gone that the only "Southern" book of any distinction published for many a year is *The Souls of Black Folk*, by that most accomplished of members of the negro race, Mr. W. E. B. Du Bois? Had the *only* focus of life then been Slavery?—from the point onward that Slavery had reached a quarter of a century before the War, so that with the extinction of that interest none other of any sort was left. To say "yes" seems the only way to account for the degree of the vacancy, and yet even as I form that word I meet as a reproach the face of the beautiful old house I just mentioned, whose ample spaces had so unmistakably echoed to the higher amenities that one seemed to feel the accumulated traces and tokens gradually come out of their corners like blest objects taken one by one from a reliquary worn with much handling. The note of such haunted chambers as these—haunted structurally, above all, quite as by the ghost of the grand style— was not, certainly, a thinness of reverberation; so that I had to take refuge here in the fact that everything appeared thoroughly to *antedate*, to refer itself to the larger, the less vitiated past that had closed a quarter of a century or so before the War, before the fatal time when the South, monomaniacal at the parting of the ways, "elected" for extension and conquest. The admirable old house of the stately hall and staircase, of the charming coved and vaulted drawing-room, of the precious mahogany doors, the tall unsophisticated portraits, the delicate dignity of welcome, owed nothing of its noble identity, nothing at all appreciable, to the monomania. However that might be, moreover, I kept finding the mere melancholy charm reassert itself where it could— the charm, I mean, of the flower-crowned waste that was, by my measure, what the monomania had most prepared itself to bequeathe. In the old Cemetery by the lagoon, to which I have already alluded, this influence distills an irresistible poetry—as one has courage to say even in remembering how disproportionately, almost anywhere on the American scene, the general place of interment is apt to be invited to testify for the presence of charm. The golden afternoon, the low, silvery, seaward horizon, as of wide, sleepy, game-haunted inlets and reed-smothered banks, possible site of some Venice that had never mustered, the luxury, in the mild air, of shrub and plant and blossom that the pale North can but distantly envy; something that I scarce know how to express but as the proud humility of the whole idle, easy loveliness, made even the restless analyst, for the hour, among the pious inscriptions that scarce ever belie the magniloquent clime or the inimitable tradition, feel himself really capable of the highest Carolinian pitch.

from *Lady Baltimore*

OWEN WISTER (1860–1938)

> Owen Wister today is known mainly for his novel *The Virginian* (1902), which was wildly popular when published and inspired a number of television and movie adaptations. He visited Charleston frequently, was well known among members of Charleston society, and was a keen observer of the unique aspects of the downtown social order. His observations became the source material for the romantic novel *Lady Baltimore* (1906), set in the thinly disguised Charleston known as "Kings Port." A close friend of President Theodore Roosevelt, Wister at one time stayed at the Villa Margherita on South Battery with President Roosevelt's party.

Thus it was that I came to sojourn in the most appealing, the most lovely, the most wistful town in America; whose visible sadness and distinction seem also to speak audibly, speak in the sound of the quiet waves that ripple round her Southern front, speak in the church-bells on Sunday morning, and breathe not only in the soft salt air, but in the perfume of every gentle, old-fashioned rose that blooms behind the high garden walls of falling mellow-tinted plaster: Kings Port the retrospective, Kings Port the belated, who from her pensive porticoes looks over her two rivers to the marshes and the trees beyond, the live-oaks, veiled in gray moss, brooding with memories! Were she my city, how I should love her!

But though my city she cannot be, the enchanting image of her is mine to keep, to carry with me wheresoever I may go; for who, having seen her, could forget her? Therefore I thank Aunt Carola for this gift, and for what must always go with it in my mind, the quiet and strange romance which I saw happen, and came finally to share in. Why it is that my Aunt no longer wishes to know either the boy or the girl, or even to hear their names mentioned, you shall learn at the end, when I have finished with the wedding; for this happy story of love ends with a wedding, and begins in the Woman's Exchange, which the ladies of Kings Port have established, and (I trust) lucratively conduct, in Royal Street.

Royal Street! There's a relevance in this name, a fitness to my errand; but that is pure accident.

The Woman's Exchange happened to be there, a decorous resort for those who became hungry, as I did, at the hour of noon each day. In my very pleasant boarding-house, where, to be sure, there was one dreadful boarder, a tall lady, whom I soon secretly called Juno—but let unpleasant things wait—in the very pleasant house where I boarded (I had left my hotel after one night) our breakfast was at eight, and our dinner not until three: sacred meal hours in Kings Port, as inviolable, I fancy, as the Declaration of Independence, but a gap quite beyond the stretch of my Northern vitals. Therefore, at twelve, it was my habit to leave my Fanning researches for a while, and lunch at the Exchange upon chocolate and sandwiches most delicate in savor. As, one day, I was luxuriously biting one of these, I heard his voice and what he was saying. Both the voice and the interesting order he was giving caused me, at my small table, in the dim back of the room, to stop and watch him where he stood in the light at the counter to the right of the entrance door. Young he was, very young, twenty-two or three at the most, and as he stood, with hat in hand, speaking to the pretty girl behind the counter, his head and side-face were of a romantic and high-strung look. It was a cake that he desired made, a cake for a wedding; and I directly found myself curious to know whose wedding. Even a dull wedding interests me more than other dull events, because it can arouse so much surmise and so much prophecy; but in this wedding I instantly, because of his strange and winning embarrassment, became quite absorbed. How came it he was ordering the cake for it? Blushing like the boy that he was entirely, he spoke in a most engaging voice: "No, not charged; and as you don't know me, I had better pay for it now."

Self-possession in his speech he almost had; but the blood in his cheeks and forehead was beyond his control.

A reply came from behind the counter: "We don't expect payment until delivery."

"But—a—but on that morning I shall be rather particularly engaged." His tones sank almost away on these words.

"We should prefer to wait, then. You will leave your address. In half-pound boxes, I suppose?"

"Boxes? Oh, yes—I hadn't thought—no—just a big, round one. Like this, you know!" His arms embraced a circular space of air. "With plenty of icing."

I do not think that there was any smile on the other side of the counter; there was, at any rate, no hint of one in the voice. "And how many pounds?"

He was again staggered. "Why—a—I never ordered one before. I want plenty—and the very best, the very best. Each person would eat a pound, wouldn't they? Or would two be nearer? I think I had better leave it all to you. About like this, you know." Once more his arms embraced a circular space of air.

Before this I had never heard the young lady behind the counter enter into any conversation with a customer. She would talk at length about all sorts of Kings Port affairs with the older ladies connected with the Exchange, who were frequently to be found there; but with a customer, never. She always took my orders, and my money, and served me, with a silence and a propriety that have become, with ordinary shopkeepers, a lost art. *They* talk to one indeed! But this slim girl was a lady, and consequently did the right thing, marking and keeping a distance between herself and the public. To-day, however, she evidently felt it her official duty to guide the hapless young man amid his errors. He now appeared to be committing a grave one.

"Are you quite sure you want that?" the girl was asking.

"Lady Baltimore? Yes, that is what I want."

"Because," she began to explain, then hesitated, and looked at him. Perhaps it was in his face; perhaps it was that she remembered at this point the serious difference between the price of Lady Baltimore (by my small bill-of-fare I was now made acquainted with its price) and the cost of that rich article which convention has prescribed as the cake for weddings; at any rate, swift, sudden delicacy of feeling prevented her explaining any more to him, for she saw how it was: his means were too humble for the approved kind of wedding cake! She was too young, too unskilled yet in the world's ways, to rise above her embarrassment; and so she stood blushing at him behind the counter, while he stood blushing at her in front of it.

At length he succeeded in speaking. "That's all, I believe. Good-morning."

At his hastily departing back she, too, murmured: "Good-morning."

Before I knew it I had screamed out loudly from my table: "But he hasn't told you the day he wants it for!"

Before she knew it she had flown to the door—my cry had set her going, as if I had touched a spring—and there he was at the door himself, rushing back. He, too, had remembered. It was almost a collision, and nothing but their good Southern breeding, the way they took it, saved it from being like a rowdy farce.

"I know," he said simply and immediately. "I am sorry to be so careless. It's for the twenty-seventh."

She was writing it down in the order-book. "Very well. That is Wednesday of next week. You have given us more time than we need." She put complete, impersonal business into her tone; and this time he marched off in good order, leaving peace in the Woman's Exchange.

No, not peace; quiet, merely; the girl at the counter now proceeded to grow indignant with me. We were alone together, we two; no young man, or any other business, occupied her or protected me. But if you suppose that she made war, or expressed rage by speaking, that is not it at all. From her counter in front to my table at the back she made her displeasure felt; she was inaudibly crushing; she did not do it even with her eye, she managed it—well, with her neck, somehow, and by the way she made her nose look in profile. Aunt Carola would have embraced her—and I should have liked to do so myself. She could not stand the idea of my having, after all these days of official reserve that she had placed between us, startled her into that rush to the door, annihilated her dignity at a blow. So did I finish my sand-wiches beneath her invisible but eloquent fire. What affair of mine was the cake? And what sort of impertinent, meddlesome person was I, shrieking out my suggestions to people with whom I had no acquaintance? These were the things that her nose and her neck said to me the whole length of the Exchange. I had nothing but my own weakness to thank; it was my interest in weddings that did it, made me forget my decorum, the public place, myself, everything, and plunge in. And I became more and more delighted over it as the girl continued to crush me. My day had been dull, my researches had not brought me a whit nearer royal blood; I looked at my little bill-of-fare, and then I stepped forward to the counter, adventurous, but polite.

"I should like a slice, if you please, of Lady Baltimore," I said with extreme formality.

I thought she was going to burst; but after an interesting sec-ond she replied, "Certainly," in her regular Exchange tone; only, I thought it trembled a little.

I returned to the table and she brought me the cake, and I had my first felicitous meeting with Lady Baltimore. Oh, my good-ness! Did you ever taste it? It's all soft, and it's in layers, and it has nuts—but I can't write any more about it; my mouth waters too much.

Delighted surprise caused me once more to speak aloud, and with my mouth full. "But, dear me, this is delicious!"

A choking ripple of laughter came from the counter. "It's I who make them," said the girl. "I thank you for the uninten-tional compliment." Then she walked straight back to my table. "I can't help it," she said, laughing still, and her delightful, inso-lent nose well up; "how can I behave myself when a man goes on as you do?" A nice white curly dog followed her, and she stroked his ears.

"Your behavior is very agreeable to me," I remarked.

"You'll allow me to say that you're not invited to criticize it. I was decidedly put out with you for making me ridiculous. But you have admired my cake with such enthusiasm that you are forgiven. And—may I hope that you are getting on famously with the battle of Cowpens?"

I stared. "I'm frankly very much astonished that you should know about that!"

"Oh, you're just known all about in Kings Port."

I wish that our miserable alphabet could in some way render the soft Southern accent which she gave to her words. But it cannot. I could easily misspell, if I chose; but how, even then, could I, for instance, make you hear her way of saying "about"? "Aboot" would magnify it; and besides, I decline to make ugly to the eye her quite special English, that was so charming to the ear.

"Kings Port just knows all about you," she repeated with a sweet and mocking laugh.

"Do you mind telling me how?"

She explained at once. "This place is death to all incognitos."

The explanation, however, did not, on the instant, enlighten me. "This? The Woman's Exchange, you mean?"

"Why, to be sure! Have you not heard ladies talking together here?"

I blankly repeated her words. "Ladies talking?"

She nodded.

"Oh!" I cried. "How dull of me! Ladies talking! Of course!"

She continued. "It was therefore widely known that you were consulting our South Carolina archives at the library—and then that notebook you bring marked you out the very first day. Why, two hours after your first lunch we just knew all about you!"

"Dear me!" said I.

"Kings Port is ever ready to discuss strangers," she further explained. "The Exchange has been going on five years, and the resident families have discussed each other so thoroughly here that everything is known; therefore a stranger is a perfect boon." Her gayety for a moment interrupted her, before she continued, always mocking and always sweet: "Kings Port cannot boast intelligence offices for servants; but if you want to know the character and occupation of your friends, come to the Exchange!" How I wish I could give you the raciness, the contagion, of her laughter! Who would have dreamed that behind her primness all this frolic lay in ambush? "Why," she said, "I'm only a plantation girl; it's my first week here, and I know every wicked deed everybody has done since 1812!"

She went back to her counter. It had been very merry; and as I was settling the small debt for my lunch I asked: "Since this is the proper place for information, will you kindly tell me whose wedding that cake is for?"

She was astonished. "You don't know? And I thought you were quite a clever Ya—I beg your pardon—Northerner."

"Please tell me, since I know you're quite a clever Reb—I beg your pardon—Southerner."

"Why, it's his own! Couldn't you see that from his bashfulness?"

"Ordering his own wedding cake?" Amazement held me. But the door opened, one of the elderly ladies entered, the girl behind the counter stiffened to primness in a flash, and I went out into Royal Street as the curly dog's tail wagged his greeting to the newcomer.

"Charleston, South Carolina"

AMY LOWELL (1874–1925)

Amy Lowell was a member of a celebrated New England family that included distinguished poets James Russell Lowell and Robert Lowell. She embraced the Imagist movement, which was led by Ezra Pound, and she promoted a renewed interest in poetry, poetics, and especially new forms.

Lowell paid several visits to Charleston and was invited as a guest reader by the Poetry Society of South Carolina, an organization which she encouraged and supported over many years. The 1921 yearbook of the Poetry Society of South Carolina includes this greeting from her: "Charleston ought to have a Poetry Society, and a poetry society which cares more for poetry than the politics thereof. For why? Because Charleston has more poetic appeal than almost any city in America. Some fifteen years ago I passed a few weeks there and those weeks have left an indelible impression upon me. It was in the spring, the azaleas in the Middleton Place in full bloom, with the sea cool, stretched blue, with the houses as lovely and fresh as their own gardens. It is a place for poets, indeed. History touches legend in Charleston; art has harnessed nature, and nature has ramped away and transcended art; the town is beautiful with the past, and glorious with the present; its wealth of folklore has been very little touched upon in poetry. What a mine for someone, what an atmosphere!" She remained a lifelong friend and confidante of local poet Beatrice Witte Ravenel.

Fifteen years is not a long time,
But long enough to build a city over and destroy it.
Long enough to clean a forty-year growth of grass from
　　between cobblestones,
And run street-car lines straight across the heart of
　　romance.

Commerce, are you worth this?
I should like to bring a case to trial:
Prosperity versus Beauty,
Cash registers teetering in a balance against the comfort
of the soul.
Then, to-night, I stood looking through a grilled gate
At an old, dark garden.
Live-oak trees dripped branchfuls of leaves over the wall,
Acacias waved dimly beyond the gate, and the smell of
their blossoms
Puffed intermittently through the wrought-iron
scroll-work.
Challenge and solution—
O loveliness of old, decaying, haunted things!
Little streets untouched, shamefully paved,
Full of mist and fragrance on this rainy evening.
"You should come at dawn," said my friend,
"And see the orioles, and thrushes, and mockingbirds
In the garden."

"Yes," I said absent-mindedly,
And remarked the sharp touch of ivy upon my hand
which rested against the wall.
But I thought to myself,
There is no dawn here, only sunset,
And an evening rain scented with flowers.

from *The Case of Mr. Crump*

LUDWIG LEWISOHN (1883–1955)

> Ludwig Lewisohn was born in Germany of Orthodox Jewish parents who immigrated to St. Matthews, South Carolina, when Lewisohn was young. They moved to Charleston in 1892, and Lewisohn spent the remainder of his youth in the city, graduating from the High School of Charleston and the College of Charleston. His first novel, *The Broken Snare*, was published in 1908. His successful autobiographies, *Up Stream* (1922) and *Mid-Channel* (1929), addressed many of the difficulties he faced growing up and seeking work as a Jew. He taught at major institutions and worked for many years as an editor and critic. His field of expertise was German literature, particularly the poet Rainer Maria Rilke. In 1926 he published in Paris the novel *The Case of Mr. Crump*, based on his early life and first marriage. Though praised by Sigmund Freud and Thomas Mann, it could not be published in America until 1947, when obscenity laws were eased. The excerpt below is clearly autobiographical, as his family lived on Calhoun Street, across the street from the Emanuel African Methodist Episcopal Church. Charleston here is known as Queenshaven.

To Herbert the word home never meant anything else than the house in Calhoun Street into which his parents moved when he was a small boy. Like all the old-fashioned Queenshaven houses it turned its gable end toward the street so that the piazzas, the upstairs and the downstairs, could face the breezes of the south and west. The house stood flush with the street. Behind it, to the very end of the deep yard, stretched a line of tiny, black, two-story cottages inhabited by Negroes. In Herbert's early boyhood Calhoun Street was still paved with half-hewn palmetto logs. Opposite the house on the other side of the street there stood, newly completed except for the steeple which was never built, the large Afro-American Methodist Church. The house next door to the Crumps, which belonged to an Irish family named Delaney, was set far back in a narrow garden, so that from his upper piazza Herbert watched all through his childhood and youth a great clear stretch of the Southern heavens and thus grew up familiar with strong blues and golds, the pomp of sunsets, the grave glitter of crowded constellations.

The visible world intoxicated him from the beginning. More clearly and elementarily the world of sound. He was four years old, as his mother told him later, and had followed his grandfather into the cool, slightly musty church one afternoon. He had climbed with the old gentleman into the organ-loft. The sonorous vibrations of sound had made the child tremble and turn pale and the ecstasy had become so insupportable that he had dropped sobbing on the floor and had had to be carried home. Herbert barely remembered this incident. But he remembered clearly, remembered with a quickening of his blood and a tingling of his skin, how music had affected him from his earliest years. At five he himself began to play. He would stop his practice, which seemed an impediment only, to strike chords, simple chords which, by their rich uncomplicated consonance, sufficed to flood him with well-being. Gradually, of course, he became more hardened to the ecstasy of mere sound. But always there recurred moments of its unbelievable poignancy. There were things that for years he could never play through to the end. They broke him. Things by Chopin, such as the "Nocturne in F," quite simple things by Schumann, certain adagios in Beethoven's sonatas. He fled to Handel and Mozart and his father thought that the boy had perhaps inherited his grandfather's sobriety of temper. But Herbert's mother always knew better. For she would sing the "*Möricke Lieder*" of Hugo Wolf and Herbert would sit in a dim corner of the room with tears streaming down his face. "*Lass, O Welt, O lass mich sein . . .*" The boy would grasp his dark tousled hair; the mother, watching him, stopped playing and drew him to her bosom.

There was another world of sound about Herbert, a world to which his father and mother paid little attention. But it thrilled and haunted him and remained forever memorable to him. There were Negroes in the back-yard, as it was called, there was the Negro Church across the street; there were Negroes all around. Herbert would go to Paul Fludd, the butcher, to buy two cents worth of meat for his cat. And the enormous black man would be singing in his vibrant bass voice: "Dee—ee—ee—eep rivah . . ." Hack! The cleaver came down on the meat and the marvelous melody was interrupted. Herbert was too shy to ask Paul to go on and finish his song. So whenever he left the house he would first go a bit eastward toward the Cooper River and listen for the singing of Paul the butcher. But that was not all. He waked up early sometimes in his garret room and would go to the window and see Queenshaven in the dawn like a city carved of mother of pearl under a sky as faintly iridescent as the inner curve of a seashell. He would watch the elderly Negresses coming from the bay. On their red head-kerchiefs they carried large flat wooden platters full of fresh, faintly coral-tinted shrimps to be boiled early and served with hominy at the white folks' breakfast tables. In their rich untutored voices the women would cry their wares: "O you shrimps! O you oysters!" And there was one old Negro man who sang up and down the scale in a dreamy, strange sing-song: "Buy fresh buttermilk . . ." Herbert caught tones and cadences in these Queenshaven streets cries of his childhood that many years later puzzled the critics in his works.

Sunday was a great day for the boy. He was permitted to attend church, not in the pew with his mother, but in the organ-loft watching his father play the handsome new triple-manual organ and treading the pedals and desperately but softly keeping the amateur choir in order. These flirtatious young persons wanted to show off; they wanted to sing new and attractive music. They thought the Lutheran Church of their fathers with German song and sermon a little common anyhow. The frowsy, freckled pale-eyed popular soprano had once turned languishingly to the stern choir-master. "Do you know, Professor Crump, what my friend Agnes Bayer sang for offertory at Grace Church last Sunday?" Crump's eyes turned severely on the fluffy, diminutive person.

"Well, what?" The girl answered with a pert gesture of the head:
"The Intermezzo from *Cavalleria Rusticana*." Herbert always
remembered with a profound pride his father's dry, infinitely
decisive: "Good; let her. Not here!" The soprano was the daughter of a very rich pew-holder. But Herman Crump was a righ-
teous man. In his small obscure place in the world he stood firm
for the good. He closed his near-sighted eyes after such an epi-
sode, leaned forward, played a Fugue of Bach and relented with
Beethoven's "*Die Himmel rühmen des Ewigen Ehre . . .*" In that
organ-loft Herbert learned both music and morals. Memories of
those Sunday mornings came to sustain him in dark and tortured
hours of his later years.

Sunday afternoons were drowsy. In the snowless Queenshaven
winters they were usually mild and golden. After dinner Herbert
would climb up to his attic and dream over a book. Above his
dream he listened. In the Afro-American Church with its stump
of a tower across the street the Sunday service was an all-day
service and people came and went and chanted and "shouted."
And now and again the sisters who had "seen Jesus" were carried into the cottages in the Crump back-yard and were prayed
and crooned over. And whatever else was going on in the church,
even during the early sermon whenever the preacher's voice fell,
the congregation chanted a single chant. Sunday after Sunday
the congregation chanted that chant, year in and year out. All
through Herbert's childhood and boyhood and youth he heard
that melancholy chant. And he used often to think, as time went
on and on and life turned out so strangely for him, that if he
could only go alone to visit Queenshaven and walk from Marion
Square eastward to Calhoun Street and stand in front of the old
house and hear the Negroes chant that chant again, that then the
foul ice which fate had made to congeal in his bosom might melt
and a miracle happen within him to placate the seemingly impla-
cable powers.

It was a very simple chant that the Negroes across the street so
tirelessly chanted. When Herbert was about fifteen it suddenly
occurred to him one Sunday afternoon that the chant must not

be lost. He wrote it down, jotted it down quite simply without any bass.

But he knew at once that the notes held neither the great resignation nor the terribly moving aspiration of simple souls that sounded in the endless, dragging, clinging chant. The C natural at the beginning of the sixth measure—did it not create an interval of infinitude? Did not the souls of the overburdened liberate themselves in it for one moment of eternity? Only to return to earth, to be sure, but with a vision and a hope that sounded full and strong and sonorous—for all its undertone of wailing—in the breadth and large peace of the final measure. Herbert, at all events, believed steadily that this chant, interwoven with all the memories of his earlier years, had an extraordinary musical value. It furnished him with the groundwork of the thematic material of the tone-poem "Renunciation" with its motto from Goethe (*"Entsagen sollst du, sollst entsagen . . ."*), the performance of which by the Society of the Friends of Music came too late to do him any good. Curiously enough, he never, during his boyhood, spoke to his parents of the absorption of so many of his hours by the magic of the Negro music. He had an obscure feeling that they might not share his taste. And then, as later, he had an unconquerable aversion from the strain and futility of disagreement and debate.

The earliest years of school were like a dream. But it was school that at last created the division between day and dream. It could be dismissed no longer, but threw its jagged shadow into the home. A little conflict arose which was symbolized in Herbert's memory by one brief colloquy between his father and his mother that took place one Friday afternoon when he had brought home a shockingly bad report of his week's work. His father arose in wrath. He could hear his mother's rich contralto speaking voice and her soft Viennese accent: *"Lass mir den Bub in Ruh, Hermann, seine Begabung liegt halt in einer andern Richtung!"* His father turned to his mother, severe and sorrowful: *"Und die Pflicht, Meta, die Pflicht?"* Then he left the room. The mother turned to the boy. "Papa is quite right—as always. You simply must do better, darling." But the boy knew that there was no real conviction behind her words. The North German conception of duty for duty's sake, irrespective of temperament or aim, was foreign to her nature. The boy perceived and, of course, passionately embraced his mother's point of view. The day came when he saw that there was much more than he had imagined to be said for his father's too.

The trouble with school, in actual fact, was not the studies. Herbert could have mastered these. It was the teachers, the atmosphere, the boys. It cannot be said that he was pampered at home. He obeyed his parents without question. He was by nature the reverse of forward. But he was, after all, an only child. There was no friction and no corrective rivalry in the home. When the little daughters of his father's sister, Flora and Annabelle Schott, came to visit, he was very gentle and polite. In fact he liked them, especially Flora, who had a long thick braid of chestnut brown hair and very red lips and liked to play a game with kisses as forfeits. Yet he was always relieved and very tired when the girls went. They were all over the house; they touched things and pulled them out of place in what seemed to him a restless and unreasonable way. It was from his father's side that he must have gotten his innate and almost pedantic love of order. It was a source of quiet amusement to his mother to see Bertie follow the little girls from room to room and with polite unobtrusiveness straighten things out after them.

School was to Herbert a leashed chaos at best, namely in the classroom, an open pandemonium before and between and after classes. The boys' spirit of raising hell for its own sake irritated him obscurely but deeply. He liked some of the teachers and studies no more than they. He would far rather have been at home or playing or walking with Ralph Greene or even with Eddie Bierfischer. But spit-balls and pea-shooters seemed to him, years before he could formulate such feelings in words, stupidly and nastily irrelevant to the situation. Ralph and Eddie more or less shared his attitude. Once in a long while the three boys would simply "play hookey"; they would quietly disappear after the noon recess. But this method wasn't satisfactory either. For the boys, in spite of the quiet bravado with which they didn't quite deceive one another, were all three darkly oppressed by a sense of the consequences of their truancy, especially of the annoyance it might cause their fathers. So they wandered rather forlornly about and ended by planning excuses to be presented at school and at home. Sometimes they envied the "Birdie" Reynolds type who, tall, wiry, sheer muscle and sinew, smote all the other boys' hip and thigh surreptitiously in the classroom, openly on the playground and lied to the teachers with an impenetrable impudence on his blue-eyed and angelic countenance. They envied "Birdie"; occasionally they tried to imitate him and always, of course, came to grief. At last one day, in the second year of high school, when Eddie and Herbert were joining in a game of fastening pins, points forward, into your shoes and jabbing the boys in front of you, Ralph, the oldest of the three, turned a disgusted face to his friends. "For Christ's sake, quit your foolishness! I want to work!" It was like a liberation to Herbert. He didn't have to pretend any more. He practiced for three hours that afternoon and that evening threw his "pony" into the attic closet and found that he could construe his thirty lines of Caesar in just about the same time that it took him to fit the pidgin English of Hinds and Noble's hacks to the Latin on the page before him. School still nauseated him often enough. But the worst was over. By applying his natural methodicalness to his actual circumstances he discovered that he could find time for school, for his music, for his play. He had to sacrifice his great secret occupation—the constant scribbling of music. With a strength of character rare in a boy of thirteen, he deliberately put it off until summer. But vacations were fifteen weeks long and seemed endless in those days.

Sometimes, of course, he broke his resolution. Strange circumstances would arise. Ralph Greene came with a flicker in his eyes that were usually reserved and steady. "Come on, Bert, let's go for a walk." "Where to?" "To Society Street." "Shucks, that isn't much of a walk." Ralph tugged at Herbert's sleeve. There was an urgency and an appeal in his gesture. "Aw, come on!" Suddenly a sense of feverish expectancy communicated itself to Herbert. His throat went hot and dry. "Oh, all right, if you want to." By a common impulse the two boys now hurried along the few blocks down Meeting Street. At the corner of Society Street stood the two Gallagher girls, slim, tall for their age, with sweet, identical, oval faces, a few freckles on their tilted noses, large, empty eyes. "How do you do?" they said in a very grown-up way. The boys lifted their caps: "How do you do?" they said in an equally seemly fashion. Ralph paired off with Kate, Herbert with Estelle. A choking silence followed. "Have you ever played circus?" Estelle asked. "No," said Herbert, "but I'd like to if"—a sudden inspiration leaped out of the hot sweetness in his belly—"I'd like to if you're in it!" The girl giggled and looked pleased and let her white sleeve brush Herbert's shoulder.

In the middle of the block they met Hen Hanahan, a boy with a curved mouth that went almost from ear to ear, and a clown-like head, round as an apple. With him was a girl who had fiercely red hair and a slatternly appearance. Estelle turned to Herbert. "Did you ever see the circus? It's in the basement of Hen's house." They were in front of the narrow four-story house. The basement could be entered from the street. Three steps down. It was an ordinary paved cellar strewn with saw-dust. The boys and girls went in and sat down on boxes ranged along the wall. The pretence at playing circus was brief and fee-ble. Hen stood on his head in the middle of the floor. Then he sprang up and slammed and latched the wooden door to the street. Silence and black darkness. Herbert thought that his heart would literally leap into his throat as he felt the head of Estelle on his shoulder and inhaled the fresh odor of the girl's hair. It was she who found his lips and pushed his hands. After that he needed no guidance. There were giggles; there were jokes. All speech was seemly and calculated to fortify the pre-tence that there was no harm in this game. Nothing fatal and ultimate did in fact happen. But these children of the South had a strong, dumb, ecstatic eroticism—fierce, earnest, almost exalted. The sharp voice of Hen Hanahan came suddenly; "Must be most supper time!" All voices babbled with a cool assumption of naturalness; the door was opened and a calming breeze swept in. The boys and girls wandered out into the dusk and separated casually. Ralph said to Herbert: "Want to come again?" And Herbert answered with the same affected carelessness: "Oh, I guess so." But that night, after the first broken feeling wore off, he covered sheet after sheet of paper with notes and dropped the sheets on the floor. In the early dawn he gathered the sheets and locked them in his little oak desk.

"A Hedonist"

JOHN GALSWORTHY (1867–1933)

John Galsworthy, a British playwright, novelist, and winner of the 1932 Nobel Prize in Literature, was known for his depiction of the English upper classes. He visited Charleston in 1919 and, from the Villa Margherita on South Battery, wrote to a friend in England: "This carries our dear love to you from a wonderful place so strangely un-American, as America is in the north. A place too of wonderful subtle colorings, and scents (not to say sometimes smells), and old time houses, and families, and dreaminess about time. To-day we went by car to the Magnolia Gardens eleven miles away—a dream of a place, really a dream. The Southern voices are very soft and pretty and the owners thereof are awfully nice." Charleston was ripe fruit for Galsworthy's social commentary. "A Hedonist" appeared in *Century Magazine* in 1921.

At the time of his visit, Galsworthy was remarkably prolific, publishing at least a book a year from 1906 until his death almost thirty years later. The first volume in his Forsyte trilogy, *The Man of Property*, appeared in 1906.

Rupert K. Vaness remains freshly in my mind because he was so fine and large, and because he summed up in his person and behavior a philosophy which, budding before the war, hibernated during that distressing epoch, and is now again in bloom.

He was a New-Yorker addicted to Italy. One often puzzled over the composition of his blood. From his appearance, it was rich, and his name fortified the conclusion. What the K. stood for, however, I never learned; the three possibilities were equally intriguing. Had he a strain of Highlander with Kenneth or Keith; a drop of German or Scandinavian with Kurt or Knut; a blend of Syrian or Armenian with Kahlil or Kassim? The blue in his fine eyes seemed to preclude the last, but there was an encouraging curve in his nostrils and a raven gleam in his auburn hair, which, by the way, was beginning to grizzle and recede when I knew him. The flesh of his face, too, had sometimes a tired and pouchy appearance, and his tall body looked a trifle rebellious within his extremely well-cut clothes; but, after all, he was fifty-five. You felt that Vaness was a philosopher, yet he never bored you with his views, and was content to let you grasp his moving principle gradually through watching what he ate, drank, smoked, wore, and how he encircled himself with the beautiful things and people of this life. One presumed him rich, for one was never aware of money in his presence. Life moved round him with a certain noiseless ease or stood still at a perfect temperature, like the air in a conservatory round a choice blossom which a draught might shrivel.

This image of a flower in relation to Rupert K. Vaness pleases me, because of that little incident in Magnolia Gardens, near Charleston, South Carolina.

Vaness was the sort of a man of whom one could never say with safety whether he was revolving round a beautiful young woman or whether the beautiful young woman was revolving round him. His looks, his wealth, his taste, his reputation, invested him with a certain sun-like quality; but his age, the recession of his locks, and the advancement of his waist were beginning to dim his lustre, so that whether he was moth or candle was becoming a moot point. It was moot to me, watching him and Miss Sabine Monroy at Charleston throughout the month of March. The casual observer would have said that she was "playing him up," as a young poet of my acquaintance puts it; but I was not casual. For me Vaness had the attraction of a theorem, and I was looking rather deeply into him and Miss Monroy.

That girl had charm. She came, I think, from Baltimore, with a strain in her, they said, of old Southern French blood. Tall and what is known as willowy, with dark chestnut hair, very broad, dark eyebrows, very soft, quick eyes, and a pretty mouth—when she did not accentuate it with lip-salve—she had more sheer quiet vitality than any girl I ever saw. It was delightful to watch her dance, ride, play tennis. She laughed with her eyes; she talked with a savoring vivacity. She never seemed tired or bored. She was, in one hackneyed word, attractive. And Vaness, the connoisseur, was quite obviously attracted. Of men who professionally admire beauty one can never tell offhand whether they definitely design to add a pretty woman to their collection, or whether their dalliance is just matter of habit. But he stood and sat about her, he drove and rode, listened to music, and played cards with her; he did all but dance with her, and even at times trembled on the brink of that. And his eyes, those fine, lustrous eyes of his, followed her about.

How she had remained unmarried to the age of twenty-six was a mystery till one reflected that with her power of enjoying life she could not yet have had the time. Her perfect physique was at full stretch for eighteen hours out of the twenty-four every day. Her sleep must have been like that of a baby. One figured her sinking into dreamless rest the moment her head touched the pillow, and never stirring till she sprang up into her bath.

As I say, for me Vaness, or rather his philosophy, *erat demonstrandum*. I was philosophically in some distress just then. The microbe of fatalism, already present in the brains of artists before the war, had been considerably enlarged by that depressing occurrence. Could a civilization basing itself on the production of material advantages do anything but insure the desire for more and more material advantages? Could it promote progress even of a material character except in countries whose resources were still much in excess of their population? The war had seemed to me to show that mankind was too combative an animal ever to recognize that the good of all was the good of one. The coarse-fibered, pugnacious, and self-seeking would, I had become sure, always carry too many guns for the refined and kindly.

The march of science appeared, on the whole, to be carrying us backward. I deeply suspected that there had been ages when the populations of this earth, though less numerous and comfortable, had been proportionately healthier than they were at present. As for religion, I had never had the least faith in

Providence rewarding the pitiable by giving them a future life of bliss. The theory seemed to me illogical, for the more pitiable in this life appeared to me the thick-skinned and successful, and these, as we know, in the saying about the camel and the needle's eye, our religion consigns wholesale to hell. Success, power, wealth, those aims of profiteers and premiers, pedagogues and pandemoniacs, of all, in fact, who could not see God in a dew-drop, hear Him in distant goat-bells, and scent Him in a pepper-tree, had always appeared to me akin to dry rot. And yet every day one saw more distinctly that they were the pea in the thimblerig of life, the hub of a universe which, to the approbation of the majority they represented, they were fast making uninhabitable. It did not even seem of any use to help one's neighbors; all efforts at relief just gilded the pill and encouraged our stubbornly contentious leaders to plunge us all into fresh miseries. So I was searching right and left for something to believe in, willing to accept even Rupert K. Vaness and his basking philosophy. But could a man bask his life right out? Could just looking at fine pictures, tasting rare fruits and wines, the mere listening to good music, the scent of azaleas and the best tobacco, above all the society of pretty women, keep salt in my bread, an ideal in my brain? Could they? That's what I wanted to know.

Every one who goes to Charleston in the spring soon or late visits Magnolia Gardens. A painter of flowers and trees, I specialize in gardens, and freely assert that none in the world is so beautiful as this. Even before the magnolias come out, it consigns the Boboli at Florence, the Cinnamon Gardens of Colombo, Concepción at Málaga, Versailles, Hampton Court, the Generaliffe at Granada, and La Mortola to the category of "also ran." Nothing so free and gracious, so lovely and wistful, nothing so richly colored, yet so ghostlike, exists, planted by the sons of men. It is a kind of paradise which has wandered down, a miraculously enchanted wilderness. Brilliant with azaleas, or magnolias, it centers round a pool of dreamy water, overhung by tall trunks wanly festooned with the gray Florida moss. Beyond anything I have ever seen, it is otherworldly. And I went there day after day, drawn as one is drawn in youth by visions of the Ionian Sea, of the East, or the Pacific Isles. I used to sit paralyzed by the absurdity of putting brush to canvas in front of that dream-pool. I wanted to paint of it a picture like that of the fountain, by Hellen, which hangs in the Luxembourg. But I knew I never should.

I was sitting there one sunny afternoon, with my back to a clump of azaleas, watching an old colored gardener—so old that he had started life as an "owned" negro, they said, and certainly still retained the familiar suavity of the old-time darky—I was watching him prune the shrubs when I heard the voice of Rupert K. Vaness say, quite close: "There's nothing for me but beauty, Miss Monroy." The two were evidently just behind my azalea clump, perhaps four yards away, yet as invisible as if in China.

"Beauty is a wide, wide word. Define it, Mr. Vaness."

"An ounce of fact is worth a ton of theory: it stands before me."

"Come, now, that's just a get-out. Is beauty of the flesh or of the spirit?"

"What is the spirit, as you call it? I'm a pagan."

"Oh, so am I. But the Greeks were pagans."

"Well, spirit is only the refined side of sensuous appreciations."

"I wonder."

"I have spent my life in finding that out."

"Then the feeling this garden rouses in me is purely sensuous?"

"Of course. If you were standing there blind and deaf, without the powers of scent and touch, where would your feeling be?"

"You are very discouraging, Mr. Vaness."

"No, madam; I face facts. When I was a youngster I had plenty of fluffy aspiration towards I didn't know what; I even used to write poetry."

"Oh, Mr. Vaness, was it good?"

"It was not. I very soon learned that a genuine sensation was worth all the uplift in the world."

"What is going to happen when your senses strike work?"

"I shall sit in the sun and fade out."

"I certainly do like your frankness."

"You think me a cynic, of course; I am nothing so futile, Miss Sabine. A cynic is just a posing ass proud of his attitude. I see nothing to be proud of in my attitude, just as I see nothing to be proud of in the truths of existence."

"Suppose you had been poor?"

"My senses would be lasting better than they are, and when at last they failed, I should die quicker, from want of food and warmth, that's all."

"Have you ever been in love, Mr. Vaness?"

"I am in love now."

"And your love has no element of devotion, no finer side?"

"None. It wants."

"I have never been in love. But, if I were, I think I should want to lose myself rather than to gain the other."

"Would you? Sabine, *I am in love with you.*"

"Oh! Shall we walk on?"

I heard their footsteps, and was alone again, with the old gardener lopping at his shrubs.

But what a perfect declaration of hedonism! How simple and how solid was the Vaness theory of existence! Almost Assyrian, worthy of Louis Quinze.

And just then the old negro came up.

"It's pleasant settin'," he said in his polite and hoarse half-whisper; "dar ain't no flies yet."

"It's perfect, Richard. This is the most beautiful spot in the world."

"Such," he answered, softly drawling. "In deh war-time de Yanks nearly burn deh house heah—Sherman's Yanks. Sueh dey did; po'ful angry wi' ol' massa dey was, 'cause he hid up deh silver plate afore he went away. My ol' fader was de factotalum den. De Yanks took 'm, suh; dey took 'm, and deh major he tell my fader to show 'm whar deh plate was. My ol' fader he look at 'm an' say: 'Wot yuh take me foh? Yuh take me foh a sneakin' nigger? No, suh, you kin du wot yuh like wid dis chile; he ain't goin' to act no Judas. No, suh!' And deh Yankee major he put 'm up ag'in' dat tall live-oak dar, an' he say: 'Yuh darn ungrateful nigger! I's come all dis way to set yuh free. Now, whar's dat silver plate, or I shoot yuh up, sueh!' 'No, suh,' says my fader; 'shoot away. I's neber goin' t' tell.' So dey begin to shoot, and shot all roun' 'm to skeer 'm up. I was a li'l boy den, an' I see my ol' fader wid my own eyes, suh, standin' thar's bold's Peter. No, suh, dey didn't neber git no word from him. He loved deh folk heah; sure he did, suh."

The old man smiled, and in that beatific smile I saw not only his perennial pleasure in the well-known story, but the fact that he, too, would have stood there, with the bullets raining round him, sooner than betray the folk he loved.

"Fine story, Richard; but—very silly, obstinate old man, your father, wasn't he?"

He looked at me with a sort of startled anger, which slowly broadened into a grin; then broke into soft, hoarse laughter.

"Oh, yes, suh, sure; berry silly, obstinacious ol' man. Yes, suh indeed." And he went off cackling to himself.

He had only just gone when I heard footsteps again behind my azalea clump, and Miss Monroy's voice.

"Your philosophy is that of faun and nymph. Can you play the part?"

"Only let me try." Those words had such a fevered ring that in imagination I could see Vaness all flushed, his fine eyes shining, his well-kept hands trembling, his lips a little protruded.

There came a laugh, high, gay, sweet.

"Very well, then; catch me!" I heard a swish of skirts against the shrubs, the sound of flight, an astonished gasp from Vaness, and the heavy *thud, thud* of his feet following on the path through the azalea maze. I hoped fervently that they would not suddenly come running past and see me sitting there. My straining ears caught another laugh far off, a panting sound, a muttered oath, a far-away "*Cooee!*" And then, staggering, winded, pale with heat and vexation, Vaness appeared, caught sight of me, and stood a moment. Sweat was running down his face, his hand was clutching at his side, his stomach heaved—a hunter beaten and undignified. He muttered, turned abruptly on his heel, and left me staring at where his fastidious dandyism and all that it stood for had so abruptly come undone.

I know not how he and Miss Monroy got home to Charleston; not in the same car, I fancy. As for me, I traveled deep in thought, aware of having witnessed something rather tragic, not looking forward to my next encounter with Vaness.

He was not at dinner, but the girl was there, as radiant as ever, and though I was glad she had not been caught, I was almost angry at the signal triumph of her youth. She wore a black dress, with a red flower in her hair, and another at her breast, and had never looked so vital and so pretty. Instead of dallying with my cigar beside cool waters in the lounge of the hotel, I strolled out afterward on the Battery, and sat down beside the statue of a tutelary personage. A lovely evening; from some tree or shrub close by emerged an adorable faint fragrance, and in the white electric light the acacia foliage was patterned out against a thrilling, blue sky. If there were no fireflies abroad, there should have been. A night for hedonists, indeed!

And suddenly, in fancy, there came before me Vaness's well-dressed person, panting, pale, perplexed; and beside him, by a freak of vision, stood the old darky's father, bound to the live-oak, with the bullets whistling past, and his face transfigured. There they stood alongside—the creed of pleasure, which depended for fulfilment on its waist measurement; and the creed of love, devoted unto death!

"Aha!" I thought, "which of the two laughs *last*?"

And just then I saw Vaness himself beneath a lamp, cigar in mouth, and cape flung back so that its silk lining shone. Pale and heavy, in the cruel white light his face had a bitter look. And I was sorry, very sorry, at that moment for Rupert K. Vaness.

"Carolina Marshes"

HERBERT RAVENEL SASS (1884–1958)

Historian Barbara Bellows has written that "among all the writers and artists associated with Charleston's cultural 'renaissance' after World War I, Herbert Ravenel Sass most fully embodied the wide range of interests, intellectual curiosity, grounding in science and literature and history that the term implies." Sass, a member of the elite class of old Charleston families, was a graduate of the College of Charleston and a founding member of the Poetry Society of South Carolina. He was a prolific and popular author, publishing both fiction and nonfiction in such magazines as the *Saturday Evening Post*, *Harper's*, and the *Atlantic Monthly*. In his fiction he often addressed major historical events, as in *Emperor Brims* (1941, about the Yemassee War), *Look Back to Glory* (1933, about South Carolina plantation life on the eve of the Civil War), and *War Drums* (1928, a pirate adventure). In 1936 he contributed a historical essay to the nostalgic book by his cousin Alice Ravenel Huger Smith, *A Carolina Rice Plantation of the Fifties*, and in 1931 he wrote the main article for and helped edit *The Carolina Lowcountry*, published by the Society for the Preservation of Spirituals.

Sass worked for the local *News and Courier* from 1908 until 1925 and for many years was the paper's main editorial writer. Not surprisingly he addressed political and economic issues more than most of the other members of the Charleston Renaissance. Like the writers in Nashville's Fugitive/Agrarian school, he thought the South's antebellum agricultural base was its greatest strength. He also published a number of books and articles on Lowcountry nature and history and for many years wrote a local newspaper column on nature and wildlife, evoking beautiful descriptions of the land around Charleston. He was nicknamed "Hobo" for his love of rambling through Lowcountry environments.

A sandy point on a lonely beach, with a little river coming down to the sea, is a spot where in March and early April I have spent many mornings watching the spring come up from the summer lands away to the south. You can see her come. She is there before you, white, radiant, graceful—a presence not only felt but, if the right mood is upon you, visible to the eye. She is not the divinity of the ancient Greeks nor the being that poets have imagined: a goddess like a lovely woman but lovelier than any woman of flesh and blood. For me she has no definite shape, yet I can see her; she is very real. She comes riding up from the summer lands on the waving, rhythmic wings of flocks of milk-white herons, flock after flock, drifting slowly along under the bright blue sky, coming nearer and nearer, shining like silver in the sun.

It is a beautiful thing to see on the wild, lonely Carolina beaches—this coming of spring. But seeing it, drinking in its beauty, rejoicing over all that it means, my thoughts fly swiftly from the open beaches and marshes along the edge of the sea to other and very different scenes. Faster than the heron flocks themselves, I am transported in fancy to deep swamps hidden in the woods, to still cypress lagoons, shaded by tall, straight trees and curtained with gray Spanish moss, where presently those heron flocks will come to rest.

For the swamps are their goal, their haven, their true home. They come along the sea's edge, following the beaches northward on their journey from the tropics and the lower South, perhaps guided at night by the everlasting music of the surf; but when they have reached the South Carolina coast, they turn inland (at least, many of them do) away from the ocean and the broad salt marshes, and, flying on and on, over forests and fields and wastes of rushes, they come down at last in the deep heart of the swamp woods and end their journey there.

That is how spring comes to the swamps. The herons bring her—the little flocks of milk-white herons in March and early April come drifting along above the palm-fringed ocean beaches like fragments of snowy, sun-lit cloud.

With her coming the swamps are transformed. They are beautiful at all seasons. Even in winter, when the cypresses are bare and there is comparatively little visible life, they are not dreary and melancholy, as many suppose. They have a gray, silvery loveliness then that, in certain moods, delights and even exhilarates; it is then that they are most mysterious, that the effect of strangeness, of unreality, as though one had passed from the world of to-day into an earlier and more fantastic epoch, is strongest. But the swamps in winter are asleep. There is a sense of waiting—waiting. At last spring touches them, and gradually, yet swiftly, they awake. It is the soft caress of a white heron's wing that brings the change.

To see the swamps at their best, to enjoy them to the fullest, one must see them in spring after the awakening has taken place. Comparatively few people know them at that season. By that time most of the thousands of visitors who come to the South for the winter are homeward bound again; and the impression that they carry away with them is an impression of gray, dismal wastes of leafless, moss-shrouded trees—silent, colorless, lifeless, fastnesses which, seen from the outside, from the window of a train or from an automobile speeding along a highway, appear both melancholy and forbidding.

Go into them and you will find, even in winter, that gray, silvery beauty and that atmosphere of mystery of which I have spoken. But there is little then to indicate what will come later; there is scarcely a hint of the transfiguration which the spring will bring—that strange loveliness of another kind which can hardly be surpassed anywhere on earth.

To reach the heart of the swamp you must paddle, sometimes for miles, in a small, flat-bottomed punt along the narrow waterlanes of a flooded forest of cypress or black gum. These waterlanes are inexpressibly beautiful. Sometimes they are straight, so that the eye, wandering down the shadowy vista ahead, looks for a great distance along a dim tunnel through the flooded woods, walled in on each side and above by the smooth trunks

and the green feathery foliage of cypresses, curtained and festooned with long, graceful pennons of Spanish moss. Sometimes
the water-paths wind in and out like serpents, so that there is
always, just in front, the mystery of the curve, a bend in the
watery road, beyond which one may see one knows not what.

For a time, perhaps, there will be little visible life. Nor will
you see, when you are afloat in the swamp woods, the brightness
and prettiness of wild flowers except the pink glow of an occasional swamp rose. There is a grander, more solemn beauty here,
yet there is nothing of melancholy in it.

There is bright sunshine and dark shadow. The cypress boughs
overhead are a vivid living green; the moss pennons, hanging
from the trees and swathing their slim trunks, are gray or silver
or ink or lavender, for the sunlight striking on it or through it
works miracles with the moss. So, too, the trunks of the cypresses,
flaring outward at the base and often hedged about with cypress-
knees, are not of one color, monotonous and unchangeable.
There also the wonder-working sunlight, pouring down through
the openings in the green roof overhead or filtering through the
tracery of the cypress boughs, changes the brown of the straight,
smooth cypress boles into many delicate tints, brilliant or soft,
varying endlessly.

Perhaps even more beautiful, the still waters underneath,
black or clear-brown like wine, are a mirror in which the world
above is not merely reflected but glorified. The darker, richer
hues reflected there, especially the many shades of green, often
appear deeper and richer, so that the watery floor of the swamp
is neither black nor brown (the actual color of the clear water)
but becomes a varicolored translucent or transparent glossy surface, as of a dark polished crystal, brighter and clearer where the
sunlight falls upon it; and in this vast crystal, luminous with
sunshine or dark with deep-green shadow, the blue sky above,
the bright green roof of cypress foliage, the exquisite tints of the
hanging moss, and the soaring tree-trunks are reproduced in
softer tones and yet with an added richness and luster.

The water-lane leads on and on. Sometimes there is only one way amid the crowding tree trunks, one narrow channel barely wide enough for the punt; sometimes the serried ranks of the trees divide and you have choice of several paths; sometimes you come to openings in the flooded forest where there are no trees at all or only a few small cypresses standing by themselves in a little lake walled in at a distance of twenty or perhaps fifty yards by the encircling woods.

These open spaces have a beauty of another kind. A bright-green carpet of duckweed spreads across the water; in shallows along the edges, beds of tall rushes, of dense telanthera and wampee and other aquatic plants flourish in the sun. Where the water is a little deeper, the lily-pads and the much larger circular leaves, often two feet in diameter, of the magnificent yellow lotus, the most gorgeous flower of the swamps, impede the passage of the boat.

All this is the background, the setting. It is, I like to think, the touch of a white heron's wing that wakes the swamps from their winter sleep; and when that awakening has taken place, when spring has fairly come, the herons are among the most abundant and most beautiful of the swamp's inhabitants.

They are of several sizes and species, but the most beautiful of them are the great white egrets—tall, graceful creatures, white as the whitest marble, adorned with long, slender plums or aigrettes which droop beyond their tails. Deep in the swamp lagoons, the egrets and herons of other kinds build their nests in the cypresses, not singly but in communities sometimes containing hundreds of birds; and in these heron cities, in late April and May, the life of the lagoons is at its crest and the beauty and strangeness of the swamps overwhelm the eye and the mind.

No one can ever forget his first visit to a heron city in one of the Carolina swamps; and the experience is all the more memorable if the city of herons which he visits is situated on one of the larger lagoons so that a considerable journey along the devious water-ways of the swamp is necessary in order to reach the place.

He passes then through scenes of indescribable beauty before attaining his goal: down shadowy, moss-tapestried water-lanes so mysteriously lovely that they are like secret byways through some Kingdom of Dreams: along broader, sun-dappled channels through the flooded woods where the magic of the sunlight in the trees, in the trailing veils of moss, and in the clear, placid water works the miracles of color; across sun-bathed openings, golden and mellow, lying like secret enchanted lakes embosomed in the woods.

Against this background he sees, as he journeys on, the abundant life of the swamp; a flash of white, slowly waving wings far ahead along a narrow water-path as an egret takes flight at his approach; the glowing orange-gold of tiny prothonotary warblers flitting here and there in the feathery green of the cypresses; wood ducks rising from the water with their high, thin notes of protest and alarm; long-necked, long-tailed anhingas or water-turkeys, strangest and most fantastic of all the swamp birds, sailing high overhead like airplanes against the blue; perhaps a flock of great wood ibises, soaring at an even greater height, their long necks and legs outstretched, their wide, white, black-edged wings rigid and motionless.

The swamp lagoons teem with life. Often it is brilliant, vivid, flashing, aglow with the rich colors of the tropics from which many of the swamp birds come. Sometimes it is fantastic, grotesque, prehistoric in its strangeness.

In all the swamp waters alligators are at home; in some of the larger lagoons and in many of the creeks and rivers they abound and attain great size, twelve feet or more in length, though these monsters are uncommon. On a trip to a heron city in one of the larger lagoons not long ago, we counted thirty alligators, none of them, however, more than eight feet long from nose to tail-tip. Terrapins of various sizes sit in rows on the half-submerged logs and dive overboard as the punt draws near. Now and again, though rarely (for, contrary to popular belief, snakes are not numerous in the cypress lagoons), a water snake, sunning himself on some log or in the lower branches of a willow or buttonwood bush, slithers downward into the depths.

The snakes are seldom seen and are most of them harmless; afloat on the lagoons there is practically no danger from them at all. The alligators, even the grim and powerful leviathans of their race, learned long ago to keep out of man's way. The life of the swamp waters, grotesque but only rarely sinister, is comparatively inconspicuous; it is the abundant life of the air that gives the lagoons their most compelling charm. The herons are the most characteristic and perhaps the most spectacular of the birds of the lagoons; and when at last the voyager along the water-paths of the flooded woods reaches the heron city for which he has been bound, he finds himself in the midst of a bewildering panorama of life such as, in all likelihood, he has never dreamed of or imagined.

The cypresses are crowded with nests, ten or fifteen perhaps in a single tree. On the nests, in the branches, in the air, herons in scores or perhaps in hundreds—herons of various sizes and hues, dark-blue or parti-colored or glittering spotless white—stand or sail in a maze of interweaving circles amid an astonishing swelling clamor of innumerable voices.

Little blue herons are there, airy, graceful Louisiana herons, burly, deep-voiced black-crowned night herons, fantastic anhingas, perhaps great blue herons also and wood ibises, the largest of the swamp birds; and, most wonderful of all, stately, immaculate great egrets, white as snow, trailing their long nuptial plumes behind them as they fly, sweep back and forth overhead or stand like tall, slender statuettes of shining marble in the green cypress tops.

Sometimes one species predominates, sometimes another. The most fascinating of the heron cities are those in which the great egrets are most numerous, for there the trees are sometimes white with the splendid showy birds, while the void above is bright with their shining, buoyant bodies, as they sail, like white stately ships of the air, above the feathery tree tops or swing slowly 'round and 'round under the blue sky on their radiant, slowly waving wings.

It is, above all else, the life of the swamps that gives them their enchantment; and since this life is most abundant on the swamp lagoons, they are always to my mind the most interesting parts of these fastnesses. The lagoons are of various kinds. Most of them are small; some are natural ponds or lakes, while others—and these include many of the loveliest—are old backwaters or "reserves" of the rice-planting days when lower South Carolina was a region of great plantations where the finest rice in the world was grown.

These were, in the beginning, artificial or semi-artificial bodies of water. A low bank thrown across a swamp would flood a large area behind it; and periodically the water from this submerged area or "reserve" would be drawn off to flood the rice fields below. The rice-planting days are over, but the old reserves remain; and in most cases nature has hidden effectively all signs of man's handiwork around them, so that they are as wild now and as beautiful as the natural ponds or lagoons.

The lagoons vary endlessly in appearance and in character. In fact, no two of them are alike; but two main types may be distinguished—those that are wooded, grown up with cypress or tupelo or black gum (or with all of these) so that the effect is that of a flooded forest, a forest whose floor is water instead of earth; and second, those that are open—that is to say, devoid of trees, though large parts of the surface are generally covered with water growths and with floating islands sometimes solid enough to support willows and low bushes.

The former are, I think, the more beautiful; but the open lagoons have their distinctive charm also. Their bird-life is of a different kind. There, for instance, in reeds and rushes and wampee pads and amid rafts of lily-pads and other aquatic plants, you will find least bitterns, king rails, and gorgeous purple gallinules, birds rarely or never seen in the wooded swamps; and in summer, when the yellow lotus is in bloom, the open lagoons and the old rice fields themselves are often scenes of unimaginable beauty.

The lotus is not found everywhere but only in certain spots. It comes and it goes mysteriously, taking possession of a lagoon or an abandoned rice field, then disappearing perhaps for years. In places only a few plans are to be seen, or, again, an acre of water may be covered with them. Occasionally these wild lotus gardens cover areas many acres in extent; and the spectacle then, in early morning or late afternoon, with white herons standing amid the great golden flowers and perhaps a pair of purple gallinules walking lightly about over the huge circular lotus leaves, is one that will never be forgotten.

The swamps are friendly, not inimical. You will not, if you will observe a few simple rules, be eaten alive by mosquitoes, poisoned by deadly snakes, or infected with prostrating fevers. You must, in the warm season, get out of the swamp before nightfall; you must, in walking through thick places, be careful where you put your foot. Once afloat on the lagoons you are safe; there is no more likelihood that a venomous moccasin will drop from an overhanging bough into your lap than there is that one of the big alligators of the lagoons will take it into his mind to climb into your boat. Nor are the swamp lagoons intolerably hot, as is commonly believed. In the dry portions of the swamps the summer heat is intense, and on the open lagoons at midday it may become actually unbearable. But on the wooded lagoons, shielded from the rays of the sun by a high canopy of boughs, the voyager, even on a sultry summer day, will suffer little or no discomfort.

And always the swamps are beautiful. There are places in the swamps of the South Carolina low country which are the most beautiful places that I have ever seen. Perhaps that is because I have lived close to them and know them more familiarly than I know the mountains or the hills; but others, seeing them for the first time in their spring loveliness, drifting along their shadowy water paths under the moss-hung cypresses, watching the living beings of many shapes and hues that make their homes in those columned solitudes, come quickly under the spell of their enchantment.

I have not begun to describe them here. I cannot put into words their loveliness as I see it, still less their mystery and their strange fascination; but in the exquisite pictures of Alice R. Huger Smith, all her life a lover of the Carolina swamps, knowing them better than any other artist who has ever tried to paint them, not only the physical beauty which the eye sees but also the very spirit of the swamps is expressed. These lovely canvases tell the story of the swamps far better than the pen can portray them.

from *Red Ending*

HARRY HERVEY (1900–1951)

Texas-born Harry Hervey is most often associated with Savannah, where he lived on and off from the early 1920s until his death and where he wrote several novels, including his best known, *The Damned Don't Cry* (1939), which is set there. But he also had many Charleston ties. Harlan Greene notes that a character in *The Damned Don't Cry* is based on Josephine Pinckney's mother. For several summers in the 1920s Hervey lived in Charleston, and wrote there the novel *Red Ending* (1929), excerpted below, based on a scandalous local story. Greene points out that Josephine Pinckney adopted the story in two of her books, though Hervey addressed it more directly, "giving it a psychological and sexual spin and, worse, naming the city." In addition to his novel, Hervey's homosexuality—he lived with his mother and a much younger lover—shocked many in the city. In Charleston he also wrote the novel *Congai* (1927), which he later turned into a play. In addition to his fiction, he wrote many plays, screenplays, and nonfiction pieces. He traveled extensively, especially in Asia, and published articles on his journeys in popular magazines.

Charleston. Soft-lipped city, slyly, expertly running its tongue along old streets cooked in the white wine of semi-tropical sunlight; pausing to stretch and flex, legs a-sprawl, as sea-winds fill its throat with crooning. Wench-born, lady-bred, it dreams in a four-poster. Aristocracy snores on the other pillow. The coverlet of respectability grows irksome—it wants to lie in a warehouse with a sailor. Frustrated, it slashes its wrists with a razor-blade—and watches the blood flow—flow—waiting for a sailor's mouth to stanch it.

Charleston. Behold it—through a peephole.

Along the waterfront, weather-peeled small craft rotting on strips of shell-sharp beach. Side-wheeler half sunk beside a barnacled dock. Red sentinel of the Standard Oil Company draining itself into the tank of a panting Ford. Fleet of tiny fishing-boats sidling up to a tug that returns these advances with a smug uplift of the bows. Out on the bay, black rigging tugging at wind-swollen sails.

Coal-dust between the tracks; silent grain-smelling freight-cars; odor of rain-soaked, heat-steamed warehouses. A stray dog pauses, tentatively friendly, gazing at a watchman who presses himself into a corner with a furtive glance over his shoulder. . . .

Clyde liner dozing at moorings; rattle of chains and the mournful chanting of black stevedores. A thin filter of tourists, knickered and spectacled, surrounded by dancing nigger children. Charleston, hey, hey! Pennies hit the sidewalk. . . .

Ferry-shed: soldiers from across the river deploying into the night, flanks restless, limbs eager. Red brick house with an iron balcony. Come in, soldier! A player-piano trilling heavily like a winded contralto, O-o-h, what a pal was Ma-r-ry...

Nigger-alleys, warm with sweat-smell and cologne-smell. High-yaller, fragile of wrist and throat, leaning in a doorway, waiting. A quick, shrill scream of laughter from black faces hanging out of windows. De buckra he don' cum tuh-night!. . .

Old Market slinking down several blocks under gray arches where a lurking urinal scent insults the flower-fragrances parading on the breeze. C.G. 3, C.G. 26 lying abreast beside the Municipal Pier. From below, rising with the odors of Life Buoy soap and oil, a good natured song: Here come a lady, she's dressed in red, I've heard them say she. . . . On deck, in the midst of sprawling gobs, a phonograph wheedling prowling thoughts into strutting words. An' I sez to the bastard, I sez, looka here. . . . Seamen's Institute. Come ye to the Lord! Dance night. Tittering, breathless girls held in sunburnt arms, the sex-whining in their minds humming a repressed obbligato to naked music. Outside, in spills of hot light, sullen-eyed, lust-bitten men staring in, now and then slouching away singly as a nigger gal drifts by. Foh a dime, boss. . . .

More tracks, more warehouses, more ships; out to the Navy Yard. . . .

Waterfront lifting its flesh-song, whispering in furled canvas, shivering in taut stays; waterfront lifting its voluptuous odor, haunting men's nostrils, men's brains; arousing them to crazy, carnal laughter, coarse nigger-laughter that derides this city lying behind it; a city no better, no worse than half a hundred other Southern seaports, part of it prancing shamelessly in the open, and the other part withdrawing into formal parlors and pre-scribed bedrooms to carry on pretenses that, after so long, have become genuine, all the while snubbing or ignoring its twin smirking and snickering at it through the windows.

Charleston. Behold it—from the Chamber of Commerce.

House where George Washington slept; church-pew where he sat. Old Powder Magazine; Fort Sumter where the first gun of the Civil War was fired. . . .

And this, ladies and gentlemen, is the Pratt House. You know who General Pratt was, of course. Now his heirs—ironic word!—will show you through it; faded and gentle ladies whose eyes look back to splendor. . . .

And don't overlook the plantations. Most of them lie to the east, along the Santee, and to the west, on Edisto and other swamp islands; the remains of great rice-plantations that now drain the sediment of past cultivation through forlorn marshes.

These vast places lie stricken during the day, awakening to a feeble glamour as night strips away their winding-sheets. A faint mortuary scent hangs over them—they have passed through cor-ruption to dust. Immense houses stare out of hollow-eyed win-dows at fields that have stolen over the surrounding walls and fences, wondering at the temerity of the soil once so obedient to their masters. At the end of long groves of live oaks dikes lie trampled; the sluice-gates have fallen into the canals they diverted in the past; the rice-land has become a refuge for heron and moccasin.

Here, in years gone (we have, somehow, strayed from the Chamber of Commerce into streets where the ancient walls whisper indiscreetly), a certain rural grandeur, an extravagance of living gave rise to the illusion that an intellectual, at least an epicurean, aristocracy flourished in this appropriate setting. In consequence, where once a cotton hoop-skirt, perhaps a little mussed, even a trifle soiled, swept polished floors, now fancy sees spotless brocade; and the verdigris on aged silver candelabra symbolizes a charming decay that achieved distinction primarily by dying.

Charleston, guarded by two parallel rivers, remains sternly set apart from this wild, desolate country, lifting its tongue visibly and audibly in numerous church-towers that daily proclaim its right to a measure of respect for having withstood vulgar Nature more successfully than its outposts. Secretly it blushes a little, realizing that its pretensions, once outside the city limits, or along the docks, suffer an embarrassing relapse into fecundity.

Nevertheless, being publicly proud of its culture, it waves an airy hand toward these plantations as proof of its genuineness. The fact that they have gone into decrepitude, that swamp-water is seeping insidiously under the foundations of the houses, merely induces a sentimental exultation in past accomplishments.

Naturally, Charleston is indignant—without becoming very active, due to climatic and financial conditions—when hordes of glorified furniture-dealers, calling themselves connoisseurs, descend upon it, paying well for the privilege of gratifying their bourgeois instinct of destruction where there is the slightest taint of aristocracy.

Fine old mantels, exquisite chandeliers, and often the paneling of entire rooms, are crated up and sent North. A few of these vandals, having at least a semblance of delicacy, content themselves with leaving these mansions intact and occupying them. Thus the tares creep in among the wheat. . . .

(The walls themselves are beginning to blanch at their indiscretions; let us return to the Chamber of Commerce.)

Yes, ma'am, there's a launch leaving the hotel-wharf in the morning for Fort Sumter; and to-morrow night the Carolina Vocal Society will give a program of Negro spirituals. . . .

Charleston. Behold it—in St. Phillip's Church.

Holy communion is being celebrated.

Outside, the city gives up a sigh from tired pavements and stares listlessly at the heavy-blooded noonday. Even the breeze, which with due observance of Sabbath decorum wanders in circumspectly from the bay, is laden with heat. From the docks it acquires the scents of hemp and cypress-shingles; from the Negro districts, the mingled smells of baking yams and fried fish; and from old walled gardens in other quarters, fragrances less pungent but equally disturbing.

To the younger people, who have remained after Sunday School as a matter of habit or compulsion, it suggests numerous lazy prospects for the afternoon: a trip to the Isle of Palms or a swim at the beach or some less innocuous opiate to deaden the fact of Sunday.

The reactions of their elders are more appropriately solid. The men, for the most part, are aware of the ghosts of food that prowl with the breeze; while the women, absorbed in simulating deeply religious natures as an example to their deficient males, hope this breath will remain and contribute to the comfort of their afternoon nap.

Of course the more conservative members—blue veins stand out on their hands like visible tracings of their heritage—are unaware of this breeze except as a feeble aid to their palmetto-fans; unless, perhaps, it is to feel a certain resentment against the profane sweetness of narcissus which it smuggles into this otherwise orthodox atmosphere.

from *Porgy*

DUBOSE HEYWARD (1885–1940)

Of the Charleston writers of the 1920s, novelist and poet DuBose Heyward remains today the best known outside Charleston, principally because of the international success of the opera *Porgy and Bess*, first performed in 1935. Born to an old Charleston family, Heyward was the great-great-grandson of Thomas Heyward, a signer of the Declaration of Independence.

In his youth, Heyward worked on the Charleston waterfront, an experience which gave him some of the source material for the life of the stevedores portrayed in his novel *Porgy* (1925). He suffered from polio at eighteen, and during his recuperation began to write. In 1922 he married Dorothy Kuhn, a playwright he had met at the Edward McDowell Writing Colony in New Hampshire. Dorothy, with her great wealth of knowledge of the theater, became his major collaborator and confidante, her influence rivaled only by that of author John Bennett. Heyward also published a great deal of poetry and with Bennett and Hervey Allen helped co-found the Poetry Society of South Carolina.

For a time, Heyward lived at 76 Church Street near the double tenement known as Cabbage Row. In *Porgy* he changed the name to Catfish Row and relocated it to Vanderhorst Wharf at the waterfront, making it the home of his central character. "Goat" Sammy Smalls, unable to walk, traveled the city in his handmade cart pulled by a goat. A 1924 article in the *News and Courier* about an aggravated assault charge against him for his alleged attempt to shoot a local woman appealed to Heyward, and the imaginative seed of *Porgy* was planted.

In 1926 DuBose and Dorothy Heyward turned the novel *Porgy* into a play by the same name. Shortly after *Porgy* went to Broadway, Heyward began a collaboration with composer George Gershwin and his lyricist brother Ira that produced perhaps the most famous American opera, *Porgy and Bess*.

The tremendous popularity of the opera has assured that DuBose Heyward will be remembered. However, his other writings, especially *Mamba's Daughters* (1929, also based on the local black population), are also worthy of attention. He was inducted into the South Carolina Academy of Authors in 1987.

"Fish runnin' well outside de bar, dese days," remarked Jake one evening to several of his seagoing companions.

A large, bronze-colored negro paused in his task of rigging a line, and cast an eye to sea through the driveway.

"An' we mens bes' make de mores ob it," he observed. "Dem Septumbuh storm due soon, an' fish ain't likes eas' win' an' muddy watuh."

Jake laughed reassuringly.

Go 'long wid yuh. Ain't yuh done know we hab one stiff gale las' summer, an' he nebber come two yeah han' runnin'.' "

His wife came toward him with a baby in her arms, and, giving him the child to hold, took up the mess of fish which he was cleaning in a leisurely fashion.

"Ef yuh ain't mans enough tuh clean fish no fastuh dan dat, yuh bes' min' de baby, an' gib um tuh a 'oman fuh clean!" she said scornfully, as she bore away the pan.

The group laughed at that, Jake's somewhat shamefaced merriment rising above the others. He rocked the contented little negro in his strong arms, and followed the retreating figure of the mother with admiring eyes.

"All right, mens," he said, returning to the matter in hand. "I'm all fuh ridin' luck fer as he will tote me. Turn out at fo' tuhmorruh mornin', and we'll push de 'Seagull' clean tuh de blackfish banks befo' we wets de anchor. I gots er feelin' in my bones dat we goin' be gunnels undeh wid de pure fish when we comes in tuhmorruh night."

The news of Jake's prediction spread through the negro quarter. Other crews got their boats hastily in commission and were ready to join the "Mosquito Fleet" when it put to sea.

On the following morning, when the sun rose out of the Atlantic, the thirty or forty small vessels were mere specks teetering upon the water's rim against the red disc that forged swiftly up beyond them.

Afternoon found the wharf crowded with women and children, who laughed and joked each other as to the respective merits of their men and the luck of the boats in which they went to sea.

Clara, Jake's wife, sought the head of the dock long before sundown, and sat upon the bulkhead with her baby asleep in her lap. Occasionally she would exchange a greeting with an acquaintance; but for the most part she gazed toward the harbor mouth and said no word to anyone.

"She always like dat," a neighbor informed a little group. "A conjer 'oman once tell she Jake goin' git drownded; an' she ain't hab no happiness since, 'cept when he feet is hittin' de dirt."

Presently a murmur arose among the watchers. Out at the harbor mouth, against the thin greenish-blue of the horizon, appeared the "Mosquito Fleet." Driven by a steady breeze, the boats swept toward the city with astonishing rapidity.

Warm sunlight flooded out of the west, touched the old city with transient glory, then cascaded over the tossing surface of the bay to paint the taut, cupped sails salmon pink, as the fleet drove forward directly into the eye of the sun.

Almost before the crowd realized it, the boats were jibing and coming about at their feet, each jockeying for a favorable berth.

Under the skillful and daring hand of Jake, the "Seagull" took a chance, missed a stern by a hairbreadth, jibed suddenly with a snap and boom, and ran in, directly under the old rock steps of the wharf.

A cheer went up from the crowd. Never had there been such a catch. The boat seemed floored with silver which rose almost to the thwarts, forcing the crew to sit on gunnels, or aft with the steersman.

Indeed the catch was so heavy that as boat after boat docked, it became evident that the market was glutted, and the fishermen vied with each other in giving away their surplus cargo, so that they would not have to throw it overboard.

By the following morning the weather had become unsettled. The wind was still coming out of the west; but a low, solid wall of cloud had replaced the promising sunset of the evening before, and from time to time the wind would wrench off a section of the black mass, and volley it with great speed across the sky, to accumulate in unstable pyramids against the sunrise.

But the success of the day before had so fired the enthusiasm of the fishermen that they were not easily to be deterred from following their luck, and the first gray premonition of the day found the wharf seething with preparation.

Clara, with the baby in her arms, accompanied Jake to the pier-head. She knew the futility of remonstrance; but her eyes were fearful when the heavy, black clouds swept overhead. Once, when a wave slapped a pile, and threw a handful of spray in her face, she moaned and looked up at the big negro by her side. But Jake was full of the business in hand, and besides, he was growing a little impatient at his wife's incessant plea that he sell his share of the "Seagull" and settle on land. Now he turned from her, and shouted:

"All right, mens!"

He bestowed a short, powerful embrace upon his wife, with his eyes looking over her shoulder into the Atlantic's veiled face, turned from her with a quick, nervous movement, and dropped from the wharf into his boat.

Standing in the bow, he moistened his finger in his mouth, and held it up to the wind.

"You mens bes' git all de fish yuh kin tuhday," he admonished. "Win' be in de eas' by tuhmorruh. It gots dat wet tas' ter um now."

One by one the boats shoved off, and lay in the stream while they adjusted their spritsails and rigged their full jibs abeam, like spinnakers, for the free run to sea. The vessels were similar in design, the larger ones attaining a length of thirty-five feet. They were very narrow, and low in the waist, with high, keen bows, and pointed sterns. The hulls were round-bottomed, and had beautiful running lines, the fishermen, who were also the designers and builders, taking great pride in the speed and style of their respective craft. The boats were all open from stem to stern and were equipped with tholepins for rowing, an expedient to which the men resorted only in dire emergency.

Custom had reduced adventure to commonplace; yet it was inconceivable that men could put out, in the face of unsettled weather, for a point beyond sight of land, and exhibit no uneasiness or fear. Yet bursts of loud, loose laughter, and snatches of song, blew back to the wharf long after the boats were in midstream.

The wind continued to come in sudden flaws, and, once the little craft had gotten clear of the wharves, the fleet made swift but erratic progress. There were moments when they would seem to mark time upon the choppy waters of the bay; then suddenly a flaw would bear down on them, whipping the water as it came, and, filling the sails, would fairly lift the slender bows as it drove them forward.

By the time that the leisurely old city was sitting down to its breakfast, the fleet had disappeared into the horizon, and the sun had climbed over its obstructions to flood the harbor with reassuring light.

The mercurial spirits of the negroes rose with the genial warmth. Forebodings were forgotten. Even Clara sang a lighter air as she rocked the baby upon her lap.

But the sun had just lifted over the eastern wall, and the heat of noon was beginning to vibrate in the court, when suddenly the air of security was shattered. From the center of town sounded the deep, ominous clang of a bell.

At its first stroke life in Catfish Row was paralyzed. Women stopped their tasks, and, not realizing what they did, clasped each others' hands tightly, and stood motionless, with strained, listening faces.

Twenty times the great hammer fell, sending the deep, full notes out across the city that was holding its breath and counting them as they came.

"Twenty!" said Clara, when it had ceased to shake the air.

She ran to the entrance and looked to the north. Almost at the end of vision, between two buildings, could be seen the flagstaff that surmounted the custom-house. It was bare when she looked—just a thin, bare line against the intense blue, but even as she stood there, a flicker of color soared up its length; then fixed and flattened, showing a red square with a black center.

"My Gawd!" she called over her shoulder. "It's de trut'. Dat's de hurricane signal on top de custom-house."

Bess came from her room, and stood close to the terrified woman.

"Dat can't be so," she said comfortingly. "Ain't yuh 'member de las' hurricane, how it tek two day tuh blow up. Now de sun out bright, an' de cloud all gone."

But Clara gave no sign of having heard her.

"Come on in!" urged Bess. "Ef yuh don't start tuh git yuh dinner, yuh won't hab nuttin' ready fuh de mens w'en dey gits in."

After a moment the idea penetrated, and the half-dazed woman turned toward Bess, her eyes pleading.

"You come wid me, an' talk a lot. I ain't likes tuh be all alone now."

"Sho' I will," replied the other comfortingly. "I min' de baby fuh yuh, an' yuh kin be gittin' de dinner."

Clara's face quivered; but she turned from the sight of the far red flag and opened her door for Bess to pass in.

After the two women had remained together for half an hour, Bess left the room for a moment to fetch some sewing. The sun was gone, and the sky presented a smooth, leaden surface. She closed the door quickly so that Clara might not see the abrupt change, and went out of the entrance for a look to sea.

Like the sky, the bay had undergone a complete metamorphosis. The water was black, and strangely lifeless. Thin, intensely white crests rode the low, pointed waves; and between the opposing planes of sky and sea a thin westerly wind roamed about like a trapped thing and whined in a complaining treble key. A singularly clear half-light pervaded the world, and in it she could see the harbor mouth distinctly, as it lay ten miles away between the north and south jetties that stretched on the horizon like arms with the finger-tips nearly touching.

Her eyes sought the narrow opening. Guiltless of the smallest speck, it let upon utter void.

"It'd take 'em t'ree hour tuh mek harbor from de banks wid good win'," said a woman who was also watching. "But dere ain't no powuh in dis breeze, an' it a head one at dat."

"Dey kin row it in dat time," encouraged Bess. "An' de storm ain't hyuh yit."

But the woman hugged her forebodings, and stood there shivering in the close, warm air.

Except for the faint moan of the wind, the town and harbor lay in a silence that was like held breath.

Many negroes came to the wharf, passed out to the pier-head, and sat quietly watching the entrance to the bay.

At one o'clock the tension snapped. As though it had been awaiting St. Christopher's chimes to announce "Zero Hour," the wind swung into the east, and its voice dropped an octave, and changed its quality. Instead of the complaining whine, a grave, sustained note came in from the Atlantic, with an undertone of alarming variations, that sounded oddly out of place as it traversed the inert waters of the bay.

The tide was at the last of the ebb, and racing out of the many rivers and creeks toward the sea. All morning the west wind had driven it smoothly before it. But now, the stiffening eastern gale threw its weight against the water, and the conflict immediately filled the bay with large waves that leapt up to angry points, then dropped back sullenly upon themselves.

"Choppy water," observed a very old negro who squinted through half-closed eyes. "Dem boat nebbuh mek headway in dat sea."

But he was not encouraged to continue by the silent, anxious group.

Slowly the threatening undertone of the wind grew louder. Then, as though a curtain had been lowered across the harbor mouth, everything beyond was blotted by a milky screen.

"Oh, my Jedus!" a voice shrilled. "Here he come, now! Le's we go!"

Many of the watchers broke for the cover of buildings across the street. Some of those whose men were in the fleet crowded into the small wharf-house. Several voices started to pray at once, and were immediately drowned in the rising clamor of the wind.

With the mathematical precision that it had exhibited in starting, the gale now moved its obliterating curtain through the jetties, and thrust it forward in a straight line across the outer bay.

There was something utterly terrifying about the studied manner in which the hurricane proceeded about its business. It clicked off its moves like an automaton. It was Destiny working nakedly for the eyes of men to see. The watchers knew that for at least twenty-four hours it would stay, moving its tides and winds here and there with that invincible precision, crushing the life from those whom its preconceived plan had seemed to mark for death.

With that instant emotional release that is the great solace of the negro, the tightly packed wharf-house burst into a babblement of weeping and prayer.

The curtain advanced to the inner bay and narrowed the world to the city, with its buildings cowering white and fearful, and the remaining semi-circle of the harbor.

And now from the opaque surface of the screen came a persistent roar that was neither of wind or water, but the articulate cry of the storm itself. The curtain shot forward again and became a wall, gray and impenetrable, that sunk its foundations into the tortured sea and bore the leaden sky upon its soaring top.

The noise became deafening. The narrow strip of water that was left before the wharves seemed to shrink away. The buildings huddled closer and waited.

Then it crossed the strip, and smote the city.

From the roofs came the sound as though ton after ton of ore had been dumped from some great eminence. There was a dead weight to the shocks that could not conceivably be delivered by so unsubstantial a substance as air, yet which was the wind itself, lifting abruptly to enormous heights, then hurling its full force downward.

These shocks followed the demoniac plan, occurring at exact intervals, and were succeeded by prying fingers, as fluid as ether, as hard as steel, that felt for cracks in roofs and windows.

One could no longer say with certainty, "This which I breathe is air, and this upon which I stand is earth." The storm had possessed itself of the city and made it its own. Tangibles and intangibles alike were whirled in a mad, inextricable nebula.

The waves that moved upon the bay could be dimly discerned for a little distance. They were turgid, yellow, and naked; for the moment they lifted a crest, the wind snatched it and dispersed it, with the rain, into the warm semi-fluid atmosphere with which it delivered its attack upon the panic-stricken city.

Notch by notch the velocity increased. The concussions upon the roofs became louder, and the prying fingers commenced to gain a purchase, worrying small holes into large ones. Here and there the wind would get beneath the tin, roll it up suddenly, whirl it from a building like a sheet of paper, and send it thundering and crashing down a deserted street.

Again it would gain entrance to a room through a broken window, and, exerting its explosive force to the full, would blow all of the other windows outward, and commence work upon the walls from within.

It was impossible to walk upon the street. At the first shock of the storm, the little group of negroes who had sought shelter in the wharf-house fled to the Row. Even then, the force of the attack had been so great that only by bending double and clinging together were they able to resist the onslaughts and traverse the narrow street.

Porgy and Bess sat in their room. The slats had been taken from the bed and nailed across the window, and the mattress, bundled into a corner, had been pre-empted by the goat. Bess sat wrapped in her own thoughts, apparently unmoved by the demoniac din without. Porgy's look was one of wonder, not unmixed with fear, as he peered into the outer world between two of the slats. The goat, blessed with an utter lack of imagination, reveled in the comfort and intimacy of his new environment, expressing his contentment in suffocating waves, after the manner of his kind. A kerosene lamp without a chimney, smoking straight up into the unnatural stillness of the room, cast a faint, yellow light about it, but only accentuated the heavy gloom of the corners.

From where Porgy sat, he could catch glimpses of what lay beyond the window. There would come occasional moments when the floor of the storm would be lifted by a burrowing wind, and he would see the high, naked breakers racing under the sullen pall of spume and rain.

Once he saw a derelict go by. The vessel was a small river sloop, with its rigging blown clean out. A man was clinging to the tiller. One wave, larger than its fellows, submerged the little boat, and when it wallowed to the surface again, the man was gone, and the tiller was kicking wildly.

"Oh, my Jedus, hab a little pity!" the watcher moaned under his breath. Later, a roof went by.

Porgy heard it coming, even above the sound of the attack upon the Row, and it filled him with awe and dread. He turned and looked at Bess, and was reassured to see that she met his gaze fearlessly. Down the street the roar advanced, growing nearer and louder momentarily. Surely it would be the final instrument of destruction. He held his breath, and waited. Then it thundered past his narrow sphere of vision. Rolled loosely, it loomed to the second story windows, and flapped and tore at the buildings as it swept over the cobbles.

When a voice could be heard again, Porgy turned to his companion.

"You an' me, Bess," he said with conviction; "We sho' is a little somet'ing attuh all."

After that, they sat long without exchanging a word. Then Porgy looked out of the window and noticed that the quality of the atmosphere was becoming denser. The spume lifted for a moment, and he could scarcely see the tormented bay.

"I t'ink it mus' be mos' night," he observed. "Dey ain't much light now on de outside ob dis storm."

He looked again before the curtain descended, and what he saw caused his heart to miss a beat.

He knew that the tide should be again at the ebb, for the flood had commenced just after the storm broke. But as he looked, the water, which was already higher than a normal flood, lifted over the far edge of the street, and three tremendous waves broke in rapid succession, sending the deep layers of water across the narrow way to splash against the wall of the building.

This reversal of nature's law struck terror into the dark places of Porgy's soul. He beckoned to Bess, his fascinated eyes upon the advancing waves. She bent down and peered into the gloom.

"Oh, yes," she remarked in a flat tone. "It been dis way in de las' great storm. De win' hol' de watuh in de jetty mout' so he can't go out. Den he pile up annoder tide on him."

Suddenly an enormous breaker loomed over the backs of its shattered and retreating fellows. The two watchers could not see its crest, for it towered into, and was absorbed by, the low-hanging atmosphere. Yellow, smooth, and with a perpendicular, slightly concave front, it flashed across the street, and smote the solid wall of the Row. They heard it roar like a mill-race through the drive, and flatten, hissing in the court. Then they turned, and saw their own door give slightly to the pressure, and a dark flood spurt beneath it, and debouch upon the floor.

Bess took immediate command of the situation. She threw an arm about Porgy, and hurried him to the door. She withdrew the bolt, and the flimsy panels shot inward.

The court was almost totally dark. One after another now the waves were hurtling through the drive and impounding in the walled square.

The night was full of moving figures, and cries of fear; while, out of the upper dark, the wind struck savagely downward.

With a powerful swing, Bess got Porgy to a stairway that providentially opened near their room, and, leaving him to make his way up alone, she rushed back, and was soon at his heels with an armful of belongings.

They sought refuge in what had been the great ball-room of
the mansion, a square, high-ceilinged room on the second story,
which was occupied by a large and prosperous family. There
were many refugees there before them. In the faint light cast by
several lanterns, the indestructible beauty of the apartment was
evident, while the defacing effects of a century were absorbed in
shadow. The noble open fireplace, the tall, slender mantel, with
its Grecian frieze and intricate scrollwork, the high paneled
walls were all there. And then, huddled in little groups on the
floor, or seated against the walls, with eyes wide in the lantern-
shine, the black, fear-stricken faces. Like the ultimate disintegra-
tion of a civilization—there it was; and upon it, as though to
make quick work of the last, tragic chapter, the scourging wrath
of the Gods—white, and black.

The night that settled down upon Catfish Row was one of name-
less horror to the inhabitants, most of whom were huddled on
the second floor in order to avoid the sea from beneath, and
deafening assaults upon the roof above their heads.

With the obliteration of vision, sound assumed an exagger-
ated significance, and the voice of the gale, which had seemed by
day only a great roar, broke up in the dark into its various parts.
Human voices seemed to cry in it; and there were moments when
it sniffed and moaned at the windows.

Once, during a silence in the room, a whinny was distinctly
heard.

"Dat my ole horse!" wailed Peter. "He done dead in he stall
now, an' dat he woice goin' by. Oh, my Gawd!"

They all wailed out at that; and Porgy, remembering his goat,
whimpered and turned his face to the wall. Then someone
started to sing:

"I gots uh home in de rock, don't yuh see?"

With a feeling of infinite relief, Porgy turned to his Jesus. It was
not a charm that he sought now for the assuaging of some phys-

ical ill, but a benign power, vaster perhaps even than the hurricane. He lifted his rich baritone above the others:

> "Oh, between de eart' an' sky,
> I kin see my Sabior die. I
> gots uh home in de rock,
> Don't yuh see!"

Then they were all in it, heart and soul. Those who had fallen into a fitful sleep, awoke, rubbed their eyes, and sang.

Hour after hour dragged heavily past. Outside, the storm worked its will upon the defenseless city. But in the great ballroom of Catfish Row, forty souls sat wrapped in an invulnerable garment. They swayed and patted, and poured their griefs and fears into a rhythm that never missed a beat, which swept the hours behind it into oblivion, and that finally sang up the faint gray light that penetrated the storm, and told them that it was again day.

At about an hour after daybreak the first lull came. Like the other moves of the hurricane, it arrived without warning. One moment the tumult was at its height. The next, there was utter suspension. Abruptly, like an indrawn breath, the wind sucked back upon itself, leaving an aching vacuum in its place. Then from the inundated waterfront arose the sound of the receding flood.

The ebb-tide was again overdue, and with the second tide piled upon it, the whole immeasurable weight of the wind was required to maintain its height. Now, with the pressure removed, it turned and raced beneath the low-lying mist toward the sea, carrying its pitiful loot upon its back.

To the huddled figures in the great room of the Row came the welcome sound, as the court emptied itself into the street. The negroes crowded to the windows, and peered between the barricades at the world without.

The water receded with incredible speed. Submerged wreckage lifted above the surface. The street became the bed of a cataract that foamed and boiled on its rush to the sea. Presently the wharf emerged, and at its end even a substantial remnant of the house could be descried. How it had survived that long was one of the inexplicable mysteries of the storm.

Suddenly Peter, who was at one of the windows, gave a cry, and the other negroes crowded about him to peer out.

The sea was still running high, and as a large wave lifted above the level of the others, it thrust into view the hull of a half-submerged boat. Before the watchers could see, the wave dropped its burden into a trough, but the old man showed them where to look, and presently a big roller caught it up, and swung it, bow on, for all to see. There was a flash of scarlet gunnel, and, beneath it, a bright blue bird with open wings.

"De 'Seagull'!" cried a dozen voices together. "My Gawd! dat Jake' boat!"

All night Clara had sat in a corner of the room with the baby in her arms, saying no word to anyone. She was so still that she seemed to be asleep, with her head upon her breast. But once, when Bess had gone and looked into her face, she had seen her eyes, wide and bright with pain.

Now the unfortunate woman heard the voices, and sprang to the window just in time to see the craft swoop into a hollow at the head of the pier.

She did not scream out. For a moment she did not even speak. Then she spun around on Bess with the dawn of a wild hope in her dark face.

"Tek care ob dis baby 'til I gits back," she said, as she thrust the child almost savagely into Bess's arms. Then she rushed from the room.

The watchers at the window saw her cross the street, splashing wildly through the knee-deep water. Then she ran the length of the wharf, and disappeared behind the sheltering wall of the house.

It was so sudden, and tired wits move slowly. Several minutes had passed before it occurred to anyone to go with her. Finally Peter turned from the window.

"Dat 'oman ain't ought tuh be out dey by sheself," he said. "Who goin' out dey wid me, now?"

One of the men volunteered, and they started for the door.

A sound like the detonation of a cannon shook the building to its foundations. The gale had returned, smashing straight downward from some incredible height to which it had lifted during the lull.

The men turned and looked at one another. Shock followed shock in rapid succession. Those who stood by the windows felt them give inward, and instinctively threw their weight against the frames. The explosions merged into a steady roar of sound that surpassed anything that had yet occurred. The room became so dark that they could no longer see one another. The barricaded windows were vaguely discernible in bars of muddy gray and black. Deeply rooted walls swung from the blows, and then settled slowly back on the recoil.

A confused sound of praying filled the room. And above it shrilled the terror of the women.

For an appreciable space of time the spasm lasted. Then, slowly, as though by the gradual withdrawing of a lever, the vehemence of the attack abated. The muddy gray bars at the windows became lighter, and some of the more courageous of the negroes peered out.

The wharf could be seen dimly extending under the low floor of spume and mist. The breakers were higher than at any previous time, but instead of smashing in upon the shore, they raced straight up the river and paralleled the city. As each one swung by it went clean over the wharf, obliterating it for the duration of its passage.

Suddenly from the direction of the lower harbor a tremendous mass appeared, showing first only a vast distorted stain against the gray fabric of the mist. Then a gigantic wave took it, and drove it into fuller view.

"Great Gawd A'mighty!" some one whispered. "It's dat big lumbuh schooner bruck loose in de harbor."

The wave hunched its mighty shoulders under the vessel and swung it up—up, for an interminable moment. The soaring bowsprit lifted until it was lost in mist. Tons of water gushed from the steep incline of the deck, and poured over the smooth, black wall of the side, as it reared half out of the sea. Then the wave swept aft, and the bow descended in a swift, deadly plunge.

A crashing of timbers followed that could be heard clearly above the roaring of the storm. The hull had fallen directly across the middle of the wharf. There was one cataclysmic moment when the whole view seemed to disintegrate. The huge timbers of the wharf up-ended, and were washed out like straws. The schooner rolled half over, and her three masts crashed down with their rigging. The shock burst the lashings of the vessel's deck load, and as the hull heeled, an avalanche of heavy timbers took the water. The ruin was utter.

Heavy and obliterating, the mist closed down again.

Bess turned from the window holding the sleeping infant in her arms, raised her eyes and looked full at Porgy.

With an expression of awe on his face, the cripple reached out a timid hand and touched the baby's cheek.

The windows of the great ball-room were open to the sky, and beyond them, a busy breeze was blowing across its washed and polished expanse, gathering cloud-remnants into little heaps, and sweeping them in tumbling haste out over the threshold of the sea.

Most of the refugees had returned to their rooms, where sounds of busy salvaging could be heard. Porgy's voice arose jubilantly announcing that the goat had been discovered, marooned upon the cook-stove; and that Peter's old horse had belied his whinny, and was none the worse for a thorough wetting.

Serena Robbins paused before Bess, who was gathering her things preparatory to leaving the room, placed her hands upon her hips, and looked down upon her.

"Now, wut we all goin' to do wid dis po' mudderless chile?" she said, addressing the room at large.

The other occupants of the room gathered behind Serena, but there was something about Bess's look that held them quiet. They stood there waiting and saying nothing.

Slowly Bess straightened up, her faced lowered and pressed against that of the sleeping child. Then she raised her eyes and met the gaze of the complacent older woman.

What Serena saw there was not so much the old defiance that she had expected, as it was an inflexible determination, and, behind it, a new-born element in the woman that rendered the scarred visage incandescent. She stepped back and lowered her eyes.

Bess strained the child to her breast with an elemental intensity of possession, and spoke in a low, deep voice that vested her words with sombre meaning.

"Is Clara come back a'ready, since she dead, an' say somet'ing 'bout '*we*' tuh yuh 'bout dis child?"

She put the question to the group, her eyes taking in the circle of faces as she spoke.

There was no response; and at the suggestion of a possible return of the dead, the circle drew together instinctively.

"Berry well den," said Bess solemnly. "Ontell she do, I goin' stan' on she las' libbin' word an' keep dis chile fuh she 'til she do come back."

Serena was hopelessly beaten, and she knew it.

"Oh, berry well," she capitulated. "All I been goin' tuh do wuz jus' tuh puhwide um wid er propuh Christian raisin'. But ef she done gib um tuh yuh, dere ain't nuttin mo' I kin do, I guess."

Battered and Primitive

GEORGE GERSHWIN (1898–1937)

Internationally famous for *Rhapsody in Blue* (1924), *An American in Paris* (1928), and a host of other jazz-age compositions, George Gershwin, along with his lyricist brother Ira, collaborated with poet and novelist DuBose Heyward on the opera *Porgy and Bess* (1935).

In the summer of 1934 Gershwin came to South Carolina to immerse himself in the culture of the sea islands: to experience the folk music of Lowcountry African Americans, and to try to capture the rhythms and the cadences of local songs for use in his "classical" operatic treatment of the story of Porgy.

Gershwin apparently created quite a sensation in both black and white society during his two months in the Lowcountry. He often visited black churches on James Island and during a "shout" (a religious service that included the singing of spirituals accompanied by loud clapping of hands and stamping of feet) Gershwin not only joined in but apparently became the most prominent shouter in the congregation. By contrast, one evening at the home of Mr. and Mrs. James Hagood at 46 South Battery, his jazz performance on the piano not only delighted his hosts but caused neighbors to come out on their piazzas in order to hear better.

Wednesday

Dear Mother,

The place down here looks like a battered, old South Sea Island. There was a storm 2 weeks ago which tore down a few houses along the beach & the place is so primitive they just let them stay that way. Imagine, there's not one telephone on the whole Island—public or private. The nearest phone is about 10 miles away.

Our first three days here were cool, the place being swept by an ocean breeze. Yesterday was the first hot day (it must have been 95° in town) & it brought out the flys [sic], and knats [sic], mosquitos. There are so many swamps in the district that when the breeze comes in from the land there's nothing to do but scratch.

If you're thinking of coming down here, consider these nuisances as I'd hate to have you make the trip & then be uncomfortable. I know you like your comforts.

We wear nothing but bathing suits all day long & certainly enjoy that part of it.

Du Bose Heyward is coming down tomorrow to spend 2 weeks & I hope to get some work done on the opera.

I'm glad I didn't bring Tony as it would have been a little hot for him. I think you should send him up to Mosbachers, if you leave town.

Please write me & I'll let you know what happens. Hope you are well & that I'll see you soon. Love to yourself and Arthur.

Your George

Roots

JOSEPHINE PINCKNEY (1895–1957)

While John Bennett, Hervey Allen, and DuBose Heyward made their literary marks primarily through their prose, the most remarkable poetry created in the 1920s and '30s in Charleston was produced by two women, Josephine Pinckney and Beatrice Witte Ravenel. Pinckney was a member of a women's literary discussion group under the leadership of Laura Bragg, the director of the Charleston Museum. This group ultimately amalgamated with a group of male writers gathered around Bennett and became the Poetry Society of South Carolina.

Pinckney's book of poetry, *Sea-Drinking Cities*, was published by Harper & Brothers in 1927; the selections below are taken from that volume. Pinckney went on to write several novels which were well received. *Three O'Clock Dinner* (1945) examines the complex relationship between a proper South-of-Broad family and a local family of humbler origin. *Great Mischief* (1948) examines a post–Civil War pharmacist who delves into the occult and establishes a romantic and sexual relationship with a beautiful young witch or "hag." The climax of the novel is apocalyptic, a vision of the end of time, reflected through images of the Charleston earthquake of 1886. The nature of the hag, as seen in local folklore, is previewed in Pinckney's poem of the same name, included below. Like many local writers, especially John Bennett, Pinckney had a great interest in the Lowcountry's version of voodoo, known as the root, or root medicine.

Josephine Pinckney was inducted into the South Carolina Academy of Authors in 1988.

Sea-drinking Cities

> Sea-drinking cities have a moon-struck air;
> Houses are topped with look-outs; as a dog

Looks up with dumb eyes asking, dormers stare
At stranger-vessels and swart cunning faces.
They are touched with long sleeping in the sea-born moon;
They have heard fabled sails slatting in the dark,
Clearing with no papers, unwritten in any log,
Light as thin leaves before the rough typhoon;
Kneels trace a phospher-mark,
To follow to old ocean-drowned green places.

They never lose longing for the never-known,
These ocean-townships moored and hawsered fast,
They welcome ships, salt-jeweled venturers
That up over the curve of the world are blown
With sun-rise in their sails and gold-topped mast;
And in the evening they let them go again
With a twisted lip of pain,
Into the cavernous fog that folds and stirs;
They have not even a faint tenderness
For their own loveliness.

Their loveliness, as of an old tale told . . .
A harbor-goblet with wide-brimming lip
Where morning tumbles in shaken red and gold,
Trinketed and sun-bedizened they sip;
Their tiny tiles all twinkle, fire-bright;
Their strong black people bargain on the docks
In gaudy clothes that catch the beating light . . .
But all bewitched, old cities sit at gaze
Toward the wharves of Mogador . . . Gibraltar,
Where the shawl-selling Arab piles a blaze
Of fiery birds and flowers on Trade's heaped altar.
Sea-drunken sure are these, —
Towns that doze—dream—and never wake at all,
While the soft supple wind slides through the trees,
And the sun sleeps against the yellow wall.

Hag!

Once when I went to see Victoria
As she sat picking shrimp on the kitchen porch—
"Yuh hear dat hollerin' las' night?" she said,
Nodding, brown-paper capped, above the shrimp
That leapt pink-striped into the yellow bowl.
"Dat was a hag; I heared 'er w'en she she jump'
Out'n de winduh en' run 'cross de roof
Scr-r-r-r-vlip!" Her tongue and eye-whites rolled
A sharp description.
        "Hags is human people,
En' dey kin ketch a ol' black cat en' boil it
En' take a bone en' hol' it in dey mout',
Den dey kin go troo any key-hole livin'.
My Gra'ma seen one w'en she was a chile
In lamp-oil times. De hag gone in de key-hole
En' step out'n 'er skin en' lef' it layin'
Down by de hearth en' gone to ride de people.

W'ite mens is scheemy, dough! Dem people come
En' fin de skin en full it full o' crumbs
En' salt en' pepper en' hide it 'hine de do',
En' time de hag git done en' start to skip
She can't git on de skin, en' den dey ketch'er.
She was a human woman, Gra'ma say,
Only she look red, like, bidout de skin,
Kind o' like flannen. Dey put 'er in de guard-house;
En' when de hangin' come a million people—
Mo' 'n a million people, Gra'ma say,
Gone out to see. De hag ain't crack 'er breath,
But she look rale mad w'en dey stan'er on de gallus;
En' w'en dey start to put 'er in de noose
Suddent she squall out—
        'Skin! Skin!
        Slip agin!'

Please Gawd! De skin come sailin' troo de air
En' slip right on 'er-vlip! En' den she *laugh*
To kill, an' ride off on de win' en' gone!
Great Day! You ought'a seen dem people run,
My Gra'ma say. Yes Ma'am, she *seen* dat hag."

from *A Short Walk*

ALICE CHILDRESS (1920–1994)

Actress, playwright, and novelist Alice Childress was born in Charleston, the great-granddaughter of a slave, but moved to Harlem at the age of five and spent most of the rest of her life in New York. Her first play, *Florence,* was performed in 1949 and published the next year. *Just a Little Simple* was produced in 1950, based on Langston Hughes's collection of stories *Simple Speaks His Mind.* In 1956 Childress won an Obie Award for her play *Trouble in Mind,* the first African-American woman to be so honored; she was also the first to have a play produced on Broadway. Other notable works include *Wine in the Wilderness* (1969), *Mojo and String: Two Plays* (1971), and *Wedding Band: A Love/Hate Story in Black and White* (1973). From 1966 to 1969 she was a writer-in-residence at Harvard and Radcliffe. In addition to her dramatic works, Childress wrote fiction for young adults, including the novels *A Hero Ain't Nothin' but a Sandwich* (1973) and *Rainbow Jordan* (1981), and for adults, including the novel *A Short Walk* (1979), from which the following excerpt is taken.

Alice Childress was inducted into the South Carolina Academy of Authors in 1990.

One morning, in the middle of the year 1900, in a two-room shack in Charleston, South Carolina, Bill James has a comforting breakfast of mackerel and hominy grits. Jesus looks down from the wall with compassion, down from his frame of pink and blue seashells. Bill is lean, good looking, and keen featured. His skin is dull, velvety, almost blue. Gently puffed lips glow grape-purple against strong white teeth. In one knotted, work-hardened hand he holds a newspaper, in the other a piece of fried fish. He shakes his head slowly, with great authority. "Etta, this world is somethin, first one thing, then another."

His brown wife peeps over his shoulder, pouring another cup of coffee, leaning in close, enjoying the odor of Dr. Alimine's

Flower Pomade. She thinks of telling him how good looking he is, but says something else.

"You like to show off, don'tcha? Just cause you can read. You oughta be thinkin' 'bout buyin another paper. All that news happen so long ago till folks done forgot."

"I'm gonna buy a new one when new things start happenin. No point in buyin the same news every day, a waste a money."

Etta takes off her apron and picks her best black skirt free of lint. Looking in the speckled, cracked mirror hanging under Jesus on the wall, she smoothes thick, bushy hair and rolls down her sleeves. "Bill, what kinda eyes I got?"

"Gingerbread eyes and stand-up ninnies."

"Shame, shame, no way to talk on the day of a funeral."

"Yeah, it is. You got pretty little feet and a nice round boonky."

"Stop talkin underneath my clothes. No shame."

"Got dimples in her cheeks, all up behind her knees and everywhere."

Her eyes light with love. They think love thoughts about how good it is to be together, how good it was each time they had it, touching hands beneath the covers even when they weren't having it. How good it is to be black and brown in a morning glory-covered house; to have mackerel and grits on a four-eyed stove; to own plates, cups, spoons and an iron bed with a big, comfortable mattress.

"Billie-boy, ain't it time we 'dopted ourself a baby?"

He lowers his head as if examining the workboots, turning his feet this way and that. "Well, folks oughta have they own chirrun and—"

"Look like we ain't gonna have any of our own. Looks like I'da got that way in five years, but no sense in accusin Gawd."

Bill carefully folds the newspaper and places it in the sideboard drawer. "Folks should be kinda well-off when they think about taking in a stranger-chile."

"We's well-off. Ain't many people got as much to show as we got. Not a meal goes by that we don't have food left in the pot. There's bedclothes in the drawer and a pump in the kitchen. We got pots, pans and dishes. How much can a baby use?"

"They don't stay little. They grow up."

"Let her grow if she wants to. That's what babies is for, for to grow."

"I gotta go to work. We gonna dig ditches behind the mill road. . . ."

"And I'm bringin Murdell's baby back after the funeral."

"But you dern well can't do it less I give the word."

"Give me your word."

"Look like Murdell's mama would keep it."

"Mrs. Johnson's gone so cripple till the next door people have to do for her."

"How come the next door people don't keep the baby?"

"Cause they got nine of they own. Haven't you been sayin and also silent-wishin for me to have a baby?"

Bill pops his knuckles and fine beads of sweat appear on his forehead. "I don't know how the baby look."

"You got eyes; come see."

"I can't look at the chile, then say I don't want it. That's rude. Bet they name it somethin I wouldn't like. Did they call her Murdell?"

"No, and you must never speak ill of the dead."

"Not speakin ill, just don't like that name."

"They gonna let me name her."

"You did it already?"

"I thought of a name and they callin her by it, but she's only three weeks old—we can change it."

"What yall callin her?"

"Cora, after your gone-to-glory mother who was born in slavery. Cora is a sound that's short, sweet and easy on your mouth."

He turns away to hide the pleasure in his eyes, having a hard time of giving in, giving up and taking in the stranger-child. . . .

"That baby is half white, Etta."

"But she's so sweetly brown, like coffee and condense milk mix together."

"But even so. . . ."

She cups his face in her hands. "Please, sweet daddy, do it just for me?"

His knees go weak. "Sure, for you and for me, too. . . ."

. . .

Cora likes the solid feel of Bill's large hand circling hers as they walk along the street. She skips a few steps, looking up to watch his velvety dark face outlined against clear blue sky.

"Papa, after I'm five, what all I'm gonna do?"

"Oh, no tellin what 'fore all this is over."

"All what?"

"Life."

"What is life?"

"Life is . . . well I heard that life is just a short walk from the cradle to the grave."

"We walkin it now, Papa-la?"

"Yes-indeedy-ree, right this very minute we livin life and on our way to the future."

"What's future?"

"Whatever comes next, Cora, everything that didden happen yet." He swings her up on his shoulder. Low-hanging, leafy tree branches brush her face. She leans against him breathing in Alimine's hair dressing.

"Girl, why you call me 'Papa-la'?"

"You always be Papa, but when it's nice, like now, then you turn into Papa-la."

"But what do la mean?"

"It's bein better than most people. One day I heard a fine 'la' sound and then I knew."

"Where did you hear it?"

"Inside a my head–'laaaaa'. The day you and me was standin on the side porch eatin grapes and you gave me the best ones and—you gonna laugh at me."

"No, I won't. If I do I'll gi'e you a dollar."

"You gave me the best grape and that's when I heard 'la'. I said it easy so you couldn't hear—'Papa-la'. You can laugh if you want and not pay a dollar."

"That's no joke. 'La' is one of the finest things I ever heard anybody relate. You can tell what you hear goin on inside a you—that's a gift. Thanks for tellin me la." He shifts her to his other shoulder as he hurries by the wrought-iron railing of the city park.

"I'm glad today's my birthday and glad we goin to Rabbit Ears Minstrel. How come Mama don't like minstrel shows?"

"Well, lotta buckin and wingin—she don't think it's fittin for nice people."

"But we think it is."

He laughs and chides her. "Girl, you talk too much."

"Papa-la, tell me what all I'm gonna be and do on my short walk."

"What short walk?"

"Life, Papa, life!"

"Well, you'll be a great lady."

"No, I mean zackly."

"Well, zackly you'll read and write."

"Like you?"

"Better than me. You gonna read and write up a blue streak."

In her mind's eye she sees the streak; it is very blue. She writes her way up the streak, then reads on the way down. The streak turns into a tree with blue branches, cool against her cheek.

"Why so quiet, baby?"

Looking over his shoulder, she sees a red, yellow and pink world on the other side of the fence. "I see flowers."

"A park."

"Who planted flowers?"

"The city. They hire men to do it."

"Let's go in."

"No, we goin to see Rabbit Ears."

"You said I can do anything I want on my birthday."

"We don't need to go in there."

"I need it, Papa-la."

"See that sign over the gate? It say 'WHITE ONLY'. We must not go in."

"You said I can do anything on my birthday."

He looks up and down the street. Not a soul in sight; the park is also clear. "We'll go for a hot minute, then right back out."

"Yessir."

They are in front of a large circle of flowers; the air is perfumed.

"Papa, is this heaven?"

"No, now let's go."

Around the turn, at the right of the gate, there is a policeman who turns red in the face at the sight of Bill. "Maybe you don't read signs, but you know niggeras not allowed to enter the park. Sign says 'WHITE'. You know what's on it even if you can't read atall."

Bill squeezes Cora's hand, the edge of his fingernail nipping into her thumb. The pinch means silence. Bill gives a hollow laugh and slightly bows his head to the policeman.

"Officer, wrong is wrong and we wrong. I come to fetch her out." His fingernail presses deeper into her thumb but she doesn't feel it.

Patrolman twirls his stick. "You niggeras don't raise your pickaninnies to respect law. Spare the rod and they'll think they white."

"Her Mama gonna put some whuppin on her. I'd do it now myself but last time I almost kill her cause I'm too heavy-handed."

"Who you work for?"

"Mr. Ray at the phosphate mill. Been there ten years without trouble."

"How come you not at work?"

"It's slack time. Colored got few days off."

"Boy, what's your name?"

"Er . . .Willie."

Policeman waves them away. "Willie, you teach that gal that she's a niggera, the same as a boy and she got no privilege to break law and enter city property, 'specially the public park. Learn her at home or we gonna teach her out here. Understand?"

"Yessir, officer."

Policeman gives her a start by stamping his feet and making a break toward her. "I'm gon' gitcha and splitcha halfin-two!"

The sound of police laughter follows them as they hurry down the street. He releases her thumb. She looks back.

"Papa, he's gone."

"Good."

"Why you afraid of him?"

His voice is dull and heavy. "Sorry you had to see me make a liar outta myself . . .on your birthday. I could whip him without puttin half my mind on it, but they got the power of life and death. Five is young but it's time for you to know that white folks got the law on their side. They can and do jail us, they can even lynch. . . ."

"What's lynch?"

"It's killin and murder, and hangin from trees, settin bodies afire. . . ."

"Why they do it?"

"We the colored, that's why he say 'niggeras'; they the white, why we say 'crackers'. The rich white man run the courthouse, the bank, the jobs . . . and the poor white cracker is mean cause he don't run nothin and is scared we gonna cut him outta what little he do get holda. They glad for any excuse to kill us off. Cora, you five and you also colored. You can't go in parks, even some stores—lotsa places."

"Why they like that?"

"Because they cruel and uphold a mean rule. In slave time they use ta cut off our ears if we learned how to read and write."

"I don't wanta read and write."

"Well, that law is over now, but they still try to hold us back on every hand."

"Why they do it? Why they so mean?"

"Make em feel biggety and strong to see us suffer, to hurt and harm. Some people's bread and butter taste better if they know somebody else is goin hungry."

"Why we lettum do it?"

"They was even worse cruel back in slavery. My poor mammy went to the grave with whip marks on her back. They holdin us down now cause they fear we will someday pay back for the wrong they done."

"Will we pay back?"

"Yes-indeedy-ree—they pushin us to it."

They fall into a long silence. She walks primly beside him, hands hidden in her dress pockets.

"You gonna like the Rabbit Ears Minstrel, baby."

"Can colored go to it?"

"Yes, it's got colored acts. We related, in a distant way, to some nice people who work in it—Uncle Sam and Aunt Francina. You'll like that, Cora-la."

Her thumb still hurts but she slips her hand back into his. "Yessir, but let's not say 'la' anymore."

"Not ever?"

"Not today."

. . .

I didn't really know we were poor until now. A war is happenin overseas and somehow it makes things more high-priced here. Hard times are harder for us Negroes. We now say "Negroes" because it is a better title and means black, while colored also means Japanese, Indian, Chinese and others who are not white. I find it hard to say "Negro" because I'm not used to it. Cecil says I must learn to say it, because our position sets us apart from other coloreds, because we were brought captive from Africa to be sold and used as slaves—not like immigrants who came to get jobs for pay. . . .

Me. I don't believe there's any war. We sure don't hear guns in Charleston Harbor. But there's plenty warships dockin. Cecil and I go down to the battery to see them and get the chance to talk to each other alone. After Cecil's father died from a weak chest, his mother soon followed from cancer. People say it in whispers cause cancer is a curse from God and the person who gets it must have done some terrible wrong. We don't say "TB" either—it's kinder to say the person is in a "decline" or has consumption. . . .

Cecil was turned over to Mr. Jenkins' Orphanage. Many homeless Negro boys were wandering the streets beggin and stealin. So, this musician by the name of Jenkins started the first Negro orphan home. His wife and friends teach orphans how to play musical instruments and do carpentry and shoe repair. Mr. Jenkins soon had so many to feed he went to the city and asked for money. They gave him three hundred dollars a year, and when that wasn't enough, he formed a band and they went on the street corners to play, then pass a tin cup to beg. People give cause they really do sound good. When that band plays, washerwomen take their hands outta soapsuds and go to the corner to listen. The hungry forget about miss-meal cramps and barefoot children hop fences and run over hot cobblestone to see and hear.

. . .

My father never had much time to himself before the illness. Now he doesn't have to go to the mill, to church, to lodge meetin, or anywhere else. He lies flat on his back starin at the ceilin, and talkin bout the Charleston slave market. "Cora, these days, Negro women go there to sell quilts and baskets, but that place is still my bad dream." He wakes durin the night and cries out about the noise in the market, his mother on a platform while men call out her price.

Kojie gives pain pills to get him back to sleep. I could have gone to Avery High School on scholarship, but it'll wait till next year, when Papa is better. Mama works and I must nurse him through this bad time. It's almost like goin to school. He talks about all sorts of things and I spend most a my wakin hours sittin on the foot of his bed.

"Papa, you lookin better."

"I'm dyin, Cora."

"Don't say that."

"I'm dyin—let's not fall out about it. Don't act like death is somethin I thought up. Help me straighten my affairs."

"Yes, Papa."

"Is my burial policy paid up?"

"It is."

"Good, now is not the time for it to lapse."

I get my copy book and write down things as he tells them. "See that your mama don't let the undertaker get everything. He put away old Miss Emily for seventy-five dollars, plus fifteen for the grave. That'll leave yall with seventy-five clear. It can last two months if she's cautious. Don't bury me in my good suit; give it to Mister July so he can go to a funeral steada hangin round outside."

"Yes, Papa."

"I leave you with this piece a knowledge: don't let the slave market have every bit of you . . . understand?"

"Slavery's over."

"Only in a way a speakin, daughter. The law still pushes us to back entrances and separate lines. But while you standin separate just keep tellin yourself that Jim Crow law is nothin but some bad echoes from a old slave market."

"It doesn't make me as mad as it use ta."

"Hang onto 'mad'. When you stop mindin, that's when they got every bit a you and have fulfill the purpose of their meaness, which is to turn us into wrung-out, tuck-tail dogs; whatcha call 'defeat'."

"I'll never act like a tuck-tail dog."

"They don't wantcha to act like one—they wantcha to be one and act like you not."

Outside of the sadness, I like the talks. Other people don't seem interested in what we go into. If they are, they keep quiet about it. When I ask folks to tell me what they think about life, it makes them uneasy. Mama says, "Love Gawd and keep goin, that's all I know." Cecil declares life is first one thing and then another. I can't dispute that, but it doesn't get down to facts. He laughed at me and tried to prove his point with a silly joke. "First it's one thing, right? Well, if it doesn't get to be another . . . you died."

Papa gives answers. "Well, honey, I still believe life is a short walk from the cradle to the grave and it sure behooves us to be kind to one another. We are born, then we begin to take notice. Noticin is not enough, so we try to find teachers to point out what we fail to notice. We begin to catch on to how things are done. We suffer some, then think we know it all . . . so that leads us to make mistakes. All such errors make us doubt our own minds. As we go along we learn not to judge people too hard but you gotta be careful who to give your deepest heart and thoughts to, because you'll carry alla those people inside for the resta your days and that can either tear you up or else make it go smoother. But with all our best figurin, somethin keeps goin wrong and we begin to think too little of ourselves. Well, trials keep comin, finally we begin to catch on to how to live . . . but by that time life's almost over." . . .

There's no way to stop him talkin and paregoric brings out crazy kinda things, more than anybody needs to hear—"And as far as you not bein our own child. . . ."—tellin me that kinda stuff till my head feels like burstin open. He'll say some, then go back to it and say more, then forget all about it. Feels like I'm dyin right long with him. I look at walls and out the window and down on the floor, everywhere but in his face cause I don't wanta believe such lies . . . yet knowin it's true.

"Papa, I don't belong to you? I'm not blood kin?"

"Course you belong to us."

"But if somebody named Murdell was my mother and some white man . . ."

"Don't tell Etta. She don't want it told."

"Papa, you scarin me."

"Truth must be told. You belong to yourself more than to any of us. Nobody is to own alla your secrets, even if they did adopt—not even me. Give me some more paregoric, please, and more pain pills."

"There's only a few pills left, you must have had four today."

"Etta and I couldn't have any of our own, you been my heart and hers. But alla your business belongs to you. Right is right."

"Yes, Papa, right is right."

The churchwomen are here to fold my father's hands, to close his eyes with pennies. Every mirror in the house is covered so his spirit won't be trapped and lose the way to the Hereafter. They pray for his soul as they lay out the suit, shirt and tie for the undertaker. The children carry messages to the neighbors and the rest of the congregation. Churchwomen wash, cook, dust and scrub the floor, always scrubbin toward the street door to drive away any evil spirit that might visit the house and claim the dead. As they work they tell good things about my father.

"Never had a harsh word, not a one."

"Was a good provider. Had not a selfish bone."

"You'll not see his like again in a hurry."

Kojie returns with the undertaker and his assistant. They carry Papa out in a long basket covered with canvas. I try to follow; the women hold me back.

I tell them, "Take the canvas off. Don't leave him in the dark. No canvas, please."

Kojie puts his arms around me. "They have to cover him, darling, because it is now raining."

Miss Odessa peeps at the street through drawn blinds. "Heaven is weeping," she says. "That's a good sign."

Miss Jenny holds my mother's hand. "We know not the day or the hour."

People, more and more people, bring sympathy. I go in his room. His bed is freshly made, as smooth as glass, empty lookin, as if he's never been in it. Kojie follows and neatly puts away bottles, spoons and medicine glasses.

"Cora, it's for the best."

"Everyone says."

"We can't question God's wisdom, dearest."

"I guess not."

"If you need anything remember I'm here, sweetness."

"Thank you."

"Not only in this hour of sorrow, but from now on."

When no one notices I go out the back door, down to the battery to find and tell Cecil. He tells me he's sorry—then we start countin how many ships are in harbor, testin to see if I remember the names and numbers. I know each navy ship, the merchant marines and the tankers. When we run out of ships, we count every sailor wearin a white cap, and when that's done with . . .

"Cecil, since you told me about your Aunt Looli, I'll tell a terrible thing Papa told before he died. I'm not theirs. My mother's name was Murdell, my father was some . . . some white man."

"I know."

"How do you know?"

"I heard it from other people."

"Well, I guess he was right to tell me if everybody else knows. Don't let my mother know that I know—it might hurt her feelings. I feel like I belong to nobody atall."

"Mr. James shouldn'ta told you."

"It was the paregoric . . . I don't wanta go back home yet . . . to all those people knowin more bout me than I do almost."

We walk past the flowery, White-only park where I once read up and down a blue streak. We walk beyond houses with double verandas, upstairs and down; past larger places smellin of gardenia and lemon leaves and magnolia; past piazzas with porch swings. Houses become scarcer and green is more. We pass a white man on the road, he waves to us, smiles, then goes in a pretty house.

from *Why We Never Danced the Charleston*

HARLAN GREENE (1953–   )

Harlan Greene grew up in Charleston and graduated from the College of Charleston. As a young man he collected the works of many Charleston authors, including DuBose Heyward, so when he was offered the chance to process Heyward's papers at the South Carolina Historical Society he eagerly accepted. Thus began a long career as archivist for a number of institutions in Charleston.

As a literary historian he is responsible for books about John Bennett (*Mister Skylark: John Bennett and the Charleston Renaissance* [2001] and *Renaissance in Charleston: Art and Life in the Carolina Lowcountry, 1900–1940* [2003], edited with James M. Hutchisson). He is presently writing a biography of novelist Harry Hervey. His archival work has led to a number of publications on Lowcountry history, and he writes extensively for the popular press on local history.

His first literary love is fiction, and his novels include *Why We Never Danced the Charleston* (1984), from which the excerpt below is taken, *What the Dead Remember* (1991), which won the Lambda Literary Award, and *The German Officer's Boy* (2005).

I was born in Savannah but spent most of my life in Charleston. Still this city never really accepted me. I was too nouveau, too outré for it; was born too far away to be taken seriously. I wish, though, that before I started on this journey, someone had told me that only Charlestonians themselves ever really arrive here. I would have gone back to Savannah, or done things differently. I see now that I was but a trespasser all along. I strayed down these streets in just the way I strayed into this story. But there is no one else who can tell it—or, at least, tell it correctly; and that is troublesome. I remember some things as clearly as my own name; others are fuzzy. So please bear with me. It is hard for an old man to begin at the beginning; to do that, I suppose I'll have to go back to Ned Grimke.

For I met Ned first. I met him years before I met Hirsch and long before any of us would ever turn up at the Battery. And even then, even that early, it was never "Ned"; it was always "Ned Grimke." My family and I spoke and thought of him that way, as if he were too frail to stand alone, as if he had no character or personality not granted him by his family. He always did seem overwhelmed by them and shadowed by their past; but that was not very remarkable: many of my friends in Charleston and even Savannah were, to a degree. History haunted us all, especially those of us born in a sleepy old southern town that had Fort Sumter for a legacy. It rose up from the harbor to stain the sky. We could see it from our school windows, red in the morning. We were used to it, the symbol of the city, its epitome. We'd stare at it in awe and reverence while we said our morning prayers, as if the ruin was Zion, as if Sumter was the Olympus hovering over us. For God, we did not doubt, did dwell in Charleston; or the Lord of the lost cause did anyway. Savannah, we were taught, was not quite so bright a star in the constellation of southern cities. Charleston was the brightest, and many of the boys I went to school with there bore holy names—names that had gathered a romantic sound to them and had garnered the prestige and patina of history—names like Laurens and Middleton and Pinckney. It was not so for Ned. There was a shame of sorts attached back then to being a Grimke, a shame that was traced to two sisters of that name, who in the early nineteenth century had believed that women were equal to men; even more telling than that, they had acknowledged a gentleman's—their father's—indiscretion, and had accepted their half-black half-brother wholeheartedly. There was something not so wonderful in being a Grimke after that; and for their ideas, for their heresies, the sisters had been forced north from the city.

Whoever you are who finds these notes, I wonder if you will believe me if I tell you that their stigma remained all those years later, and that the stain of their name was still there when I was growing up. Something peculiar and unclean seemed to lurk even in its pronouncing; I think I can remember, even as a child, how strange it sounded—as if it were a word from another language. I remember a chill running down my spine as my mother checked my nails and behind my ears and turned me over to my Dah to take me to meet Ned Grimke.

"What's that?" I remember asking my mother.

"He is a boy, just like you," she said. "Take him, Dah."

"I don't want to go," I cried. I was scared by one of those irrational fears in which childhood specializes.

"You must," my mother said; she kneeled beside me to pat my hair. "And you must be kind to him and make him feel welcome while he is here."

My Dah pressed my fingers together. Tightly. When she did that I knew there was no chance. I looked at my mother and waved as if going to Europe. She waved back. My Dah took me down the street to meet Ned Grimke.

That was the beginning. It was the same year that Miss Wragg first came here. I don't even recall if I liked Ned Grimke at first: if we became friends, it was out of necessity, for it seemed that summer that we were the only two boys in the whole city.

Like every summer, heat had laid its siege and people refugeed as they had after Sumter; they went to Flat Rock, and to the mountains of North Carolina, as my family and I did usually. But the summer Ned and I first met, my grandmother lay ill and we could not leave. We were left in Charleston in the heat, and Grandmama lay gasping for breath, like a mullet out of water in a shuttered upstairs room. I tiptoed up to her doorway to listen to her inhales and her gasps as if they were the pronouncements of some deity. Dah would shoo me away if she saw me playing with my puppets in the doorway. I had several. The gendarme my grandmother had given me was the angel of death.

"He's coming for her," I told Dah.

"Boy," she warned, "don't even think those things."

She was scared of puppets and glass-eyed doll babies.

Often the doctor would appear. In a gloom that gripped the house as tensely as hands held in prayer, my parents spoke to him in whispers and interpreted every tiny change: was it a sign that the end was near, or did it signal a rally? They could not tell top from bottom in their weariness and so they felt cross and guilty in the heat. Lost in the shuffle of emotions, I slipped through people's fingers. Dah, my black nurse (and that was their generic name, Dah being an African word for mother, and one that best summed up their tragedy—that of those black women doomed to raise white babies), took me out for walks once in a while; but she spent most of her time with my sickly brother, Hal, who had been born in April. So I was free to wander the city.

I found Charleston a ghost town that summer—the houses hollow and the streets empty; the Charlestonians who could just went to cooler places before air-conditioning. The fact that we were left in town and were from Savannah was not lost on the other families. Grass grew up in the streets, and every afternoon the streetcar came by, depositing my father for his dinner, which we ate at three: cold potato salad, cutlets and shrimp, tomato sandwiches, okra or green beans. While we ate, the shutters of the nearby houses rattled like dice in the breeze and petals of overblown roses fell in green gardens abandoned to the ravages of creepers and ivy. The talk was sparse, mostly of my grandmother—what she had eaten that morning—and of the stranger's fever that had appeared here and there in the black sections of town. Passing a shack on the way home, my father said he had heard a scream and a black woman's malarial delirium. "New York," she had cried, "New York City." Later, nearly every afternoon, purple storm clouds came up from the sea and it rained and thunder boomed in the deserted streets; the old roof tiles were washed in a rainbow, a pigeonlike sheen. On Sunday, we could hear St. Michael's chimes throughout the whole city.

Time was a tunnel that summer, like the one I entered under the cool trees of Broad Street, to be passed through listlessly until September would bring its storms and October would arrive, leading people back to the city. It was halfway or so through that tunnel of summer (I think the hurricane lilies were out and wisteria was blooming again) when my mother came looking for me one morning; she examined me with a look of pride and inevitability. She sighed and suggested with a false brightness in her voice—as if she were suggesting something to which she had been forced to concur—that I go off and visit Ned Grimke.

There was no use resisting; Dah was the disciplinarian in our home and made me do everything my parents said; so we went, Dah and I, passing slowly down the streets, she matching her rhythm to mine. Going through the throbbing heat, we passed the hucksters calling out their wares, singing out for she-crab or "weggutubles" or shrimp; on a corner the ground-nut mauma dipped into a sweet grass basket and gave me a taste of her goods for free; and I thanked her.

"Thank *you*, white gentleman," she said.

They all tipped their hats out of respect for Dah—no mean feat, for some carried their wares on their heads. Though Standard Oil moved my father and us back and forth between Charleston and Savannah, the Charlestonians, all in all, considered us almost quality; Dah was attached to us and so she held the same ranking.

Finally we drew up in front of a dark green door, so dark it was almost black, and stopped. I lost my nerve. Both of us were scared, I think; both of us had heard tales of what went on behind these walls, but neither of us had ever entered the Confederate Home before that morning. It loomed up above us on Chalmers Street.

It seemed huge that day, the building, as it always did; and eternal; and gray, reaching up to eclipse the sky. Rust-stained and rain-streaked, the earthquake-bolted façade seemed clasped in some iron-clad bitterness; the three-storied back (the front is on Broad Street) rose like a medieval fortress, so abruptly, that I had never known until we summoned up our courage and

entered that the building was arranged around an open courtyard, in the middle of which grew a huge and balanced cedar
tree. Once we opened the door to the passageway, we could see
the tree waving in front of us, green and dazzling, so that it
seemed like sunlit water at the end of the dark walkway.

When we reached it, we looked up with eyes blinking: there
were porches atop porches surrounding the courtyard; and on
them, we could see, watering flowers in tin cans, or sitting in
green wicker rocking chairs, or just pausing to look out over the
railings, countless old ladies, looking like aged Juliets on their
balconies.

"Do, Jedus," Dah moaned.

I said nothing.

They made sounds like bees humming. If they waited up there
for their beaux, they waited in vain; for only death would ever
come calling. I think they must have realized this, for all the
ladies wore black, and it was that fact that frightened me most.
To me, they looked like those ominous nuns I had seen circling
in front of St. Mary's; my friend Dwin had told me that all nuns
carried guns under their black habits, guns that had been issued
to them by the Pope for each newborn Catholic baby.

I was scared of them and tried to call to my Dah but my mouth
was dry; she stood rooted and all the ladies ignored us. We were
mesmerized by them, so that we were surprised when Ned
Grimke suddenly appeared.

We had heard him, without knowing that the sound heralded
his coming—a funny scraping noise against wood, as if someone
were coming downstairs dragging something metal, like a scythe,
behind him. He was coming down one of the many ramshackle
staircases that seemed to have been added as an afterthought to
the building.

Because of the angle of the sun, he was half in and half out of
the shadows; like a magician's saw, white light sliced him diago-
nally. He stood there on the bottom step, holding on to the newel
post.

His head was in the sunlight; he was so blond it was almost
blinding; and his pale skin was nearly the color of an albino. His

eyes were the same blanched blue of the burnt-out sky that hot July morning. He seemed to gleam in the light, all thin elbows and knees. But he had a look my grandmother would have called "lively." We looked him up and down as if he were some vision; and I held onto Dah's hand. His shoes were peculiar: one was normal, while the other's sole was thicker by an inch or two; both were black and shiny.

Ned Grimke looked us over, too, surprise widening his eyes; he hung back, reaching for the banister, and tilted his head to one side, studying us.

Dah pried her fingers free from my moist hand and gently pushed me forward.

"Manners," she whispered.

"Hello," I responded, like her pet monkey.

Ned Grimke held tighter to the post and backed away.

With another prod from Dah, I held out my hand to shake, telling Ned my name and how my mother had sent us. He became solemn; he chewed his lip, clasped his own hand behind his back, and stared at mine, outstretched, as if it were something peculiar, a fish, I was offering.

He worked his jaw; his eyes drew light. He seemed to listen; then he reached out his hand and we shook; he bent from the waist in an old-fashioned bow, all the while saying not a thing.

"Cat got your tongue?" Dah asked.

He smiled, hung his head a little, and shyly shook it. His silence gave him a serious air. He blushed.

And no one moved or said a thing; we were suspended there in the wilting silence, oppressive as the temperature. It came from all around, in waves, like heat; all you could hear were insects shrilling. Some folks said they were so loud that year they drove two colored people crazy.

"Where are your people, boy?" Dah asked gently.

Ned just turned his head to one side and whispered something to no one we could see; then he paused again and seemed to be listening. We were impressed by that—as if it was a sign of wisdom or maturity; he was unlike anyone I had met before and had roused my curiosity if not my sympathy. We knew (only because my mother had told us) that Ned was an orphan—or half a one: his mother was dead and his father had moved away after Ned's birth to Walhalla, South Carolina. I had never met an orphan before that I could remember and wondered if that thick shoe had anything to do with it—a mark of it, a badge, maybe.

"Where are your aunts?" Dah asked.

Ned spoke to his shoulder; his eyes turned down, and Dah warned, "Boy, doan you make fun o' me. Where they be?"

We knew he was here visiting his father's two aunts, who lived in the Confederate Home. Those gaunt gray women, Azalea and Eola, though they did not like children, nevertheless insisted that Ned spend as much time as possible with them in his native city. This was not a wish—the thin old women did not give into whims—it was an abstract idea, inbred, against which there was no struggling. For, to them, Walhalla might just as well have been Africa. Azalea and Eola and all their family believed that true civilization existed only in Charleston and the low country, that thin strip of alluvial soil about forty miles in from the sea: plantation country—encompassing a few other populated areas—Richmond, Savannah, and by the grace of geography alone, New Orleans. Civilization existed only where it smelled of salt and seaweed; an almost underwater world in which moss dripped down from the trees; a damp and moist atmosphere that mildewed and moldered everything, one that had molded all of us—the Grimke sisters and all the other old ladies, Ned, my Dah, and me.

We stood there at the foot of the stairway, frozen in a tableau like wax figurines.

"Whooh!" Dah waved a handkerchief under her arm; she was sweating profusely. "I declare," she shook her head and muttered, "you too strange, boy." She looked along the walls of the porch—a chafed pink. There was no one around on the ground floor to appeal to; there were only the ladies on the porches hovering above us and we did not want to ask them anything. They were above us, like insects or chimney swifts swirling across the sky in the evening. There were steps leading up there, but they were useless. We knew the ladies were removed from us by more than mere height; they seemed as evanescent as light, as unearthly. They had been transported up there by their dreams; bereft, they were the wives, daughters, granddaughters, and great-nieces of those men who had fought for the Confederacy. Flesh may have withered; tints had changed from pink to lavender; but the unvanquished ideas of a vanished world still reigned here.

All of us children in Charleston knew of others, maiden aunts and spinster cousins, who had pressed their blossoms, shut them up and lovingly consigned them to where we found them on rainy days (in Bibles or albums), but they—the ladies of the Confederate Home—still clung to them like bridal bouquets, eternal Miss Havershams. They were vestal virgins.

They were not women, they were ideas; each obsessed with an individual past, each a small taper burning in memory:

"I am Richard Henry Duprée, cut down at First Manassas."

"I am my great-uncle Huger."

"I am chivalry."

We suspected them of taking such vows, and accused them of rituals and bizarre ceremonies. My Dah and I knew we had set foot on foreign soil when we entered; and we got no help at all from Ned Grimke. He hung there between the shadow and the light. "What do you think?" he asked himself out loud. "No! I won't!" he answered himself defiantly.

Dah was by now getting nervous—looking about for whom Ned was talking to. She was always on the lookout for plat eye, ghosts, and zombies; I saw her touch the match she kept in her hair, knowing the sulfur would keep haints at bay. Ned spoke more to himself, and then with a lurching and not ungraceful movement, he came off the bottom step towards us.

Before we could do anything there was a movement on the stairs and Ned's own Dah appeared; she must have come down with him from the upcountry. She stood behind him and put her hands on his shoulders protectively. She was tall and thin, statuesque, part Indian perhaps; with her scarlet turban on her head she moved with great dignity. Then she mopped her hands on her white apron and, although she and my Dah had never met before, after dropping each other a curtsy, they immediately started speaking to each other in Gullah, their stark and grotesque patois.

She gave Ned a look that between those two, and those two alone, held a meaning. Each nodded slightly. The two black women moved off, speaking together.

Now Ned stood right in front of me. "Hello," he said.

"Who were you talking to?" I asked.

"A friend."

"Who? I didn't see anyone."

"He's tiny."

"Can I see him?"

He nodded.

I stood still, fascinated, as Ned pinched the air above his shoulders as if he were lifting something off that he then put in his other palm, offering it open and flat to me.

"It's Jervey."

He came over and lifted his palm to right in front of my eyes.

"I don't see a thing."

"He's invisible." Ned then cocked his ears and listened. "Jervey says he's pleased to meet you."

"Oh." I was taken aback. "Can I hold him?"

Ned looked at his palm and then up at my eyes. He hesitated. "Okay."

I opened my hand next to his, our two index fingers touching in a bridge. "Here he comes," Ned said. "Hold still."

I waited with baited breath. I could feel him. I said, "It tickles like a cricket!"

"He's dancing in your hand. But be careful," Ned worried; he dragged his foot and hovered nearby.

I was not about to admit that I didn't see anything. Jervey, in Ned's behalf, seemed to be some sort of half man, half sprite, with wings.

"Where did he come from?" I asked.

"I found him."

"Where?"

"Over there." He pointed to a patch of deeper green under the cedar tree. "He may have belonged to one of the ladies."

"Why don't you ask?"

"Because then I'd have to give him back." He looked up at them. Ned was thoughtful about that for a while and said, "Jervey's tired."

"How do you know?"

"He told me."

"I didn't hear anything."

Ned snatched him up quickly from my hand and put him in the hollow under his arm. "He likes it under there. He's sleeping."

"I'm gonna see if I can find me one." I ran over to the patch of clover and Ned followed me. With his hands, he lowered himself to the ground.

"What's wrong with your foot?" I asked. "Why's your shoe so big?"

Ned did not answer. He had turned to Jervey again, having wakened him up and transfered him to his ear. "You can't make me," he said.

I was poring through the clover and Dah called, "You git outta there, boy! Ain't I tell you not to play wit dem stink bugs?"

"I'm not, Dah."

But having issued her warning she paid no attention to me. She and Ned's Dah were already thick as thieves.

All I found in the clover that morning was a dried-out cocoon—some shell an insect had left behind after molting; it was Jervey's, Ned told me; his carriage. "Give it to me," he demanded.

I did. "Why does he need a carriage when he has wings?"

"It's a secret," Ned said.

We were in Hibernian Hall, that white Ionian temple at the foot of Chalmers Street, at some ball, maybe even our grandest of the

season, the St. Cecilia; or it might have been the debutante party.
I can't remember that; but I can remember that it was a splendid
evening. And what with all the candles on the walls and the old
gas-light fixtures above us and some of the old gowns, you could
almost believe it was the nineteenth century. My father's business contacts, I suppose, had gotten us in here. The Charlestonians
did not like that in the least, and they blamed us for their pov-
erty that made this a necessity. The musicians played only
waltzes and reels and quadrilles, no modern themes; it was a
ritual. The dancers could have been their own ancestors; times
mixed; young men danced with old ladies. With the great oaken
doors of the hall rolled shut, they could feel that there was nothing else transpiring in all the world. All that mattered was here.
A young and foolish boy from Savannah could pretend that he
belonged as well. And then, in a flash, in the whirr of the
moment, it was all changed, shattered, like a champagne glass,
with a sound that was shrill and disconcerting.

I had been standing along the wall watching the believers
dance, trying not to be seen by anyone, when one of the manag-
ers silently whisked by. That usually meant some newspaperman
was trying to break in to take photographs—a taboo thing by
the by-laws of the Society—or some dowager had fainted, or a
poor debutante had been caught smoking. That night, it was
none of those things. The manager had not been quick enough
to stop a couple from committing the unpardonable sin that has
ever since been called "fast dancing."

Back then it was shocking. People nearly screamed as suddenly, without warning, as if having fits, Lucas Simons and
Suzanne Pinckney broke into the Charleston, the dance that had
been spawned on our street corners by colored children and
would soon be mimicked across the country. As soon as Lucas
and Suzanne began there arose a cry; other couples ran from the
floor, holding their hands over their eyes, as if they were afraid
they would be blinded by gazing at such deviltry. Lucas just
smiled with his hands going wild on his knees and Suzanne
reached for the heaven like a Jesus-crazed black lady. You almost

expected to hear the screech of whistles or to see the police; but like reporters, they were not allowed in here. The believers had their own watchdogs of society. Men in evening dress quickly pushed past us and ushered the culprits off the dance floor; no one swooned, though many had seemed capable of it; there was a lot of fan snapping and tut-tutting among the old ladies. They issued dark prophecies and there were at least two fates sealed that evening—Suzanne and Lucas were expelled for their heresy; two positions in the elect became open in the St. Cecilia Society.

In the confusion of their dancing and being led away (I watched them as they walked out, heads up and wrists together, unrepentant and proud, as if being led to the guillotine), Lila Lesesne lowered the bodice of her gown and smiled at me. But I had had my fill of debutantes that night; and I was not going to volunteer for any extra duty if my name was not already on a dance card and no dowager sailed up to claim me for a visiting niece. I pretended not to see her. So Lila, undaunted, set her green eyes on Ned, and licked her teeth. He had been following me. I saw him blush bright red and immediately turn his eyes downward. He backed against the wall and tried to disappear. He was slightly taller than me, but still so bleached out, white as a skeleton, so skinny. He seemed out of place here; as if he had just dropped to earth and was not used to this atmosphere. Lila came his way; he gulped and blushed and chewed his lip. He looked to me to save him but I looked away. And that made me wonder if he were not like me. I started to blush too and suddenly was hot; I looked around to see if anyone noticed. As Lila spoke to Ned I slipped away to the punch bowl, and returned armed with two glasses. Ned looked up hopefully, but they weren't for him; people would think I was retrieving for some young lady, so I could wander about freely.

I walked about pretending I was looking for my girl; everyone I passed was whispering about Lucas and Suzanne. Would they leave town? Would they get married? The musicians started up a waltz; and after that, as if regrouping after a battle, people assembled for a Virginia reel. So they had arrived; Charlestonians celebrated their own hardihood; it took more than one assault to destroy society. Lila Lesesne came my way with her arm linked through Winfield Huger's, and as they passed, I bowed and presented them with my two cups of punch. Winfield saluted, but Lila ignored me. I stood in the middle of the floor.

In a second, my friends came up; Hilary and Dwin came out of a corner looking like Jack Sprat and his wife, or Laurel and Hardy, Dwin thin and dried up, Hilary pink and pudgy with blond hair. They were always together.

"Where's Swinton?" I asked.

He was our best and we always gravitated to him; he was older than us by a few years; we felt somehow grander in his company. He was slim and dark; there was already some gray in his black hair and he had a refined face, a "French face," we said in Charleston, and an elegant body. We saw him across the room and he motioned us to silence.

The colored waiters in their white jackets were still whispering and flashing their white teeth as Swinton moved behind them and surreptitiously lifted a bottle of champagne from an ice bucket. He wiped it with a napkin and winked. He quickly put it under his coat, became solemn, and crossed the ballroom. In a flash I saw Ned marooned along the wall looking at us longingly with his blanched blue eyes. I looked away.

In the vestibule, I found my father helping my mother into her coat and I told them not to wait up. My mother blew me a kiss; we boys went out into the freezing night; and St. Michael's rang as we ran toward it, hooraying in victory as Swinton lifted the bottle. He held it up in tribute to the white church that loomed up at us like a wedding cake, tasteful and chaste under excesses of decorative white filigree. We went reeling and hallooing under the portico to Swinton's parents' house on Tradd Street. It *must* have been the St. Cecilia ball, for lights were on all over the city.

from "Finisterre"

LOUIS D. RUBIN, JR. (1923–)

Louis D. Rubin, Jr. is University Distinguished Professor of English Emeritus at the University of North Carolina, Chapel Hill. Over the years his students have included Clyde Edgerton, Annie Dillard, John Barth, Lee Smith, and Kaye Gibbons. The founder of Algonquin Books of Chapel Hill, Rubin was born and raised in Charleston. He attended the University of Richmond and received his Ph.D. from Johns Hopkins University. Rubin, one of the most distinguished men of letters in the South, is the author of many critical essays on southern literature. His seminal *The Edge of the Swamp: A Study in the Literature and Society of the Old South* was published in 1989. He has also written a number of works of fiction, ranging from *The Golden Weather* (1961) to *The Heat of the Sun* (1985). He is a founding member of the Fellowship of Southern Writers and was inducted into the South Carolina Academy of Authors in 1987. In recent years, he has written a number of autobiographical pieces, including the excerpt from his short story "Finisterre" below, about his fascination with boats as he grew up in Charleston.

The city of Charleston, South Carolina, is bounded on three sides by rivers and the harbor. In such a place, with ships and tugboats and small craft always moving about, I was very much aware of the water and wanted to go out on it. But except on very rare occasions when my uncle would take me sailing, I never got the opportunity. No one else that I knew owned a boat of any kind. My father was not an outdoorsman and was utterly uninterested in boats or in fishing. For me to have proposed that we acquire a rowboat would have been as far-fetched as to suggest the purchase of an airplane or a railroad locomotive. Moreover, I had been declared by my mother to be ineligible for going out on boats except under the most reliable of adult supervision such as my uncle's, because of my failure to learn how to swim.

When we had lived downtown on Rutledge Avenue I was only a few blocks from the Ashley River, and it was a walk of ten blocks down Tradd Street to Adger's Wharf and the Cooper River waterfront, but I seldom thought to go there. Not until we moved far up to the northwest end of town did I begin to get interested in the waterfront.

I was fourteen years old that fall, and on Saturday mornings after the movies I would set off down King Street for the water-front, pausing to examine the postage stamps, Confederate army buttons, insignias, and belt buckles, and the swords and pistols on display in the window of Bruchner's Antique Store. . . .

After looking at the window display I would walk on to Broad Street and then eastward toward the Cooper River. Usually I would stop in at the law office where my Aunt Ellen was employed as a secretary, spend a little while there, and then proceed across East Bay Street and along Exchange to the shore. The *Cherokee*, one of the coastal passenger ships of the Clyde-Mallory line, would usually be tied up alongside the pier just upstream, in full sight.

Compared to the Transatlantic liners that put in at ports such as New York and Boston, I knew, the *Cherokee* was no doubt a very small ship, but she seemed enormous to me. Her great black hull took up the entire length of the pier from close to the shore all the way to the end, where her stern protruded out into the ship channel, while her cabins and superstructure, painted white and gold, towered above the two-story warehouse on the dock. The *Cherokee* arrived early in the morning, lay alongside the dock while her passengers were off touring the city, and departed in mid-afternoon. While in port the ship was festooned with pennants and flags, and appeared altogether glamorous.

I would remain there for a while to watch, then I would walk southward along the shore. Just downstream, next to a marine railway, there were the remains of several old wooden boats partly buried in the mud and marsh grass, with the weathered ribs and timbers protruding up like arms and legs. At high tide the harbor water would wash about the old hulks, but when the tide was out they were imbedded in the mud, with fiddler crabs scurrying about the surface of the black, viscous tidal flat. There was a salty fragrance in the air that seemed to be part of the scene. No doubt the old craft had been towed there years ago and left to disintegrate gradually in the heat and moisture of the marsh. Once my Aunt Ellen walked down to the waterfront with me, and referred to the place as a "ship's graveyard."

I would pause there briefly, then proceed along the shoreline to Adger's Wharf. It was actually two wharves, and was home port for a variety of shrimp boats and small working craft, several of which were in freight service between Charleston and the various sea islands up and down the coast. There was a packing house, situated on the land side of the north pier, with a tin-covered roof beneath which black women worked at sorting and packing shrimp brought in from off the various boats. Meanwhile the crews of the shrimp boats were working aboard their craft, hosing down the decks and the hold, repairing nets and adjusting lines. The shrimp boats were of all shapes and sizes. Some were painted in bright blues, reds, and greens; others were unpainted and drab. But all held their attractions for me, for they were seagoing boats, and went out beyond the jetties at the harbor mouth and into the ocean.

By far the most interesting craft berthed at Adger's Wharf, however, were the tugboats of the White Stack Tugboat Company, which occupied the far end of the south pier. There were three of them, the *Cecilia*, the *Robert H. Lockwood*, and the *James P. Congdon*. They were painted brick red, with glossy black hulls and white trimming, and their smokestacks were white with black rings. They were kept in prime condition, and when not at work somewhere about the harbor lay waiting alongside the pier, their boilers always kept fired, with wisps of smoke trailing from their stacks. It was always my hope to see one of them departing or returning, for it was a formidable sight to view the sturdy craft in action, their powerful propellers churning the harbor water at the stern into foamy little hills, as they maneuvered confidently alongside the dock, while crewmen waited to tend the lines. They were owned by the Lockwood brothers, the eldest of whom, Captain Tunker Lockwood, was mayor pro tem of the City of Charleston and had lived next to us on Rutledge Avenue. My father had told me once that the two Lockwood boys, Henry and Edward, would one day succeed to command of the tugboats, and I always viewed them with awe and envy. They were several years older than I, and hardly knew me, but I watched them from afar, as among the more fortunate of the earth.

Berthed at Adger's Wharf along with the shrimp boats, cargo launches, pilot boats, and the White Stack towboats were a few small open boats with make-and-break gasoline engines and several rowboats. They were used for fishing or for work about the waterfront, and sometimes while I was watching, the owner of one of them might show up, climb down to where his boat was moored alongside the dock, and after a time cast loose the lines and proceed out into the harbor. I was deeply envious, for I could envision myself as someday being able to actually own a boat of that size, and the idea of heading out into the harbor in a boat of my own, rowing along the waterfront past the Clyde Line docks and up toward the Cooper River Bridge, or else downstream past the Carolina Yacht Club and along the sea wall of the High Battery, was marvelous to contemplate. Even better, if more remote, was the hope of possessing one of the larger craft with gasoline engines. With such a boat I could go out to the center of the harbor, explore the wooden shoreline along the southern rim of the harbor up to Fort Johnson and beyond, or even head upstream on the Ashley River, rounding the point of the Battery and up along the Boulevard past the lighthouse station at the head of Tradd Street, to where the river widened and the Intracoastal Waterway entered it at Wappoo Creek across the river. . . .

In June school ended, and there was no longer anything to prevent me from sometimes riding my bicycle downtown to the waterfront and spending all morning there, returning only in time for two o'clock dinner. I would take along a pair of inexpensive binoculars that my father had bought for me to observe the occasional ships that moved up the Ashley River past our house. I would ride all the way to the High Battery at the very tip of the city. From there I could see all the way across to where the low form of Fort Sumter lay near the harbor entrance, so that most of the activity in the lower harbor was visible to me. When a ship came into the view, she was first a smudge of smoke and a dot of superstructure far out beyond Sumter.

With binoculars I could observe her all the way in until she disappeared behind Sumter, and afterwards reemerged, much larger in visible size, along the Fort Moultrie side of the fort.

The next minutes were crucial. For if she were a ship from a foreign port she would anchor out in the Roadstead for customs inspection and come no closer that morning, while if she were bound up the Cooper River she would move along the Rebellion Reach channel on the far side of the harbor, pass out of sight beyond Castle Pinckney, which was on an island in the harbor, and at no time come closer than three or four miles from where I stood. But if when the ship rounded Sumter and moved toward the inner harbor she neither anchored nor swung northward, then I knew that I would soon be able to observe her from close by, for the destination would be either the downtown waterfront or else up the Ashley River, and in either event she would pass within less than a half-mile of the High Battery. What I most hoped was that the ship was headed for the Cooper River waterfront, for then she would move right across my line of vision, in front of me, no more than a few hundred yards away, and I should not only be able to observe her every detail but also get a long look at the White Stack tugboat that had gone out to meet her and guide her in.

The tug designated to receive the ship would make its rendezvous with the visitor well out in the harbor. The ship would have stopped her engines to await her escort. There would be a ceremonial (as I thought) exchange of whistled salutes, the tug's high-pitched whistle signal answered by the deep-voiced note of the ship. I would watch through the binoculars to try to catch sight of the passing of the towline from tug to ship, but it was too far out to see. Eventually, however, the tug would take up its position in front and the procession would head for port, the tug in the lead, followed by the much larger ship. As they neared the point at which the Cooper River waterfront channel veered from the Ashley River channel there would be more whistle signals, and then first the tug and then the ship would make the turn, and come slowly, massively toward the waterfront. Past where I stood watching they would steam, the sturdy red tugboat in the lead, the huge freighter or tanker following obediently behind, still under her own power but linked to the tug by the manila towline that was to be used in the docking operation. The White Stack tugboats never looked more capable and confident than at such times. As they churned their way past the Battery they seemed to be aware of their own importance as worthy stewards of the port, and without ostentation but in entire self-possession and pride they would lead the visitor to the wharf and the waiting slip.

Meanwhile a second White Stack tugboat would by then have cast off its lines from its berth at Adger's Wharf and be waiting off at the far side of the channel, ready to follow along upstream and assist in the docking. As the first tug and its tow moved by, it would take up its station abeam and proceed upstream too, and I would watch until finally the ship and her escorts passed out of view, and only the tall masts of the ship were now visible above the low roofs of the warehouses along the shore.

What I would have liked to be able to do was to own a small boat, so that I could row upstream to where the freighter was being docked, take up a position safely out of the way, and observe the entire operation. As it was, I could only look enviously at the occasional small craft that did come moving along the waterfront. If, as sometimes happened, the occupants of such craft were not adults but boys seemingly only a little older than myself, then my envy was almost beyond bounds. To have to stand there on the Battery, looking out at the harbor, while some fortunate boy was out on the water in a boat, rowing along in splendor past me, perhaps even glancing up, as I imagined, in momentary pity for such as myself, but for the most part too satisfyingly engaged in rowing his boat to have time for mere landlubbers—it was a mournful business.

from *The Last Gentleman*

WALKER PERCY (1916–1990)

> Walker Percy was born in Birmingham, Alabama, attended the University of North Carolina, and received a Doctor of Medicine degree from Columbia University. He left medicine early, turning to writing, and was successful in having his work accepted in the *Partisan Review, Sewanee Review,* and other major literary magazines. He won the 1962 National Book Award for his first novel, *The Moviegoer,* and thereafter was widely considered one of America's most important authors. His other novels included *The Last Gentleman* (1978, from which the excerpt below is taken), *Love in the Ruins* (1971), *Lancelot* (1977), *The Second Coming* (1980), and *The Thanatos Syndrome* (1987). He wrote a number of essays and books on nonfiction topics, including philosophy, language, and faith.

They didn't, the engineer and Jamie, quite cut loose after all, or detour through Norfolk (did Rita mean he should take Jamie to a whorehouse?) or feel any beloveds' warm mouths on theirs. But they had a good time and went their own way for a day or two at a time, wandering down the old Tidewater, sleeping in the piney woods or along the salt marshes and rendezvousing with the Cadillac in places like Wilmington and Charleston.

The camper was everything he had hoped for and more. Mornings on the road, the two young men sat together in the cab; afternoons the engineer usually drove alone. Well as he looked, Jamie tired easily and took to the bunk in the loft over the cab and either read or napped or watched the road unwind. They stopped early in the evening and went fishing or set up the telescope on a lonesome savanna and focused on the faraway hummocks where jewel-like warblers swarmed about the misty oaks.

Nights were best. Then as the thick singing darkness settled about the little caboose which shed its cheerful square of light on the dark soil of old Carolina, they might debark and, with the pleasantest sense of stepping down from the zone of the possible to the zone of the realized, stroll to a service station or fishing camp or grocery store, where they'd have a beer or fill the tank with spring water or lay in eggs and country butter and grits and slab bacon; then back to the camper, which they'd show off to the storekeeper, he ruminating a minute and: all I got to say is, don't walk off and leave the keys in it—and so on in the complex Southern tactic of assaying a sort of running start, a joke before the joke, ten assumptions shared and a common stance of rhetoric and a whole shared set of special ironies and opposites. He was home. Even though he was hundreds of miles from home and had never been here and it was not even the same here—it was older and more decorous, more tended to and a dream with the past—he was home.

A déjà vu: so this is where it all started and which is not quite like home, what with this spooky stage-set moss and Glynn marshes but which is familiar nevertheless. It was familiar and droll and somehow small and curious like an old house revisited. How odd that it should have persisted so all this time in one's absence!

At night they read. Jamie read books of great abstractness, such as *The Theory of Sets*, whatever a set was. The engineer, on the other hand, read books of great particularity, such as English detective stories, especially the sort which, answering a need of the Anglo-Saxon soul, depict the hero as perfectly disguised or perfectly hidden, holed up maybe in the wood of Somerset, actually hiding for days at a time in a burrow of ingenious construction from which he could notice things, observe the farmhouse below. English men like to see without being seen. They are by nature eavesdroppers. The engineer could understand this.

He unlimbered the telescope and watched a fifty-foot Chris-Craft beat up the windy Intercoastal. A man sat in the stern reading the *Wall Street Journal*. "Dow Jones, 894—" read the engineer. What about cotton futures, he wondered.

He called Jamie over. "Look how he pops his jaw and crosses his legs with the crease of his britches pulled out of the way."

"Yes," said Jamie, registering and savoring what the engineer registered and savored. *Yes, you and I know something the man in the Chris-Craft will never know.* "What are we going to do when we get home?"

He looked at Jamie. The youth sat at the picnic table where the telescope was mounted, stroking his acne lightly with his fingernails. His whorled police-dog eye did not quite look at the engineer but darted close in a gentle nystagmus of recognitions, now focusing upon a mote in the morning air just beside the other's head, now turning inward to test what he saw and heard against his own private register. This was the game they played: the sentient tutor knowing quite well how to strike the dread unsounded chords of adolescence, the youth registering, his mouth parted slightly, fingernails brushing backward across his face. *Yes, and that was the wonder of it, that what was private and unspeakable before is speakable now because you speak it.* The difference between me and him, thought the engineer and noticed for the first time a slight translucence at the youth's temple, is this: like me he lives in the sphere of the possible, all antenna, ear cocked and lips parted. But I am conscious of it, know what is up, and he is not and does not. He is pure aching primary awareness and does not even know that he doesn't know it. Now and then he, the engineer, caught flashes of Kitty in the youth, but she had a woman's knack of cutting loose from the ache, putting it out to graze. She knew how to moon away the time; she could doze.

"Why don't we go to college?" he said at last.

"It's forty miles away," said Jamie, almost looking at him.

"We can go where we please, can't we? I mean, do you want to live at home?"

"No, but—"

Ah, it's Sutter he has in mind, thought the engineer. Sutter's at home.

"We could commute," said the engineer.

"Then you'll go?"

"Sure. We'll get up early in the morning."

"What will you take?"

"I need some mathematics. What about you?"

"Yes, me too," nodded the youth, eyes focused happily on the bright mote of agreement in the air between them.

It suited them to lie abed, in the Trav-L-Aire yet also in old Carolina, listening to baseball in Cleveland and reading about set theory and an Englishman holed up in Somerset. Could a certain someone be watching the same Carolina moon?

Or they joined the Vaughts, as they did in Charlestown, where they visited the gardens even though there was nothing in bloom but crape myrtle and day lilies. Evil-tempered mockingbirds sat watching them, atop tremendous oily camellias. Sprinklers whirled away in the sunlight, leaving drops sparkling in the hairy leaves of the azaleas. The water smelled bitter in the hot sun. The women liked to stand and talk and look at houses. They were built for standing, pelvises canted, and they more or less leaning on themselves. When the men stood still for thirty minutes, the blood ran to their feet. The sun made the engineer sick. He kept close to the women, closed his eyes, and took comfort in the lady smell of hot fragrant cotton. A few years from now and we'll be dead, he thought, looking at tan frail Jamie and nutty old Mr. Vaught, and they, the women, will be back here looking at "places."

It was like home here, but different too. At home we have J. C. Penney's and old ugly houses and vacant lots and new ugly houses. Here were pretty, wooden things, old and all painted white, a thick-skinned decourous white, thick as ship's paint, and presided over by the women. The women had a serious custodial air. They know the place was theirs. The men were not serious. They all but wore costumes. They plied their trades, butcher, baker, lawyer, in period playhouses out in the yard.

Evening the Vaughts sat around the green chloriniferous pools of the California motels, Rita and Kitty swimming and minding their bodies, Mr. Vaught getting up often to monkey with his Cadillac (he had installed a top-oiler and claimed he got the same mileage as a Chevrolet), Mrs. Vaught always dressed to the nines and rocking vigorously in the springy pool chair and bathing her face with little paper pads soaked in cologne. When she was lucky, she found some lady from Moline who shared her views of fluoridation.

Kitty avoided him. He sought her out, but she damped him down. She must think badly of him, he decided, and quick as he was to see as others saw, was willing to believe she was right. Was it simply that she took the easy way: she was with Rita and not with him and that was that? At any rate, if she didn't love him, he discovered he loved her less.

When they met by chance in motel passageways they angled their shoulders and sidled past like strangers. At Folly Beach they collided at the ice dispenser. He stood aside and said nothing. But when she filled her pitcher, she propped it on the rim of her pelvis and waited for him, a somewhat abstracted Rachel at the well.

"It's a lovely night," she said, stooping to see the full moon through the cloister of the Quality Court.

"Yes," he said politely. He didn't feel much like waiting upon her. But he said, "Would you like to take a walk?"

"Oh yes."

They put their pitchers in the chest and walked on the beach. The moonlight curled along the wavelets. She put her hand in his and squeezed it. He squeezed back. They sat against a log. She took her hand away and began sifting sand; it was cool and dry and left not a grain on the skin.

He sat with his hands on his knees and the warm breeze flying up his pants leg and thought of nothing.

"What's the matter, Bill?" Kitty leaned toward him and searched his face.

"Nothing. I feel good."

Kitty shifted closer. The sand under her sheared against itself and made a musical sound. "Are you mad at me?"

"No."

"You act mad."

"I'm not."

"Why are you different then?"

"Different from what?"

"From a certain nut who kissed a very surprised girl in the automat."

"Hmm."

"Well?"

"I'm different because you are different," said the engineer, who always told the exact truth.

"*Me!* How?"

"I had looked forward to being with you on this trip. But it seems you prefer Rita's company. I had wanted to be with you during the ordinary times of the day, for example after breakfast in the morning. I did not have any sisters," he added thoughtfully. "So I never knew a girl in the morning. But instead we have become like strangers. Worse, we avoid each other."

"Yes," she said gravely, conscious, he could not help but notice, of saying it so: gravely. "Don't you know why?" she said at last.

"No."

She sifted the cool discrete sand into her palm, where it made a perfect pyramid, shedding itself. "You say you never had sisters. Well, I never had a date, boyfriends—except a few boys in my ballet class who had foreheads this low. Rita and I got used to living quietly."

"And now?"

"I guess I'm clinging to the nest like a big old cuckoo. Isn't that awful?"

He shrugged.

"What do you want me to do?" she asked him.

"What do I want you to do?"

"Tell me."

"How do you feel?"

"How do you feel? Do you still love me?"

"Yes."

"Do you? Oh, I love you too."

Why did this not sound right, here on Folly Beach in old Carolina in the moonlight?

One thing I'm sure of, thought he as he held her charms in his arms: I shall court her henceforth in the old style. I shall press her hand. No more grubby epithelial embraces in dogbane thickets, followed by accusing phone calls. Never again! Not until we are in our honeymoon cottage in a cottage small by a waterfall.

But when he kissed her and there she was again looking at him from both sides at once, he had the first inkling of what might be wrong. She was too dutiful and athletic. She worked her mouth against his (is this right, she as good as asked).

"Wonderful," she breathed, lying back. "A perfect setting."

Why is it not wonderful, he wondered, and when he leaned over again and embraced her in the sand, he knowing without calculating the exact angle at which he might lie over against her—about twenty degrees past the vertical—she miscalculated, misread him and moved slightly, yet unmistakably to get plainly and simply under him, then feeling the surprise in him stopped almost before she began. It was like correcting a misstep in dancing.

"What is it?" she whispered presently.

"Nothing," he said, kissing her tenderly and cursing himself. His heart sank. Was it not that she was right and that he made too much of it? What it was, though, was that this was the last thing he expected. It was part of his expectations of the life which lay before him that girls would be girls just as camellias were camellias. If he loved a girl and walked with her on Folly Beach by moonlight, kissed her sweet lips and held her charms in his arms, it should follow that he would be simply he and she she, she as complete as a camellia with her corolla of reticences and allurements. But she, Kitty, was no such thing. She didn't know any better than he. Love, she, like him, was obliged to see as a naked garden of stamens and pistils. But what threw him off worst was that, sentient as always, he found himself catching onto how it was with her: he saw that she was out to be a proper girl and taking every care to do the right wrong thing. There were even echoes of a third person: what, you worry about the boys as good a figure as you have, etc. So he was the boy and she was doing her best to do what a girl does. He sighed.

"What?" she asked again.

"Nothing," he said, kissing her eyes, which were, at any rate, like stars.

He sighed again. Very well, I'll be both for you, boyfriend and girlfriend, lover and father. If it is possible.

They stirred in the musical sand. "We'd better go back," said the gentlemanly engineer and kissed her somewhat lewdly so she wouldn't feel she had failed. It seemed to be his duty now to protect her non-virtue as best he could. After all, he mused, as he reckoned girls must have mused in other ages, if worst comes to worst and all else fails I can let her under me—I can't begrudge her the sacrifice. What ailed her, him, them, he wondered. Holding her hand as they returned to the Quality Court, he flexed his wrist so that he could count his pulse against her bone.

Mainly their trouble—or good fortune, as the case might be— was that they were still out of phase, their fervors alternating and jostling each other like bad dancers. For now, back at the cooler and she then going ahead of him with her pitcher on the rim of her pelvis, desire like a mighty wind caught him from behind and nearly blew him down. He almost fainted with old motel lewd-longing. "Wait," he whispered—oh, the piercing sorrow of it, this the mortal illness of youth like death to old age. "Wait." He felt his way along the blotting-paper wall like a blind man. She took his outstretched hand.

"What is it, dearest?"

"Let's go in here," he said, opening the door to a closet which housed a giant pulsing Fedders.

"What for?" she asked. Her eyes were silvery and turned in.

"Let us go in the service room." For it is here and not by moonlight—he sighed. Her willingness and nurse-tenderness were already setting him at naught again.

"There you are," said Rita, opening the door opposite. "Where in the world was the ice machine?"

And off he went, bereft, careening down the abstract, decent, lewd Quality corridor.

"The Salt Marsh"

JAMES DICKEY (1923–1997)

James Dickey, Georgian by birth, is one of the most distinguished southern poets of the last fifty years. He was professor of English and poet-in-residence at the University of South Carolina until his death. *Drowning with Others* (1962) earned him a Guggenheim Fellowship, and *Buckdancer's Choice* (1965) a National Book Award. After serving as poetry consultant for the Library of Congress, he gathered together his previous poems in the volume *Poems 1957–1967*. He read "The Strength of Fields" at the inauguration of President Jimmy Carter in 1977. His best-selling 1970 novel, *Deliverance*, was made into a popular motion picture that still sends shudders down the necks of viewers. Inducted into the South Carolina Academy of Authors in 1986, Dickey wrote the posthumous induction of Henry Timrod into that body in 1992.

Once you have let the first blade
Spring back behind you
To the way it has always been,
You no longer know where you are.
All you can see are the tall
Stalks of sawgrass, not sawing,
But each of them holding its tip
Exactly at the level where your hair

Begins to grow from your forehead.
Wherever you come to is
The same as before,
With the same blades of oversized grass,
And wherever you stop, the one
Blade just in front of you leans,
That one only, and touches you
At the place where your hair begins

To grow; at that predestined touch
Your spine tingles crystally, like salt,
And the image of a crane occurs,
Each flap of its wings creating
Its feathers anew, this time whiter,
As the sun destroys all points
Of the compass, refusing to move
From its chosen noon.

Where is the place you have come from
With your buried steps full of new roots?
You cannot leap up to look out,
Yet you do not sink,
But seem to grow, and the sound,
The oldest of sounds, is your breath
Sighing like acres.
If you stand as you are for long,

Green panic may finally give
Way to another sensation,
For when the embodying wind
Rises, the grasses begin to weave
A little, then all together,
Not bending enough for you
To see your way clear of the swaying,
But moving just the same,

And nothing prevents your bending
With them, helping their wave
Upon wave upon wave upon wave
By not opposing,
By willing your supple inclusion
Among fields without promise of harvest,
In their marvelous, spiritual walking
Everywhere, anywhere.

from *And I'm Glad: An Oral History of Edisto Island*

NICK LINDSAY (1 9 2 7 –   )

Nick Lindsay has lived most of his life on Edisto Island, South Carolina, south of Charleston, where he has involved himself intimately in the local community. A poet, novelist, and historian, as well as a carpenter and boatbuilder, Lindsay spent a number of years as a professor at Goshen College in Indiana, where he continues to lecture and teach courses. He is well known for his readings of the poetry of his father, Vachel Lindsay.

In the 1970s Lindsay brought to fruition two volumes of oral histories from Edisto Island. The first presented the words of Sam Gadsden, a social historian who was principally concerned with an accurate rendition of the origins and development of Edisto; the second featured Bubberson Brown, a true storyteller, who was concerned with myth making and the creation of fiction. The two volumes were combined and republished in 2005 as *And I'm Glad: An Oral History of Edisto Island*. The first section below contains excerpts from Gadsden, and the second is from Brown, whose narrative takes on the dimensions of James Joyce: prose so dense that it approaches poetry. In particular, the end, included here, is apocalyptic, looking forward and backward to the beginning and end of time.

The world was full of pirates in those days. Nobody should admit to pirate blood, because the character of a pirate is so bad. It's worse than an animal's. They would take the goods and the ship and all, and haul them about, kill the people or sell them into slavery. If anybody resisted, they would kill them and throw them into the seas.

In the beginning, when my people immigrate to America, it was a Dutchman who brought them. He was a pirate. He had colored pirates with him. All of them been working in piracy on the high sea. He had the colored pirates go and get the Negroes from Africa and make a trade of them. They brought them back into America around this section where there were plenty of new plantations being built, plenty of work going on. That Dutchman was a salesman: he taught the settlers that these Negroes from Africa knew more about cleaning up land than any of the white people did no matter how they would try. The country was wild then and they needed help. He told them, "Let those Africans come; they will make good laboring people for you. I will bring them here; you can put them in slavery and let them do all the rough work."

Soon every man was in the race to see how many Africans he could get to bring over and sell. They sold them by the head, just like you sell cattle. Some of the white people who came over from Europe used these slaves with a good result. They were cleaning up America, and they were mostly good, only just the one thing: they treated them like slaves. They had guards and patrols and watched them all the time so they wouldn't run off.

The masters would buy these people from the slave trader by the dozen head. They didn't buy them at any auction sale; they bought them right off the boat at a place they call Bohicket Creek on Wadmalaw Island right up here. That is where the market was.

The boat would come in, then all the masters go there to buy. Maussa So and So would buy so much, then Maussa So and So would buy so much, and Maussa So and So would buy so much, and they would carry them on to their plantations. They would put them in a little cabin and make them work.

The people would clean up the land, dig ditches for rice fields and put up dams and learn off the kingdom. They treat the people as slaves, but they give them rations, give them meat and give them cloth.

Some of them live better and some of them live worse; it all depends on the master. Some masters treated their slaves well. They would let them do their own work in the evening and make their own little crop, and they could load it and sell it and make a little money. My grandmother told me these things.

That Dutchman kept bringing them in. He made a regular trade of them. He would come in here with a load, sell them, turn around and go out there and fool them niggers and round up and load his boat again. He fooled them with red cloth, beads, and promises. The Africans liked things like that.

They were easy to fool because they didn't have much education. The Dutchman was able to fool them because he did. He found out a way he could get rich off of them.

The old time Africans were not savages, not the Ibo people. They were a peaceful and industrious people. They studied how to clear and plant there in the jungle, how to harvest their crops and raise their children peacefully. They were no savages, but they had never yet run across clothes made out of cloth. This was the reason the things the Dutchman brought to them there pleased them so much.

My great grandfather was named Kwibo Tom. He was the main chief of a tribe in Nigeria, in Africa, a tribe of Ibo people. The Dutchman had been dealing regularly with the old man. Old Tom would lead the Dutchman in to find ivory, gold, diamonds, elephant tusks—whatever it was he wanted. In return for this, the Dutchman would bring the people clothes. This trade had been going on for years, for many years.

The chief's oldest son was named Kwibo Tom just like his daddy. One day he took a notion, "Why shouldn't I be going out there and trading? We could be trading out there on our own account."

This would have been a very profitable trade if he had managed to do it, for the Dutchman was getting rich off of those people even without selling them as slaves. Young Tom could have bought ten boats like the one the Dutchman was using after they made just one load of ivory, gold, and diamonds and sold them at market price. Tom got with his brother, Wallie, and they spoke to the Dutchman about it. That Dutchman answered, and told those two brothers, my great-grandfather Kwibo Tom and his brother, Wallie, that he would bring them here to the place where those trinkets came from; and if they would bring a cargo of trade goods and trade for themselves for these things, they could gather up a boat load and take them back to their tribe. Yes, he said he would bring them back, in his own boat. And they could give him a proportion of their trade goods to pay him for his trouble and the use of his boat. Tom and Wallie could then bring that cloth and those trinkets back to their daddy and their tribe and they would receive a laurel. Their daddy was the main chief and this made Tom a young chief of the tribe there. Both he and his brother were married; Wallie had about four children, Tom had about twelve. They all agreed to that and Tom and Wallie went aboard with their trade goods and their families.

When they go to America, the Dutchman sold both the wives and all the children into slavery, right there at Bohicket, on Wadmalaw. Tom and Wallie never did work as slaves, but they came and went freely about these islands; there may have been some special arrangement about them. Among Tom's children was my grandmother, Rebecca.

They did not come in at the Customs House in Charleston. The Dutchman was a pirate and it was an illegal trade anyhow, so they came in at Bohicket. He told those two brothers how much better off they would be here, how they could go from place to place in these islands and have as many wives as they wanted—be a rich man here. Why would they want to go back to Africa?

What became of the ivory and trade goods I don't know. Maybe those brothers made a deal with the Dutchman, the pirate! But it might be he had them where he wanted them and they couldn't do anything but go along with what he said, once they were out at sea. Anyhow, after they got here and got settled in, the planters liked the kind of children they made, and they told them to make as many as they wished. Tom, he was the Big Chief.

The whole family—the two brothers, their wives and children—went to Mr. Clark over on Wadmalaw. Wallie's people were settled at a place they call Clark's, here on this island [Edisto]. Clark had all that then. My grandmother and her brothers and sisters and their father, Tom, came first to a place they call

Legree's, over near Oak Island Plantation on this island, then from there they went to Murray's place, when her father gave all that family—Tom's family, not Wallie's—to his daughter, Liddy, as a wedding portion when she got married. That was in 1825.

Major William Murray, when he married for the first time, married Lydia Clark from Wadmalaw, and all that stock of colored people came to him along with her. They were not his property, but they came to stay on his place. They belonged to Miss Liddy. In those days the master had his own slaves and the missus had her own. Murray didn't rule them; Miss Liddy did. Only in this one thing Murray had the say so: he told Tom, "You go ahead: get as many wives as you want. We need the same kind of people as your children are."

On some islands and in some parts of the country there is a wild part and a tame part. In the wild part there are hobos and murderers and people the law wants, there are jailbreakers and gamblers. They go in to the closed places in the swamp and they hang around there hiding from the law. Where there are no churches? All the bad people go there. But where the churches are, there is the place where there are civilized people. This island has always been as one, one Christian people, the white and the colored. There are two swamps over on the mainland where wild people live to this day: Four Post Hole Swamp reaches all the way up nearly to Columbia, near about a hundred miles, and then there's Caw Caw in around Hollywood and Summerville. The Indians used to live in there, and a people they call the Brass Ankle people. The Brass Ankle people are a mixture of British Revolutionary soldiers with Catawba Indians and then those people mixed with colored people who ran away from these plantations along the coast. The colored people went to live with the tribes in the swamp. Those British soldiers were called the Hessians; they were some kind of Germans. There is no plain record of the Brass Ankle people, since they are the only ones who know their own story and they are not telling it. They were a private people and pretty wild according to some of the stories.

The Catawba Indians used to rule in South Carolina. They traveled to Edisto to make their summer resort here. They would . come to the point above Edingsville on John Jenkins' land and eat sea oysters every summer. When commercial oyster fishing began it destroyed all those sea oysters.

The old chief of the tribes who used to come here in the days when Kwibo Tom first came was called Edisto, Chief Edisto of the Catawba Indians. They had an Indian settlement here until quite late. There is one in York still, a couple of hundred miles up the country there by the North Carolina line. . . .

The colored people, after Peace was declared, they covered the island with churches. They never stop building churches; they are building a church right now. There are four AME churches here: Calvary, which was started by John Wesley, then Bethlehem, which is on the land where the white Episcopal church from the beach was put, then Bethel, and Allen. Allen had a missionary bishop in Africa for years and years, Doctor William Beckett. He died in 1925. The AME Church has had missionaries in Africa since Reconstruction times. . . .

Everybody agrees that the Africans believed in witchcraft. Their religion was half witchcraft. When the white man came into Africa preaching against witchcraft, the Africans listened and believed what he said. But then, when the test came, it turned out that the white man's witchcraft was worse than any they had before then. He bought them and sold them and cheated them and beat the poor fools every way.

Witchcraft had power. Let no one deny that it has power, but there is a power which is far above any small power such as witchcraft can have. The power of the Good News. If a man knows the way of Jesus, there is no need for him to study any spells or any antidotes to spells, death charms or life charms. He is free. The only person who is subject to those spells is the one who believes in them, he is the one who thinks he needs to study them, and he is a fool. The only one who will believe in them is the one who doesn't know the truth.

Witchcraft is a heavy charge to lay against any person. To some of the white people who write books, it is some kind of biological curiosity, they say, "Look what jigs these monkeys are playing now," but they all have witchcraft in their own people just a hundred or so years ago. The Salem Witchcraft trials were about people who practiced and believed in witchcraft. In Europe and in England, the thing was going on too. There is no way they can put on airs of superiority except just if they are ignorant of what their great-great-grandpeople were doing.

Some of the books about the island name the names of living people and say they are using witchcraft against one another when they were not. The charge of witchcraft is a bad slander against sensitive and intelligent people, the leaders of the older community here, people who have fought against it all their lives. . . .

The most important lesson of life is the relationship between the spiritual and the temporal powers and fruits. An education can be of great value to you if you can learn the spiritual arts from it. Most people waste their time on the temporal. They study and they study and after a long time they gain the temporal arts—how to steal, how to lie, how to gain power over the other people. Then, if they are lucky, they become dissatisfied with what they have learned and they go to work and learn the spiritual arts. It is then that they find they had no need of the temporal arts: all the power they ever could need comes to them through the spiritual arts, which put the temporal in the service of the Lord. . . .

I remember [John Townsend's] old granddaddy used to sail in a sailboat all up and down there where we would fish. The colored people used to fish plenty back then, but we didn't use boats for that. Each person had his own catch. He would use a cast net back in the creek. And there is an inlet over there where old Mr. Townsend used to be sailing called Jeremy Inlet, and another one further down called Frampton Inlet. In those inlets you could catch fish by the load at certain times. And if you went out on the beach there you could fish for sea bass in the ocean.

For sea bass you use a long line, swing it round your head two or three times, then let go, and it will sail out way beyond the breakers and you can catch those bass out there. Maybe two or three in a day—that's a cart load. Big old bass! Red channel bass maybe five feet long.

I have caught him many times out there on Edingsville Beach. By now that's about the only place left where you can catch him, because a bass is a scary fish and the people have scared him away from the beaches further down. You can't catch him where the real estate people have developed the place, you must come further down this way where the people aren't mixing up the water.

Sam Gadsden

Care for your own, that's the best thing to learn or know. Care for your own people. I stay with mine—Daddy, Granddaddy, Grandmother, and all—until I bury them. I walk with them, I plant and plow for them, gather the crop. When Daddy ain't home, my mother work right with Granddaddy. Granddaddy, he crazy about them daughter. He plant six task of cotton for each of them, plant tater and all. And he cultivate it too. He care for us.

You must care for your own. My wife tell them children we need wood here, tell them cut wood. And then they ain't done nothing but slip off! My own grandchildren! You better believe I tell them a good warning. "I work for you, I care for you myself all these years. When you see me come to the place where I can't do it no more and your grandmother tells you, ain't nothing to do but go and do it." I tell them so. That's the best thing they could learn and know. . . .

I could do it, I could work in New York. I have a first cousin there. I took care of her, minded her from the time she was a baby. She's the grandchild of Bella, the daughter of Christian, and the only one left out of her family. Mother and father and all died. She has come to own five houses. She can supply me with work there every day. I have been up there and worked as a carpenter three times since nineteen twenty-five, but by now it's too rough. You need a bodyguard just to walk in the streets. . . .

When you live in the country, you can help yourself. I raise hogs, raise poultry of all kinds. I have a big hog here, and one up yonder, she is in pig right now. She'll have pigs here in the next two or three weeks. I fish sometimes, but not this month. By next month the bass will bite. In August and September you can always catch a good fish. But in July, this time of year, you go out there, and set down two or three hours and come back with two or three little fish. Why do that when I could go and catch eight or nine quarts of shrimp and put them up? I went out and got three quarts of shrimp this morning. I work around here all the time, go in the creek, come out with some fish or oysters. I take on little jobs here or there, yarn a net or nail up some screens or jack up a sill of a house. I keep on doing something all the time, make myself useful. If I sit down long, it gets painful.

This is better, home here. Me and my wife been together all these years now, sixty years. Long water run out me eye how thankful the Lord been to me! I sleep so good here, the world turn over. Like I sleep in that dark rain way back yonder, I was a boy. Such a terrible thunder shower. Middle of the afternoon, it was a Friday. Dark, dark, dark. That same lighting strike a woman, Old Man Lestin daughter, over the other side of the creek. I come in the house, my grandmother house. Lay down, gone to sleep. Done night time for me. Later on, I wake up, sunshine, bird sing. I get up. I gone out, start my Saturday work. "How come? Sun in west? World been turn upside down while I been asleep?" But they show me: sun in the west cause it still Friday. I done the same today. Sleep so good, wake up at two o'clock this afternoon, I figure I done sleep around the clock, couldn't make it out no way, got to call my wife in here, "Hey, old woman! Come here, get me some sense into my head!" She must tell me what day it is. Sleep so good the world turn upside down.

And now I have been living here for the last lifetime, a three and three quarter, a four score of years, a quite a while. I ain't been up to New York from Edisto now for over two straight years. That's all.

Bubberson Brown

"Coley Moke"

WILLIAM PRICE FOX (1926–   )

William Price Fox lives in Columbia, South Carolina, where he serves as a writer-in-residence at the University of South Carolina. Fox's first book, *Southern Fried*, a collection of humorous short stories that had originally appeared in the *Saturday Evening Post*, *Sports Illustrated*, and other popular magazines, was published in 1962 in paperback. Not for Fox the usual author's schedule of publishing first in cloth, then paper. In 1968 the book was expanded to *Southern Fried Plus Six* and finally released in a hardback edition. It has stayed in print ever since. "Coley Moke," below, appeared in that volume.

Fox followed with several novels, including *Moonshine Light, Moonshine Bright* (1967), *Ruby Red* (1971), *Dixiana Moon* (1981; according to some sources the inspiration for Bruce Springsteen's song "Darlington County"), and the semi-autobiographical *Wild Blue Yonder* (2002). His novel *Doctor Golf* (1963) has become a golfer's classic. Fox has also published a number of essays and books of nonfiction including *Lunatic Wind: Surviving the Storm of the Century* (1992) about Hurricane Hugo and *Satchel Paige's America* (2005).

In order to get back to Coley Moke's place outside Monck's Corner, South Carolina, you have to run down a Peevy or a Taylor or another Moke and make him take you back. Charley, Jim, and I got us a Taylor and went back one day.

There were too many dogs in the yard to count, but there were four runty gray pigs who'd been talked into believing they were hounds. When we petted the dogs we had to scratch the pigs. It was hot and the dogs were panting so Coley led us into his front room. There was a bed and a wood stove in the room and nothing else. No tables, no chairs, no lights; it was the only room in the house.

"Make yourself to home."

And then, "You bring any funny books?"

Charley pulled a roll out of his back pocket. Coley thumbed through them and said, "Fine."

He emptied a Mason jar of corn whiskey into a water bucket, placed a tin dipper in the bucket and set it down on the floor.

Three of the older dogs got up on the bed with Coley. One of the little razorbacks tried to make it but couldn't.

We sat down against the wall near the bucket and when we started drinking, Coley started talking.

"See this dog here . . . his name's Brownie."

He was a long thin brown dog; his eyes were closed.

"Well, when I tell him the law is coming he picks up that steel bucket and runs into the swamp, and I mean he doesn't come back until I call him. Couple of the others would do that for me but they got so they were spilling too much.

"Brownie here knows I got me only one small still going now and he doesn't waste a drop. One old timer—Trig—he's gone now—would take it out there by the creek. He was a mess. He'd drink a while and then swim a while and then sleep until he was sober and then start it all over again. . . ."

Charley nudged Jim and Jim nudged me. We drank some more.

Coley laughed and rasseled the head of the red bone hound on his left. "This here's Bob, and they don't come any smarter than him. One day he convinced these Federal men he would lead them back to the house. And they followed him. He led them poor bastards between the quicksand and the 'gators and showed them every cottonmouth moccasin in the swamp. He got them so scared they were just begging him to lead them back on the road—any road. They promised him steaks and that they'd never raid me again. Well, sir, Bob kept them going until it was dark and after he walked them over a couple long 'gators that looked like logs he finally put them up on the road. It was the right road but it was about twelve miles from their car. Old Bob sure had himself some fun that night. He told Brownie here all about it and Brownie told me."

Charley took a big drink; Jim and I took a big drink. There was more. About how Spot and Whip would team up on a moccasin or a rattlesnake and while one faked the snake out of his coil the other would grab him by the tail and pop his head off like a buggy whip.

Jim said, "Man, that is some dog to do that."

Coley began to drink a little more and when he started talking about his wife his voice changed. "Yeah, I suspect I miss that old gal. Wonder what she looks like now. She was something, all right. Up at dawn, cook a first-class meal and then go out and outplow any man and mule in the county and every Sunday, rain or shine we had white linen on the table and apple pie . . . ain't nothing I like better than apple pie.

"Sometimes we didn't speak for a week. It was nice then, real nice. As long as I kept quiet and minded the still and my dogs everything was fine. But we started talking and then the first thing you know we were arguing and then she began to throw the dogs up in my face. Let's see . . . it was right in the middle of the Compression. Right here in this room. She had to go and try and turn me against the dogs. . . . Well, the Compression hit us bad—real bad. I had no money, no copper for the still, and no way of getting any up. I was doing a lot of fishing and hunting then. . . . Yeah, right here . . . oh, it was different then. There were four cane chairs and a dresser and a mirror from Sears Roebuck against that wall, and there was a couple insurance calendars from the Metropolitan Insurance Company hanging over there."

He took a big drink. The light was fading but we could still see his face. A bull alligator deep in the swamp rumbled once and decided it was too early.

"Yeah, I was lying here with old Sport. He was Brownie here's father. He was young then and high-spirited and, you know, sensitive. When Emma Louise got up from her chair and came over he must have seen it in her face. They never had gotten along. He crawled off the bed and went outside. If I live to be two hundred, I'll never forget those words. . . .

"She said, 'Coley Moke, you are the sorriest man on God's green earth. Here it is almost winter, we got no money, we got no food, and you just lay there and stare up at that leaky roof. And what's more, you've gone out and taken our last hog and traded it for another dog.'"

Coley smiled and leaned forward. Then his face set mean and hard. "'Emma, Emma Louise,' I said, 'if I told you once I told you a hundred times. . . . But since you seem to not hear I'm going to tell you one more time. I traded that hog and I got me a dog for the plain and simple reason that I can't go running no fox with no hog.'

"Come on men, drink her up. When that's gone there's more where it came from. And if we get too drunk to walk we can send my old buddy Brownie here."

He rasseled the dog's head. "How about it, boy, what d'you say?"

We drank until it was time to eat. Coley lighted a fire in the wood stove and warmed up some red-horse bread. He served it on folded newspapers and with the little light from the stove we sat back down where we had been sitting and ate.

Later he chased the two pigs outside and we heard their hooves clopping down the porch and on the steps. The pigs slept under the house with the dogs. Coley said they generally got to bed a little earlier than the dogs.

An owl sounded, a bull alligator answered, and the moon glided out of the tall cypress trees in the swamp and the room began to streak with silver light. We slept. . . .

It was raining in the morning and all the dogs and hogs were in the living room. Spot, Trig, and Buckles were on the bed with Coley. The two hogs were under the unlit stove and the rest of the dogs were against the wall. Charley, Jim, and I were sitting on the floor.

Coley was talking. "Bob's father—that was Earl Brown—he's been dead a long time now. Let's see, next month it'll be eleven years. It doesn't seem like it was that long ago. Eleven years, man, but don't it drive by?"

Charley took a drink and handed me the dipper. I took one and gave it to Jim.

"Buried him out on that hill knuckle in front. He always liked it up there. Some mornings I'd wake up and look out and there he'd be sitting up there just as pretty as you please. All the other dogs would still be sleeping. But not Earl Brown, he was always the first one up.

"He wasn't like the others. Now I ain't saying the others weren't smart but it was a different kind of smartness. You know how it is with hounds. They'll do anything you tell them. But there's a lot of them that just doesn't have any initiative. Now that's right where Earl Brown was different. Earl Brown was always trying to better himself, trying to improve himself, you might say.

"I could tell it when he was a pup. The other dogs would fall all over one another getting at the food and when they'd get to it they'd bolt it down like they hadn't eaten in a month. But not Earl Brown, no sir. He'd wait and let them take their places at the trough. Then he'd walk over, slow-like, and commence eating. He wouldn't rush. He even chewed his food longer."

Coley got down off the bed and took a drink. He studied the bottom of the empty dipper.

"Yeah, they don't make any finer dog than Earl Brown."

He put the dipper in the bucket of whisky on the floor and sat back down on the bed.

"That dog was a loner, too. The others would all sleep in the wood box. Sometimes there'd be as many as seventeen all flopped in there on top of one another. But not Earl Brown. From the day that scutter was weaned he slept by himself outside the box.

"I guess I miss Earl Brown as much or more than any of them. He was a marvelous dog, all right. Marvelous, that's what he was.

"I told you how he'd sit up on the hill early in the mornings. Well, he wasn't out there lapping the dew off the grass for nothing. He was working on something.

"Boys, I want you to know what that dog was working on. I couldn't tell this to just anyone else. They'd say that fool Coley Moke has gone slap out of his mind, living out there with all them dogs.

"First of all I wouldn't have known a thing if it hadn't been for the chickens. But they started a lot of noise during the night. I thought a weasel or a snake was getting at them so I started watching from the window. It wasn't no weasel and it wasn't no snake. It was two foxes. Big red ones, long as dogs, and five times smarter. But those foxes didn't go inside the coop. They just stood there. They must have been there five minutes and then I thought I saw another fox. I looked again and you know who it was?

"It was Earl Brown. Well sir, those two red foxes and Earl Brown stood outside that chicken coop for ten minutes. My other dogs were all inside the house and they were going crazy. The poor hens were clucking and screeching for help. I didn't know what to do. Finally I heard Earl Brown growl and then the next thing you know the three of them ran off into the woods.

"I kind of figured Earl Brown was setting those foxes up for me to shoot, so I decided to wait until he gave me some kind of sign. Well, next night it happened again. Same time, right around three o'clock they came out of the woods. Well, they had their little meeting right outside the coop and then they ran off again.

"Of course, during all this I had to make sure Earl Brown got out at night and my other dogs stayed in. That took some doing. The others all knew that Earl Brown was getting special treatment and they got mad as hell. And they smelled those foxes on him and they wouldn't have a thing to do with him.

"But Earl Brown didn't care what they thought about him. He even liked it better that way. But he got to looking peaked and red-eyed. Like he wasn't getting any sleep. I put a couple extra eggs in his rations. That boy was on a rough schedule. He'd go to sleep around ten with the others but he'd be up at two and off with his friends.

"Things began looking bad. My dogs were giving me a fit to be let out at night. I wasn't getting any sleep. And those hens. Lord, those poor hens were going right out of their minds. They got so nervous they were laying eggs at midnight. The rooster worried so he began losing weight and limping. He got so he wouldn't even crow. They were one sad-looking sight in the mornings. Wouldn't eat, couldn't sleep. I mean it got so bad them hens were stumbling around and bumping into one another.

"I decided to give Earl Brown two more nights and then end it. I was determined to shoot those damn foxes and get my chickens back on some decent schedule.

"And that was the very night it happened. . . .

"Earl Brown stepped aside and let one of those foxes go into the coop. Those poor chickens were so scared and tired. I guess they were relieved when that fox walked in and picked one out. He took a Rhode Island Red. That hen didn't even squawk. Just hung there in his mouth and across that red fox's back like she was glad it was all over. Those chickens slept the rest of the night. It was the first good night's sleep they'd had in three weeks."

Coley stopped. "You boys ain't drinking."

Charley said, "I just this minute put the dipper down."

Coley drank again and hunched himself back up between the dogs. "Well, I figured that was the end for Earl Brown. I saw where he had thrown in with the foxes and I knew it would be best if I shot him and the foxes. I had it worked out in my mind that those three were going to take a chicken a night until I was stripped clean. So I loaded up my four-ten over and under and got the four-cell flashlight ready and waited. I was praying Earl Brown wouldn't run off that night. But two o'clock came and he sneaked out and lit out through the woods. . . . You know what happened?"

"What?"

"They never showed up."

"Never?"

"Never . . . but still every night Earl Brown would leave the house at two. About a week later, I followed that dog out through the woods. I was downwind and I stood behind a big sweet gum and watched them.

"They were out in this little field and the moon was good and I could see everything. They were playing some kind of game out there in the moonlight. The foxes would run and Earl Brown would chase them back and forth. And then it all ended and Earl Brown started back through the woods home.

"Mind you, I said 'started back.' Because the minute that rascal figured those foxes figured he was going home, he doubled back. I tell you that was one funny sight. Here I'm behind one tree and Earl Brown is behind another tree and we're both watching those foxes.

"They were running around in circles and making little barking sounds like they were laughing. I tell you, I don't know when I've been so fascinated. I shore wish I had had me a camera about then.

"All of a sudden it hits me what was going on. Old Earl Brown was picking up the foxes' secret about running. That rascal had paid them foxes to show him something. He'd paid them with that Rhode Island Red and now he was checking out the foxes to make sure he'd got his money's worth. Well, by God, I thought I knew something about hounds and foxes but I was shore learning something that night out behind that sweet gum tree. And Earl Brown not twenty yards away tipping his head around his tree . . . man, that was one funny night.

"Well, that running secret ain't easy and Earl Brown had to go back several nights. And every night he went, I went. It took him, all told, about three weeks but I'll be dogged if he didn't finally get it."

Coley got off the bed and squatted down by us. He took another drink and we followed. He spoke lower now.

"I don't want them dogs hearing the rest of this. They'll get out and try it out and wind up breaking their necks. It's too tricky. As smart as Earl Brown was he had a hard time learning it. He took a few pretty bad falls himself before he got it."

Coley stopped and let the bait trail. . . .

Charley rose to it. "Learned what, Coley?"

Coley spoke even lower than before. "How to run like a fox, that's what. Oh, that was one fine dog. He set his mind to it and he learned it. He was marvelous."

Charley was getting jumpy. "What did he learn, Coley? What did he learn?"

"Don't rush me, boy. You don't know much about foxes, do you, boy?"

"I guess not."

"Well you know a fox can outrun any living dog if he feels like it, don't you?"

"Yes."

"Usually they don't feel like it. They're too smart to just do straight running. Most of the time they work in pairs and they get the dogs so confused they don't know what's going on. They'll be running one way and then all of a sudden the other fox will pop up from another direction. Hell, they have signals. Sometimes they'll run the dogs through briar patches, skunk cabbage, anything, and lots of times round and round in the same circles. A good fox will give a pack of dogs a fit. Lots of times a fox will hide and when the dog pack comes by he'll jump in and run along with them. He'll be barking and carrying on and having himself a marvelous time and the dogs won't know a thing.

"Oh, them red foxes are smart. And a good running fox on a straightaway, I mean, no cover, no nothing, can burn a dog down to the ground. He can run that hound right into the ground and he'll be as fresh as when he started. He won't even be breathing hard. You think back. You ever seen a tired fox? No. They don't get tired. And it's all because they got this secret way of running."

Coley was whispering. He really didn't want the dogs to hear. "It's like this. When a fox runs he only uses three legs. Next time you see one running, you watch. You gotta look close, those reds are smart devils. They keep it secret and they only do it when they're off by themselves or when they get in trouble. Kind of emergency you might say."

Charley said, "Whoa now. What do you mean three legs?"

"They rotate, that's what they do. They rotate. They run on three and keep rotating. That way they always got one resting. That's why they give the impression that they're limping all the time and got that little hop in their run."

"Coley," Charley said. "I just can't believe that one."

Coley jumped up and walked across the room twice. He raised his hand. "The Lord will snatch out my tongue and strike me dead right here and now if that ain't the God's truth."

It continued raining . . . and the Lord didn't make a move. . . .

from *The Trembling of a Leaf*

ROBERT W. MARKS (JOHN COLLETON)

(1907–1993)

In the early 1970s Charleston native Robert W. Marks had already established a remarkable writing career, publishing dozens of books and hundreds of magazine articles on a dizzying range of subjects. He covered mathematics, philosophy, psychology, music, hypnotism, wines, and more. His biography of Buckminster Fuller was particularly well regarded. He wrote a profile of photographer Alfred Stieglitz for *Coronet* magazine and followed up with a series of articles that ran for several years on other early twentieth-century photographers. The publisher of *Esquire* told him, "If you can write about automobiles the way you write about photography you can be automotive editor"; he could, and he was.

In his sixties Marks decided for his own entertainment to write a novel based in Charleston. His wife convinced him to share the manuscript with his agent, who sold it to a paperback publisher as *The Trembling of a Leaf*, a title he stole from W. Somerset Maugham. It was a huge success—and a scandal, described alternately as "racy," "dirty," "erotic," and "filthy." The *News and Courier* ran an article puzzling over who the author could be, as it was published under the pseudonym John Colleton (the name of one of the seventeenth-century Lords Proprietors of Carolina), but Marks was more than willing to acknowledge his authorship. He then moved back to Charleston and published six more volumes with many of the same characters. The books balance philosophical discussions (Marks had taught philosophy at the New School for Social Research in New York), which often take place in bed, with steamy sex scenes and evocative descriptions of Charleston.

The only member of this friendship's garland I could persuade to go sailing with me was Larrine. She was a natural sailor. She could handle the ropes like a man. She loved the high waves; she leaned against the wind, and her strong body, stripped to a bikini, blazed in the sun like palmetto leaves.

She would dive overboard when mermaid impulses moved her and sing to me like the Lorelei. Sometimes, after anchoring off a sandbar, we would snorkel together or scuba dive, and I would enjoy her unleashed bronzeness as it slithered through the sparkling water. Sometimes we spent the day in simple, talk-free delight, sailing up the coast beyond the Isle of Palms, or down beyond Kiawah.

When the swells rose and the boat careened, when the wind set the sails humming and the whitecaps lapped at the hull there was little we cared to say to each other. Our bond was the coast and its waters, the spume and blue.

Late one bright afternoon, when the boat was neatly moored and both of us were softened by the sun and sea, we walked together hand in hand through City Hall park. The late wind blew high on the trees. The wind whistled in the vines lying prone on the broken glass which topped the cracked wall separating the park from the old Confederate School for Young Ladies, whistled in the wisteria twined among the wrought-iron traceries which joined City Hall with Robert Mills's Palladian Fireproof Building. Benches, untenanted, unwarmed, stood stolidly in the screaming night. . . .

She held tight to my hand; the language of nerve-endings told me more than her clipped speech. A light went on in one of the law offices facing the Broad Street gate of the park; to our left, the bronze bust of William Pitt, Revolutionary America's one friend in Britain, glowered. . . .

We passed through the Broad Street gate, turned left, walked down the deserted pavement. Above us shingles emblazoned with lawyers' names swung frenetically in the wind. Iron staircases led up, in alleys, to the shabby offices where vested attorneys supported their families by hallowed exercises in the practice of injustice. A block farther down was State Street, where the ancestors of these gentry had private jails for the safekeeping of slaves put up in escrow, or to be auctioned because of the foreclosure of a lady's mortgage.

Along these streets ancient evils somehow compounded into current poetry. Morality and poetic fancy, I had slowly learned, have little in common, except, perhaps, in the sense that beauty, by giving pleasure, creates another morality. The two codes, the two sets of value, are not competitive.

The doges, who tortured prisoners in the Venetian dungeons, were also the patrons of Titian. The second is not a justification of the first. But others—say the Bulgars or the Turks—also tortured prisoners in or out of dank dungeons, and they commissioned no Titians. No Grand Canal, no Rialto, no Piazza San Marco was offered the world as a bribe to overlook ancient evils. Evil and beauty do not come into the world as either-or alternatives. Our heels clicked on the paving stones; echoes bounced from the Flemish-bond brick walls. Shadows from the floreate ironwork entangled our feet.

She unlocked the front door, massive, well-mortised, crowned with twin sunbursts. Her jumbo key slithered into the polished brass plate. The wild wind sweeping from the sea rocked the bell buoy which bobbed between Fort Sumter and the Battery, and the steady gong-gong paced our steps. We clicked across the checkered terazzo of the entrance hall, climbed the winding staircase, her young ass swinging in front of me, honeysuckle sweet. "Amy will be very jealous," she said. Such a simple announcement. She assumed what was to be assumed.

The canopied four-poster, ocean wide, looked through open French windows, through filigreed ironwork, across the oyster-scented harbor to the barrier islands. Distant lights flickered among the dense pines, now black serrations against luminous clouds; lights of river boats blinked as they rounded the island spits or weaved through marsh creeks. "Lie here, my love, and wait for me." She emerged from her dress, instantly opened, like a heron rising from marsh, all grace and assurance. Her browned blonde body flashed past me on its way to the bathroom. I heard the shower splash, and the St. Michael's clock chime another segment of an unnumbered hour.

Slim, exuberant, naked, her skin all sun and morning dew, she knelt at the side of the bed. Without preamble or coyness she opened my zipper. Certain of herself. Little Jack Horner. She put in her thumb and took out a plum. . . .

"Love (Prime)"

ANDY WARHOL (1928–1987)

Andy Warhol was born in Pittsburgh and graduated from the
Carnegie Institute of Technology, after which he centered his
attention on New York City. During the 1960s and '70s he
became the principal artist of the Pop Art movement, producing a hugely popular series of paintings and prints of everyday
objects such as Campbell's soup cans. Later he took on images
of celebrity figures, ranging from Elizabeth Taylor to Mao
Zedong, on which he splashed bright colors. His work can be
found in many of the most important art museums in the world.

In addition, Warhol worked as an avant-garde filmmaker,
record producer, and rock band patron (Velvet Underground).
He became one of the most noted figures in the world, and
lived, worked, and traveled with a group of bohemian eccen-
trics that he promoted. In 1975 he wrote *The Philosophy of
Andy Warhol (From A to B and Back Again),* from which the
excerpt below, about a Charlestonian, is taken.

A: Should we walk? It's really beautiful out.
B: No.
A: Okay.

Taxi was from Charleston, South Carolina—a confused, beautiful debutante who'd split with her family and come to New
York. She had a poignantly vacant, vulnerable quality that made
her a reflection of everybody's private fantasies. Taxi could be
anything you wanted her to be—a little girl, a woman, intelligent, dumb, rich, poor—anything. She was a wonderful, beautiful blank. The mystique to end all mystiques.

She was also a compulsive liar; she just couldn't tell the truth
about anything. And what an actress. She could really turn on
the tears. She could somehow always make you believe her—
that's how she got what she wanted.

Taxi invented the mini-skirt. She was trying to prove to her family back in Charleston that she could live on nothing, so she would go to the Lower East Side and buy the cheapest clothes, which happen to be little girls' skirts, and her waist was so tiny she could get away with it. Fifty cents a skirt. She was the first person to wear ballet tights as a complete outfit, with big earrings to dress it up. She was an innovator—out of necessity as well as fun—and the big fashion magazines picked up on her look right away. She was pretty incredible.

We were introduced by a mutual friend who had just made a fortune promoting a new concept in kitchen appliances on television quiz shows. After one look at Taxi I could see that she had more problems than anybody I'd ever met. So beautiful but so sick. I was really intrigued.

She was living off the end of her money. She still had a nice Sutton Place apartment, and now and then she would talk a rich friend into giving her a wad. As I said, she could turn on the tears and get anything she wanted.

In the beginning I had no idea how many drugs Taxi took, but as we saw more and more of each other it began to dawn on me how much of a problem she had.

Next in importance for her, after taking the drugs, was having the drugs. Hoarding them. She would hop in a limousine and make a run to Philly crying the whole way that she had no amphetamines. And somehow she would always get them because there was just something about Taxi. Then she would add it to the pound she had stashed away at the bottom of her footlocker.

One of her rich sponsor-friends even tried to set her up in the fashion business, designing her own line of clothes. He'd bought a loft on 29th Street outright from a schlock designer who had just bought a condominium in Florida and wanted to leave the city fast. The sponsor-friend took over the operation of the whole loft with the seven seamstresses still at their machines and brought Taxi in to start designing. The mechanics of the business were all set up, all she had to do was come up with designs that were basically no more than copies of the outfits that she styled for herself.

She wound up giving "pokes" to the seamstresses and playing with the bottles of beads and buttons and trimmings that the previous manager had left lining the wall. The business, needless to say, didn't prosper. Taxi would spend most of the day at lunch uptown at Reuben's ordering their Celebrity Sandwiches—the Anna Maria Alberghetti, the Arthur Godfrey, the Morton Downey were her favorites—and she would keep running into the ladies room and sticking her finger down her throat and throwing each one up. She was obsessed with not getting fat. She'd eat and eat on a spree and then throw up and throw up, and then take four downers and pop off for four days at a time. Meanwhile her "friends" would come in to "rearrange" her pocketbook while she was sleeping. When she'd wake up four days later she'd deny that she'd been asleep.

At first I thought that Taxi only hoarded drugs. I knew that hoarding is a kind of selfishness, but I thought it was only with the drugs that she was that way. I'd see her beg people for enough for a poke and then go and file it in the bottom of her footlocker in its own little envelope with a date on it. But I finally realized that Taxi was selfish about absolutely everything.

One day when she was still in the designing business a friend and I went to visit her. There were scraps and scraps of velvets and satins all over the floor and my friend asked if she could have a piece just large enough to make a cover for a dictionary she owned. There were thousands of scraps all over the floor, practically covering our feet, but Taxi looked at her and said, "The best time is in the morning. Just come by in the morning and look through the pails out front and you'll probably find something."

Another time we were riding in a cab and she was crying that she didn't have any money, that she was poor, and she opened her pocketbook for a Kleenex and I happened to catch sight of one of those clear plastic change purses all stuffed with green. I didn't bother to say anything. What was the point? But the next day I asked her, "What happened to that clear plastic change purse you had yesterday that was stuffed with money?" She said, "It was stolen last night at a discothèque." She couldn't tell the truth about anything.

Taxi hoarded brassieres. She kept around fifty brassieres—in graduated shades of beige, through pale pink and deep rose to coral and white—in her trunk. They all had the price tags on them. She would never remove a price tag, not even from the clothes she wore. One day the same friend that asked her for the scrap of material was short on cash and Taxi owed her money. So she decided to take a brassiere that still had the Bendel's tags on it back to the store and get a refund. When Taxi wasn't looking she stuffed it into her bag and went uptown. She went to the lingerie department and explained that she was returning the bra for a friend—it was obvious that this girl was far from an A-cup. The sales lady disappeared for ten minutes and then came back holding the bra and some kind of a log book and said, "Madame. This bra was purchased in 1956." Taxi was a hoarder.

Taxi had an incredible amount of makeup in her bag and in her footlocker: fifty pairs of lashes arranged according to size, fifty mascara wands, twenty mascara cakes, every shade of Revlon shadow ever made—iridescent and regular, matte and shiny—twenty Max Factor blush-ons . . . She'd spend hours with her makeup bags Scotch-taping little labels on everything, dusting and shining the bottles and compacts. Everything had to look perfect.

But she'd didn't care about anything below the neck.

She would never take a bath.

I would say, "Taxi. Take a bath." I'd run the water and she would go into the bathroom with her bag and stay in there for an hour. I'd yell, "Are you in the tub?" "Yes, I'm in the tub." Splash splash. But then I'd hear her tip-toeing around the bathroom and I'd peek through the keyhole and she'd be standing in front of the mirror, putting on more makeup over what was already caked on her face. She would never put water on her face—only those degreasers, those little tissue-thin papers you press on that remove the oils without ruining the makeup. She used those.

A few minutes later I'd peek through the keyhole again and she'd be recopying her address book—or somebody else's address book, it didn't matter—or else she'd be sitting with a yellow legal pad making the list of all the men she'd ever been to bed with dividing them into three categories—"Slept," "Fucked," and "Cuddled." If she made a mistake on the last line and it looked messy, she'd tear it off and start all over. After an hour, she'd come out of the bathroom and I'd say, gratuitously, "You didn't take a bath." "Yes. Yes I did."

I slept in the same bed with Taxi once. Someone was after her and she didn't want to sleep with him, so she crawled into bed in the next room with me. She fell asleep and I just couldn't stop looking at her, because I was so fascinated-but-horrified. Her hands kept crawling, they couldn't sleep, they couldn't stay still. She scratched herself constantly, digging her nails in and leaving marks. In three hours she woke up and said immediately that she hadn't been asleep.

Taxi drifted away from us after she started seeing a singer-musician who can only be described as The Definitive Pop Star—possibly of all time—who was then fast gaining recognition on both sides of the Atlantic as the thinking man's Elvis Presley. I missed having her around, but I told myself that it was probably a good thing that he was taking care of her now, because maybe he knew how to do it better than we had.

Taxi died a few years ago in Hawaii where an important industrialist had taken her for a "rest." I hadn't seen her for years.

"Charleston, Charleston"

ALBERT GOLDMAN (1927–1994)

> As Albert Goldman acknowledges in the following essay, first
> published in *Esquire* in 1977, he was an unlikely enthusiast of
> Charleston. He had already published a well-received biogra-
> phy of Lenny Bruce (1974) and a New Journalism–type review
> of the counterculture; he wrote extensively for *Esquire* maga-
> zine. But he had not yet produced the two books he would be
> most noted for: controversial biographies of Elvis Presley
> (1981, and another about Elvis's last days in 1990) and John
> Lennon (1988). Nonetheless he cast an insightful eye on the
> city, which seems to have welcomed him warmly. He wrote of
> a Charleston that didn't often appear in magazine pieces: of
> Jimmy Dengate's private restaurant and Gordon (or Dawn)
> Simmons's wedding, of the Carolina Yacht Club's coed cruise
> to Rockville and the tradition of driving to a party with an
> open drink. Indeed, Goldman arrived at a turning point in
> Charleston's history: the two o'clock dinner was still common-
> place and Spoleto Festival U.S.A. had not yet started. Inevitably,
> many Charlestonians expressed outrage when the article was
> published, but in 1994, when John Berendt's *Midnight in the
> Garden of Good and Evil* exposed many bizarre details about
> Savannah to an audience of millions, some locals remembered
> Goldman's article about Charleston, which was read by many
> fewer readers.

When the downbeat is given for Spoleto U.S.A., this May 25, the
moment will mark not only the establishment of a famous
European arts festival in the United States but, more importantly, the awakening of that Sleeping Beauty of American cities:
Charleston, South Carolina. This legendary town, renowned for
its role in American history, myth and culture, has resisted for
over a century the life of the modern world. It has become a
social and cultural museum, a time capsule stuffed with antiqui-

ties and old-timers. Eighteen months ago, I succumbed to the spell of Charleston and took up residence in this city at the end of the world. Not a week has passed since then that somebody has not demanded my reasons for deserting the avant-garde for the rear guard of American society.

"You, Albert! The Lenny Bruce man! The rock critic! The big expert on dope smuggling!" Thus they reproach me, and I always feel obliged to defend myself, as if I'd done some crazy, self-destructive deed or yielded at last to syphilitic insanity. If my interrogator is a typical New Yorker, someone who has never been south of Chinatown or north of Zabar's, I struggle to convey the beauty of this ancient American city. Imagine, I croon, the delicious sensation of stepping into a waking dream that paints in all the freshest, most springlike colors, all the balmiest airs and most melodious chimes and chirps, the quintessential fantasy of the Old South. Picture stately Georgian mansions flaunting triple tiers of white-columned piazzas, soaring eighteenth-century church steeples ringing down silvery showers on an Easter morning, the heady aroma of oleanders or tea holly as you open the heavy wrought-iron gate and crunch down the gravel path beside some tall, silent house, until suddenly there is revealed to you, as if by magic, an enchanting little eighteenth-century garden, its paths bordered with carefully trimmed box hedges and topiary trees, its voluptuously blooming flowers dropping their petals into a tiny reflecting pond, its atmosphere that of a dreamy retreat from the world, guarded by high brick walls and soaring old magnolias that offer their white satin blossoms high above the ground as if to consecrate them to astral rather than earthly presences.

Or imagine the effect of wandering for hours, lost in the mazy English gardens of the neighboring plantation, Magnolia, acclaimed by John Galsworthy as one of the six great gardens of the world, an astounding spectacle in the spring, when twenty-six acres of azaleas, including every subtly shaded, waxy petaled exotic known to man, blaze up in simultaneous bloom. To soothe your senses from such an overdose of chromatic stimulation, you must steep them in the moody depths of that most beguiling of Southern glades, Cypress Gardens, where you enter Edgar Allan Poe's "misty mid-region of Weir." Here the native glamour of the Low Country has been concentrated into a single sheet of black water studded with a thousand cypress trees, whose knobby knees protrude above the surface like wickedly turned elves' stools, while their towering trunks rising precipitately to the blue sky and floating clouds, repeat themselves with eerie effect to the very depths of this mirror-smooth lake. To step into the little gondola-like skiffs that ply this dark tarn (propelled by silent black punters), to abandon yourself to the fascination of this looking-glass world that puts the treetops, the sky and the clouds far beneath your feet or within grasp of your hand as it trails in the water, is to experience an enchantment just as great as that afforded by a nocturnal journey through the narrow back canals of Venice. Ah, how I labor to seduce my dear old friends from that filthy necropolis, New York, to the eternal blooming of my new home in the Southland. They laugh and nod and sigh and exclaim with delight as I paint my extravagant pictures with all the lyric colors of a born enthusiast. But then, when I am out of breath, they shake their heads as if to say, "Oy! He's crazier than ever!" and reply, in the tone of a man who has enjoyed himself but must now attend to reality: "Albert, what do you do down there when you want to talk to someone? Isn't it all old ladies and closet queens and retired admirals? Don't they hate Jews and drink a lot? Don't they wonder what you're doing there? What are you doing there? There isn't much to do, is there?"

Admirals? Old ladies? Nothing to do? What nonsense! It's true, my next-door neighbor on Tradd Street is General Westmoreland. What of that? I don't see any more of him than I did of my next-door neighbors on Eighty-second Street and Fifth Avenue: Punch Sulzberger, Ved Mehta, Bob Scull (the taxi czar and Pop Art freak) or Baby Jane Holzer (Tom Wolfe's onetime Girl of the Year). So far as old ladies go, I'm not ashamed to say that like most middle-aged Jewish intellectuals and writers, I

have a lot of old lady in me: to be precise, a lot of my dreadful
mother. When I'm in Charleston, I indulge my passion for house-
keeping, fussing over those ancient floors that demand to be
exposed but are so hard to keep shining, unless you have them
polyurethaned (which I despise).

In fact, when I survey my little garden house, my "depen-
dency," so neat and shipshape, with its decks that list about five
degrees to starboard; when I let my gaze fall on its fine antique
furniture or its big modern kitchen (formerly the kitchen of the
big house); or when I sit inside my brown nutshell-like study,
focused on a fine old brick fireplace, at which I gaze for hours
every night in winter—while the oak logs flame yellow-orange
and shoot off spectacular sparks when the fire hits a vein of fragrant sap; when I sip from my tinkly glass of Black Label Scotch
or puff on the fine Santa Marta Gold (which my boys in the
"game" always send me), I feel a sense of profound contentment, of richness and repletion that I never experienced anywhere else in my entire life. You think that's bad?

So far from having nothing to do, I have everything to do,
from running a house, to writing a menu, to instructing the cook
on how to make the salad a subtle entr'acte in the meal—not a
Holiday Inn Fourth of July—to ordering the wines, pastas, and
chocolates from New York, to worrying whether the frost will
blight the camellias, to reviewing, writing and re-reading the
entire course of my life to date. I wouldn't say that I was exactly
idle. Yet when I am at leisure here in the Deep South, I do enjoy
a very deep feeling of contentment. In fact, I'm so laid-back that
for the first time in my life I've become a listener instead of a
compulsive talker. Albert Goldman, the great-listener. Wouldn't
my analyst be proud?

My only complaint against Charleston is not that it lacks the
intellectuals, restaurants, stores or theaters of New York—all of
which are only about ninety minutes away by air—but that
Charleston lacks the people and institutions that would enable it
to capitalize on its own very great and unique resources. When
you first discover Charleston, you can't believe that it hasn't

been discovered by thousands upon thousands of other people before you and that these thousands haven't included numerous artists, writers and people of intellect and culture, who have fled to this favorable environment the way creative people once fled America for Europe or the way so many leave the big bankrupt metropolises today for cities like San Francisco, Santa Fe or Key West. You can't believe, in short, that any place with such an ideal climate, with such a rich store of historical and cultural materials, with the very stuff of art and literature practically popping out of the paving stones (think how Charleston inspired George Gershwin, who arrived in the summer of 1935 with a few sketches for an opera about a local goat beggar and left the city five weeks later with most of the ideas for the greatest masterpiece of the American musical theater), how such a classic site should not have become at the very least a notable art colony or, pricing the article at its full value, a distinguished center for art, culture and education, perhaps the Cambridge of the South.

Yet when I looked about me after my first infatuation with the city had faded, I began to recognize that Charleston presented a profound and dismaying paradox: though it offered one of the richest soils for the imagination in America, it was intellectually and culturally one of the most poverty-stricken of our famous cities, especially when you measured the local culture by the basic standards of ambition, initiative, enterprise or simply energy. Charleston, I recognized, was not just vacant to the eye, its immaculate and picturesque streets largely devoid of people or events; it was enervated, or "effeminate," to recollect Henry James's description of the city. It reminded me at times of those mummified medieval towns in Germany, Rothenburg and Dinkelsbühl, where not a stone has been changed since the Canterbury pilgrims set out upon their journey.

Such "living museums" strike me as being in contradiction to themselves. What is the point of preservation if it does not foster fresh life and growth, if it does not transfuse into the blood and brain of a living generation the genius of all the dead generations that tilled this ground and left it so rich and fertile? This is the problem, the paradox of Charleston. Not until I had resided in the city for many months and begun to understand what had produced this unhappy state of affairs did I begin to realize what would have to be done to awaken Charleston and make it play the part (and assume the honor) it so richly deserved.

The first thing you recognize when you study the history of Charleston, either from books or from the eloquent record afforded by the city's richly suggestive physical fabric, is that the Charleston everyone prizes—the city of the magnificent homes and public buildings and palatial country estates—was not built by the cautious curatorial types who now inhabit these splendid lodgments. Charleston was built by a totally different society: a wealthy, gay and boisterous plantocracy that relished horse racing, cockfighting and dueling. These gentlemen, many of whom had either been born or bred in England, envisioned their city as the second metropolis of the British empire. They laid out its streets and erected its first public buildings along the lines of Christopher Wren's Palladian and imperial London. They imported shiploads of silver, furniture, crystal and wall hangings; they built splendid town houses, which they sometimes designed themselves, exhibiting both good taste and architectural imagination. When the malarial fevers rose in the marshes, the planters would install themselves in their mansions and while away their time with balls, routs and concerts of fine music.

The economic basis of this resplendent society was the triple economy of indigo, rice and cotton. So long as these crops were raised on its neighboring plantations and shipped through its port, Charleston flourished. Long before the commencement of the Civil War, however, the sources of Charleston's short-lived wealth began to dry up. Indigo was replaced by chemical dyes like Prussian blue; rice was grown farther south and shipped out of Savannah, Charleston's commercial rival; and cotton, king of the Southern economy, proved to be a soil waster that demanded ever fresh conquests in the virgin lands to the west and south, especially in Alabama and Mississippi. You can see the cutoff point for Charleston's affluence in the city's architectural record;

practically all the good building was done before 1840; from that year on, Charleston and her fortunes evidently began to languish.

Charleston was spared the worst ravages of the Civil War, the fires that leveled Atlanta and nearby Columbia, South Carolina's capital. The economic disruption and depression that followed the war were so extreme, however, that the city never really recovered. For three generations the utmost that Charlestonians could hope to accomplish was to hold fast to their patrimonies—their houses, lands and domestic possessions—through the practice of the most stringent parsimony. It was in this long interregnum that Charleston became the castle of Sleeping Beauty or the cave before which the dragon Fafner snores as he guards the Rheingold.

Eventually, the stimulus of the World War II economy was felt in even so remote a backwater as Charleston. After the war, the congressional seniority system elevated Mendel Rivers to the chairmanship of the Armed Services Committee and the senior representative from South Carolina began funneling back to the desiccated metropolis the vast sums required to enlarge the mighty naval base and shipyard, to build the Polaris submarine base, establish the Air Force reconnaissance squadron, and the various Army installations that have appeared and disappeared in the region. Charleston had always held on to its position as a regional center for banking, insurance and law; it modernized eventually its ancient port facilities to accommodate container technology. When agribusiness became America's principal source of foreign income, the old city that had always lived by shipping American farm produce abroad gained a second lease on life.

Paradoxically, the years of impoverishment had made the city the richest lode of urban antiquities in the Western World. Lacking the sort of industry that has to destroy in order to create, lacking the kind of ready money that tempts householders to modernize, lacking even that close contact with the modern world that sends trends and fads rippling, sometimes with destructive effect, across the face of the urban landscape,

Charlestonians preserved their city almost entirely. As early as the 1920's, when the whole emphasis of America was upon being a booster and a builder—and consequently an obliterator of the American heritage—Charleston established a historic preservation society, which went to work quietly and tactfully to save the city's architectural heritage. Striking a chord in the deeply conservative souls of native Charlestonians, this foundation and a sister organization gradually turned the tide of urban decay and desuetude until Charleston became the mecca of urban conservationists.

Today, Charleston is a Janus-faced city that looks simultaneously back toward the easygoing, if essentially hopeless, life of the old days and forward into the uncertain future, where the growing power of the black vote and the tourist dollar portend profound changes in this archaic society. For Charleston is, in many ways, still its old, sleepy nineteenth-century self. The black street vendors of Porgy and Bess no longer break the morning stillness with their cries of "Shwimp!" and "Stwawbehr-reeees!", but the classic institution of the two o'clock dinner, the main meal of the day, is still maintained in many families. Though the women now go out in the morning to exercise classes or to courses in flower arranging at the Gibbes Art Gallery, they still play bridge in the afternoon, sipping bourbon and indulging in the timeless Southern appetite for gossip and scandal.

Indeed, nothing is more characteristic of Charleston than the fondness for drink, talk and idleness. When I first arrived from New York, supported by a brace of friends and carrying in my luggage a symbolic property—a dozen fine fluted champagne glasses from The Four Seasons—I was very uncertain of my capacity to meld with the local society. Charlestonians had been described to me as the most profoundly insular, snobbish and exclusionary people in the South. Yet from the night of my arrival, and on for many months, I enjoyed a nearly ceaseless round of parties and good times that made me regard (rather naively, I realize today) all these notions of Southern folk as Northern prejudices.

Partying is a way of life in Charleston; you don't have to teach them how to do it. All you need to hold a party is a room and a bottle. (You also need a supply of cocktail napkins because the local decorum requires that every glass be neatly swathed before it is handed to the guest.) The bottle is the symbol of sociability in the South and especially in Charleston, whose people are famous drinkers. Some people have their first martini at ten in the morning. Others take a liquid lunch. Many Charlestonians fortify themselves with a drink for every drive, even the short hops; their cars are equipped with glass holders on both the driver's and the passengers' sides, though some citizens will place the glass right on top of the dashboard and then drive so slowly and smoothly with their big hog cars that the glass remains steadfast, a juggler's trick. This practice of drinking as you drive even has a name: it's called taking a "traveler." (The drink you have while dressing is called a "dresser.") I remember once receiving a call from a man who was going to drive me to a party. "I'll be over in fifteen minutes," he said. "Shall I bring you a traveler?" I thought he was already drunk until we straightened out the nomenclature.

Charlestonians are a convivial and enormously sociable race. Yet it is not just their social vivacity or gregariousness that makes them exemplary guests; they are also the world's most accomplished mixers. After spending a lifetime in New York trying to push one cranky egotist into the conversational circle of another, I was astonished and relieved when I gave my first party in Charleston. My guests took to each other like long-lost brothers. Indeed, the analogy is not entirely fanciful. Most Charlestonians can discover, if they try hard enough, some degree of relatedness between themselves and their fellow citizens, even if it be only a third cousin twice removed in a collateral line. This sudden metamorphosis of total strangers into kissin' cousins is but one of many ways in which you see how incredibly inbred the population of Charleston is.

Another is the endless repetition of the same quaint names: Rhett, Ravenel, Manigault, Pinckney, Heyward, Gibbes,

Rutledge. Yet another sign is the physical homogeneity of the local population. I wouldn't say that if you've seen one, you've seen them all, but after you've seen enough Charlestonians, you understand the meaning of the term "gene pool." Charlestonians start off small, neat folk, with short legs, long torsos and duck asses, and spread by middle age into Queen Anne chairs. Their pink skins, blond polls and comely snub-nosed faces suggest the fair, fleshy look of their English or Barbadian ancestors.

Sometimes the ancestral look is so strong that you feel a stiff old portrait has stepped down from the wall, wrapped a paper napkin around its glass and turned to smile and talk to you in precisely the same accent and the same wry-necked, stiff-backed attitude that you see in eighteenth-century engravings or porcelain statuary. This archaic look was snapped into startling focus last year when Americans began dressing up like their Colonial ancestors. In most parts of the country this assumption of old clothing was ridiculous; big post-hippie lops and beer bellied businessmen, clowning around like the cast of burlesque musical comedy. In Charleston, the effect was so becoming that I felt for the first time I was seeing my neighbors correctly dressed.

Charlestonians are proud of the fact that they do not talk with a Southern drawl. After alcohol, speech is the South's greatest addiction, and styles of speech count for as much in this part of the country as do styles of dress in New York. The first thing that impressed me, as an English professor, about the speech of Charlestonians was that it was colored by long, close-mouthed vowels that are known in the trade as "continental" vowels. The English student learns about these vowels, comparable to those hard to pronounce French vowels and German umlauts when he studies Chaucer, but of course the sounds continued into the early modern English of the seventeenth century, when the first colonizers arrived in this country. When a Charlestonian speaks with this classic accent—which makes English "house" rhyme with French "mousse"—the effects are of a very gentle stroking and soothing of the auditory nerve. The voice is invariably low, resonant and well modulated; the tempo is best described as largo.

After the nervous impatient speech of New York, especially the fast-talking worlds of Broadway and Madison Avenue, it is at first astonishing and then utterly exasperating to hear anyone speak at this sedan-chair pace. You find yourself constantly smirking and interjecting little signs of agreement or surprise, or practically dancing a jig in your head as you wait for this honey dipper, this mortar spreader, to round his period and wind up his yarn. (If you're really desperate, you may even find yourself interrupting rudely, just to allow yourself to breathe.)

Charlestonians do not all speak in this solemn plainsong (which makes a woman of twenty-eight sound on the phone like a middle-age matron): there are those who have a totally distinct manner of speech, which is all hill and dale, start and stop, quirk and grimace; a jumpy, twitchy, witty patter that is liberally interspersed with golly's and eye pops. Nor should one overlook the more rustic and rambunctious type of speaker, the Squire Western sort, who, especially when in his cups, will essay to speak in a voice that is all husk, phlegm and Holy Roller: "I swear to Jesus, Ahbert, he was knee walkin', shit-faced drunk!"

As for the substance of all this well-lubricated talk, it is invariably gossip and scandal. When the sin is fresh and savory, it is offered and consumed with the maximum possible horror: gasps, oaths, eyes cast heavenward, attest to the marvelous potency of the stuff. After the story has grown old and hoary and the characters banished to another part of the country, the same shocking tale appears again as an uproariously funny anecdote. As Lenny Bruce used to say: "Comedy is tragedy plus time."

The greatest, most earthshaking scandals are those that entail sexual transgressions. A priest is found abed with one of his married parishioners; a member of the Yacht Club is discovered in flagrante delicto with another member's wife on the annual "coed cruise" to Rockville; a wealthy old gentleman in his seventies suddenly decamps with a young matron; a grave young woman is sued for adultery with a prestigious landholder, who is also taken to court—for alienation of affections. Charleston is a city of lawyers and the populace is highly litigious; it is a rare scandal that does not entail enough legal complications to make your head spin.

Another sort of scandal entails mismanaged money. Another, bribery of public officials. Another, some crazy scheme to defraud. Many impostors, ranging from fake Italian counts to spurious Yankee capitalists, have appeared in Charleston over the years and practiced successfully upon the credulity, snobbery and greed of the local people. Perhaps the most marvelous of all the scandals that have shaken Charleston in recent years was one that involved sex, deceit, imposture and even perversion!— all wrapped up into one howling tale that never fails to bring down the house.

The protagonist of this farce was a rather effete young man who claimed kindred with an illustrious English actress. He appeared in Charleston one season, and opened an antique shop. At once, he ingratiated himself with the local society and especially with the old ladies who relished his conversation and his knowledge of heirlooms and bric-a-brac. After a season in town, he suddenly disappeared. When he returned, he thrilled the old dames by inviting them to his wedding. When the great day arrived and the staid, genteel guests had been seated in the parlor, tastefully decorated and furnished with all things requisite to a wedding, including a priest, the bridal march blared forth and down the fine old staircase came the bridal party. As the elderly guests turned in their chairs to smile benignly on the happy couple, a gasp of horror filled the room—the long, ecstatic breath of SCANDAL. The bride, decked out in white and dripping orange blossoms, was none other than the antique dealer (who had undergone a sex change operation). His groom was a black chauffeur! After that, what did it matter that the bridesmaids were two lace-ruffled poodles!

When the Charlestonian is not partying, he is working, often with loud complaints about the killing pace he is forced to maintain. I took these complaints at face value, being a workaholic myself, until gradually I realized exactly what the office day comprised. Judge for yourself whether these men are courting coronaries from overwork. The Charleston professional man or merchant will go to work at nine, a half hour after the clerical help arrives. Then, after one hour on the job, it's time to knock off and go across the street to the local coffee shop, where, between plastic-coated sips, the men talk over the news of the day or the latest scandal or the chances that South Carolina will beat Clemson, the usual front-page story in the Sunday *News and Courier*. ("The South's Oldest Newspaper": everything in Charleston is the "oldest," from the Dock Street Theater to the Charleston Library Society to the weather reports kept by Dr. John Lining in the eighteenth century.) After an hour of talk, the weary slaves of commerce repair to their quaint offices in buildings that bear plaques testifying to their origins ("Built in 1822 by Isaac Goldberg, merchant") until it is time to go home for dinner at one.

Now for the classic institution of the two-o'clock dinner: "In the old days, Ahbert, you could heah that two-ah-clock dinnah bell ringin' all oveh this town." As the bankers, the lawyers, the cotton factors, the merchants, the planters, the marine surveyors, got in their buggies and drove home comfortably down Church or King or Legare (pronounced "Legree") Streets, a mere four or five blocks, where they put up before their single or double houses. When they entered their dining rooms, their noses were assailed with the odors of okra soup or gumbo, creole shrimp or rice pilau, guinea squash (eggplant) and sieva beans (limas) and, for desert, a fragrant Huguenot torte. The lady of the house presided over the gleaming board set with Spode or Wedgwood, as the little angelic children, fresh from school, bowed their heads for grace. Then, the big colored cook brought forth the dishes and the family enjoyed the principal meal of the day.

This was the old Charleston and this is the Charleston that still persists, though every year it retreats a step in the face of modern business routine and rising servant costs. ("I'm not paying any two dollars and twenty-five cents an hour to those lazy maids settin' there watchin' television," as one matron remarked apropos the recent boost in the minimum wage. How else could she feel when she recalled that twenty years ago, as a young mother, she paid only fifteen dollars a week for a maid and had two of them, one arriving at seven-thirty a.m. to cook dinner, the other coming on duty at three p.m. to take charge of the children until she and her husband returned at midnight from their supper party. Now, the men folk are liable to take a stag lunch at the bar of the Yacht Club or even adjourn to Jimmy Dengate's, a joint—"Ah mean uh joint!"—a key club in the colored quarter on the west side of town—founded upon the belief that friends with mutual ties desire an exclusive place to enjoy lunch and fellow-ship—where, if you're white and right, you can fall by at any hour and enjoy a nice cheap plate of boiled shrimp, red rice, maybe even a delicious deviled crab—plus a couple of "shooters" or "burners"—while enjoying the raunchy laid-back, down-home, rustic atmosphere that so many men crave after living for years in a house/museum where every move upsets the wife, who is trying to get the place into mint condition to put it on show when the historic tours come through in the spring.

After work, the men still repair to their favorite haunt, the mighty heart that keeps the social blood pumping through old Charley Town (as the CB boys handle it): the Carolina Yacht Club. The Club is the supreme institution in a town whose citizens are the most clubbable in America. (Other clubs include St. Andrew's, the St. George's, Hibernian, New England, German Friendly and the fancifully titled Piping and Marching Society of Lower Chalmers Street.)

Charleston men love to draw apart from their women and enjoy a life of male camaraderie. They drink, talk and play cards together; shoot, fish and sail; and travel abroad in groups. They hug and kiss each other; needle and play practical jokes on one another; or come to the rescue of members threatened by job or family crises. Always together from their earliest years in the old neighborhood or school to their last days as elderly gentlemen seated in a corner of the club, these men develop a touching and generous sort of friendship that runs much deeper in many ways than does conventional marriage, that often acrimonious partnership, which is weakened rather than strengthened by its carnal foundation. It's not hard to understand why some men are never home, spending virtually their entire lives in the company of their friends at the club.

The women of Charleston appear to have drawn the short straw. Their lives impress one as being less satisfying emotionally and more filled with the sort of busywork that compensates for inner frustrations and emptiness. The ladies are always in motion: working as guides, docents, teachers; preparing their homes for holidays and special occasions like the annual candlelight tours of historic houses; attending meetings of the Junior League, the garden club, the church organizations and supervising the upbringing of one, two or three children. Such pretty, innocent-looking children in their Charleston bonnets and smocks, their little storybook suits, toddling when they're tiny in the grip of some big jovial black maid, rushing home from school on their bikes in later years, gathering on the corner to deliver the newspaper (enclosed in a plastic baggie when it rains) or going to that other great Charleston institution: the Wednesday afternoon dancing school, where the little girls wear white gloves and sit with crossed ankles until the whistle is blown and the boys come stampeding across the floor to claim their partners, the best-looking girls receiving a swarm of boys while the homely child is condemned to dance with her teacher. These are those forgotten children, who, when addressed by an adult, answer, "Ma'am" or "Sir." In later years some of these girls will put on white gowns and come out at an enormous debutante party. A few of them will even attend the ball of Charleston's—and America's—oldest and most exclusive society: the St. Cecilia.

Established in 1762 to give concerts of fine music, the society is notable today for two things: (1) restriction of membership to the sons of current members, and (2) the annual ball, which is conducted along strict nineteenth-century lines. The decorum of the ball demands that the men wear tails, the ladies have their partners scheduled on a dance card, that there be no close or "jukey" dancing (monitors are employed to enforce this rule) and that there be no smoking or drinking save sherry during the dance and champagne during the supper. The ball also entails such quaint customs as the practice of having one cotillion led by the most recently married member, whose wife must appear in her bridal gown.

The St. Cecilia Society provides an extreme illustration of that exclusionary mania that is so prominent a feature of Southern society. It has many less extreme parallels in Charleston social life, which are not apparent when one first arrives in the city but which gradually emerge once one settles in. Charlestonians are exceptionally gracious and hospitable people. They leave their doors open in every sense of the word. What gives them the confidence to welcome strangers into their lives, however, is the knowledge that no outsider can ever truly penetrate their society. Fortified by this faith, they can afford to throw open their gates and entertain even the most eccentric alien types with ease and charm, although woe betide the incautious visitor who mistakes these signs of affability for the sort of genuine social acceptance that such behavior might signal up north.

The exclusionist character of Southern society has been discussed too much in terms of race and politics and too little in terms of art and culture. By turning in on themselves, the older, more genteel members of Southern society have lost both the capacity to appreciate or communicate with men of imagination and intelligence. They have likewise lost the capacity to produce such men out of their own ranks. Charleston, for example, has never been noted for its writers, painters or composers, though in its three-hundred-year history, there have been more than a few individuals who have assayed each of these arts. Other sections of the South have been far more productive of good literature and have patronized the performing arts much more generously. The fact is that many writers and artists would welcome an opportunity to work and reside in the South but fear that they would not meet with many fellow spirits.

Recently, however, Charleston has begun to stretch and yawn and wake up. In the next few years it may be transformed from a sleepy old town in the South to the latest discovery of the American tourist industry. It has been a case of everybody getting the same idea at the same time, whether they be the Kuwaiti government, building a new Hilton Head on Kiawah Island, or the state of South Carolina expanding its college and medical school facilities or Gian-Carlo Menotti discovering the American counterpart of his atmospheric medieval Italian hill town at Spoleto. Overnight, Charleston is being transformed from the town DuBose Heyward described on the first page of Porgy as an "ancient beautiful city that time forgot before she destroyed," to the latest in the succession of re-discovered "authentic" American cities, right up there behind Key West.

Charleston has already a few good pieces to put into its tourist package. Some years ago, the New York investment banker Richard Jenrette endowed the city with a gem of a hotel, the Mills Hyatt House, a reconstruction of a classic old building from the time of Edgar Allan Poe with beautifully decorated period rooms, and an arched, mirrored, fanlighted and candlelit dining room, that evokes Charleston's Barbadian past in a flickering, glamorous night setting that is on another plane from every other public facility in this intensely private city.

Now the developers are hard at work turning Charleston's historic long-shed open-air farmer's market into a one-story version of Ghirardelli Square. Boutiques and quickie ethnic food counters and all the hip, fern-hung amenities of American tourism now confront the Gullah-talking black farmers who bring their melons and vegetables into the city from sea islands that are still redolent of Africa, the plantation and slavery.

Keeping pace or even outstripping the race of the tourist entrepreneurs have been the bureaucrats of the state medical university and liberal arts college. Overnight they have transformed a medical school that rated a sarcastic snort in New York into a research institution that boasts a faculty with big stars like Albert Sabin. At the same time, the College of Charleston, a parochial little school with an enrollment of three hundred students, has been jacked up to a full-scale city college with five thousand students and a whole neighborhood of beautifully restored houses.

Spoleto will be the heaviest thing to hit Charley Town since the earthquake of 1886. From May 25 to June 5, the Holy City, with its one good hotel and its one old hotel, its handful of motor inns and its slow-motion restaurants—to say nothing of the jitney cab service and the fifteen-cent buses, which are patronized almost exclusively by black domestics—will play host to an estimated fifty thousand tourists. While Tchaikovsky's Queen of Spades is being performed at the Gaillard Auditorium and Peter Serkin's chamber music group is banging out Mozart's piano quintet at the Dock Street Theater and the Eliot Feld dance group is camping it up on the campus of the college, thousands of people will be plodding up and down Charleston's dreamy streets, trying garden gates, rubbernecking house-fronts, hauling around town in mule-drawn surreys with thickly accented guides and gradually wearing down in that thick, hot summer weather that the local folk call "gummy." It will be an important trial for the new order. If it works, Charleston will be launched on a new career, a new course of history. If it bombs, the boys at the club will blame it on all "the women," and Charleston will go right back to its own interpretation of the cult of St. Cecilia, patron saint of music.

"Charleston, South Carolina, 7 P.M."

WENDY SALINGER (1948–)

Wendy Salinger, a native of Durham, North Carolina, graduated from Duke University and received a master's degree from the University of Iowa. She has lived in New York for many years, where she works at the 92nd Street Y's Unterberg Poetry Center. She spent several years in the 1970s living on Folly Beach, teaching at the College of Charleston, and working as poet-in-residence for public schools throughout the state. During that time she created the poems that would make up *Folly River*, including the one included in this collection. Her manuscript won the National Poetry Series open competition, which led to the book's publication in 1980. Salinger's poetry has appeared in the *New Yorker*, the *Kenyon Review*, and the *Paris Review*.

She is also the author of *Listen* (2006), a poetic memoir, and the editor of Richard Wilbur's *Creation* (1983). Salinger has received a Guggenheim Fellowship and a National Poetry Series award. She served previously as a lecturer in English at Columbia University's School of General Studies and as a visiting professor at Sarah Lawrence College.

Vapors of musk and oyster rise,
a fine perspiring from the streets.
Blue bends toward purple:
a voice growing husky.
Things seek their silhouettes.
Green gathers darkness into the palm trees,
and the houses seem to rush out.
How whitely the stucco flowers and the pillar
that wavers as if seen through water.

So it is with consequences, the sun's aftertaste,
its resonances pool out in clapboard and stone.
Light hesitates between the streetlamp and the sky,
and distance is palpable as it is between those
who turn to each other with eyes downcast.

We lean from our bones but we don't leave,
we hang about, we hover at the edges,
we live in our mouths, heaviness on our tongues.
The tongue could do all the work tonight
of sight and sound and most surely of thought.
We hover at surfaces like moths
at our white linen, our moon silks,
at our own flesh. Surely under the fresh
ironing our genitals are cool and strange.
Surely they are fronds and gardenia flowers.

A weedy draft of ocean floods our lungs.
I know this now. How the past waits
coiled in an odor,
wet for the drinker of a limpid sound,
to be unbottled, to assail the blood.
I know the past exists.
And I could enter anywhere and find you, arranged
in the mime, for example, of just such an evening,
when lifting the cigarette through its steam
your arm inscribes forever that arc in space.
I know the rich molecules collect.

But who can court a balcony that commands
the bay to shine from its dark height?
My music's wrong, I'm not my own
bent low in the folds of a polished gown,
bowing to a man whose forehead shames the moon,
whose wrists flash steel.
A moisture films his formal lip

and sticks the shirt to the moving chest
and lifts the light on the beaded glass.
Is it possible that other histories covet us?

A stray dance can find our forms,
an incomplete gesture usurp our arms.
We shudder against the humid seizures
that wrestle us out of modern motion,
curve us, bow us,
wheel our waists through the watery air
where the ocean lives in its altered state
of brine and oyster musk, and smoke
from the factories braids with the swerve
of the black kids on their bicycles
who criss-cross the northend traffic.

from *Edisto*

PADGETT POWELL (1952–   )

Padgett Powell, born in Gainesville, Florida, graduated from the College of Charleston in 1975. The Lowcountry gave him many of the settings for his first, highly successful novel, *Edisto* (1984). He later studied at the University of Houston with Donald Barthelme before teaching creative writing at the University of Florida. Many of his writings are humorous, mixing high art with low camp. One reviewer described his style as "goofy, white-trash sensibility mixed with an ornate, almost Latinate syntax." In addition to *Edisto*, Powell has published novels—*A Woman Named Drown* (1987), *Edisto Revisited* (1996), and *Mrs. Hollingsworth's Men* (2000)—and collections of short stories—*Typical* (1991) and *Aliens of Affection* (1998). His stories have appeared in the *New Yorker*, *Harper's*, the *Paris Review*, *Grand Street*, *Esquire*, the *New York Times Book Review* and *Magazine*, and the *Oxford American*. Powell has won the Prix de Rome and a Whiting Writers' Award.

Then we went to town one last time, for no reason other than the good old days, which you could taste suddenly getting closer to their end and sweeter, like the last pieces of candy. We got up early on a Saturday I was not scheduled for a custody junket. Taurus had his car idling by the shack, mumbling little piffs of hot smoke into the cool cloud of fog which held everything still like a sharecropper photograph. We closed the green shutters on the sea window and one of them fell off, about breaking my foot. I said before they were sorry shutters anyway, which he got from Charleston, and they were sorry even though no dime-store stuff. Each weighed about a hundred pounds, which is why the one fell and why they never departed this world in the hurricanes which probably took a house or two out from under them. That's why Taurus could come to find them out of service yet still for sale, shutters stouter than planters' summer homes and stronger than a cotton economy. When that one fell in the sand, old and spent as it had to be, with scaling paint so thick it could cut your fingers like can lids, it looked like the top of a treasure chest to me. It was green and crooked, with sand already drifting into the louvers.

"Theenie's going to pitch a fit about cutting her wall open," I said.

"We'll put it back later."

"It won't matter," I said. "When she gets back and sees that hole, she'll put a mattress in it until we get a professional carpenter with tar paper and tin tabs and real lumber to shore it back up *right*."

"Hmmp," he said, just like Theenie. He was a cool jake to the end. We took off.

We had breakfast at an old hotel on the Citadel Square in Charleston. John Calhoun's out there in bronze about forty feet tall, and it seems he's doing something about the Confederacy by standing up there so very proudly, but I don't know what, because I don't know what he did, if he was a decent Reb or a bad one or anything. Looking out the cool dewy windows of the hotel, feeling the cold glass, I could still see that sad shutter in the sand.

We order these country-gentleman breakfasts, and this other waitress than ours comes to the table. She just comes up very close to it, even presses it with her front, and just kind of turns her lips or bites the inside corner of her mouth, tucking her lips to one side.

"Hey," she says to Taurus, but then she looks quickly at me, too. It's a funny way to show them, but I get the idea this girl has manners.

Taurus stands up and takes her hand and bows to kiss it, and she snatches it away with a laugh and sort of slow-motion socks him in the arm. Then she wiggles around like a tail wagging a dog. Her uniform rear had some jelly on it, which she might have already had or got wiggling, I don't know, but it was funny the way she moved sideways to him but watched him straight with large eyes. In fact, they were the largest eyes I had ever seen that weren't in a calf, and very blue or gray. I think I had a romantic stirring.

"Are we all set?" Taurus asked.

"I don't know," she said.

He doesn't say anything. She fiddles with the table a bit. "She's never been on a date, T."

Who? T.? I was figuring a bunch of things at the time, like the eminent sensation I had that this female third party had a lot to do with me, so I missed for a time the significance of "T." That's what she called him for short, I guessed, and it became my only clue to his real name, because that's all she called him and I never asked. But could he really *have* been named Taurus?

"Well," he says. "Simons here is just starting out himself."

"Oh, good." Then she adds, "That's romantic," almost so quiet you can't hear her.

"You get off at eleven? We'll be down there on the green."

We got those country-gentleman breakfasts with pork chops that had about an ounce of paprika and pepper on them, very tasty, and cut them up in white-sided chunks and pushed the rich broken egg yolks around, making the meat yellow. I was all of a sudden hungry as hell.

"What's happening?"

"We're going sailing," he told me. "With a boatful of willing gentlewomen from the low country."

"Holy God."

"Holy God is right."

Suddenly great old patinaed John Calhoun and the green shutters all vanished before what I was sure was the dawning of the real, present South, a new land full not of ghosts but of willing gentlewomen.

It didn't turn out so marvelous. It's like water-skiing, which is no fun until you know what you're doing. Same with kissing, etc. We picked up this girl from a house on the Battery. She was cute all right, a regular button of a girl. She jumped down the steps

in blue tennis shorts and a white cotton shirt with a tiny mono-
gram, her hair pulled back, making her face shinier than it might
have been without the tension, which was, I suspected, plenty
shiny. She had on blue Keds that looked tight too and little pom-
pom socks. She jumped in the car. For some reason, before I
could look at her face all I saw was those cinched-up shoes,
brand-new and looking as firm as shoe forms or hooves. I wondered if I was going to be a blockhead.

The trouble was, Taurus's girl was shabby where mine was
shiny, loose where mine was tight, and I had already taken a
heavy fall for her because of those jaw-breaker eyes. And she
was developed out. Now, I didn't hold that against mine, because
my burning worm was nothing to call the bureau of standards
and measures about either, but the whole effect of this big-eyed,
wobbling, nervous girl with giant bazongas had got to me, and
what I wanted was a little one just like her. What I had looked
like something at a recital.

"Oh, wait!" she cried, clapping her hand to her mouth. "Hi"
to me. "I forgot" to them. She dropped a pink orthodontic
retainer from the roof of her mouth and was out of the car and
up the steps and back, smiling, in one motion. "All set."

She and I got through names and grades before we reached the
water. We were about even on names—she was a double Jenkins
and I had my one-"m" Simons, plus the Manigault—but on
schools she had the edge, being at Mrs. Oldfield's famous institution for landed white girls, while I was in Bluffton Elementary
with the people. I was going to display some Great Books stunt-
work if she pressed about my not going to Cooper Boyd
Academy. But she didn't. She was nervous and smiling so hard
about nothing at all that every time I looked at her, it sort of hurt
my face. I hoped a little weather and salt on the boat would
knock the shine off and we could be regular. Her name was
Londie. Short for Altalondine Jenkins Jenkins.

At the yacht club we met a gigantic fat dude who was breathing with difficulty. He outfitted us with his boat, an air of a favor
he owed Taurus about the proceedings. He made sure to impress

Taurus with how irregular lending his boat was without *his* going. And then Taurus's girl came out of the yacht club changed into a purple swimsuit with plenty of everything very obvious and she a little self-conscious, which made her smile and do that dog-wobble ever so slightly. On the front of the suit was a brilliant whale dancing on its fluke and spouting white spume, the figure made of inlays of nylon stitched together in colors resembling a parrot. The fat guy stopped talking when he saw her.

I watched him while Taurus rigged the boat. He had been blubbering about tightening this and battening that and rules of the road, but now he was mostly pointing and grunting, half at Taurus and half at this girl. His wheezing picked up.

He stepped over to Taurus and said, "My health."

Taurus looked up.

"I'm worried about my health."

"What about it?" Taurus said.

He sucked in a big load of wind and said, "It's *deteriorating.*"

Taurus was holding a broken halyard and standing in three inches of stinking bilge water in the open ribs of the cockpit.

"What *isn't?*" he said.

"Good point! Very good point! Ah, sir!" shouted the wheezer. He laughed and then charged Taurus's girl, virtually shouting, "Young lady! There's a *whale* on your stomach!"

She bit her mouth sideways, stretched her suit outward a bit, and looked down at the colorful whale.

"Are you a"—he almost choked—"a *swimmer?*" With reverence in that word.

She looked at him and then at herself again, up and down, her legs, the whale, the bosom she could hardly see over. Now I was excited too, but the big guy was, I swear, fixing to collapse drooling, and she was getting red in the face. He was about two inches from her and standing like Santa Claus, rocked back on his heels with an enormous gut stuck out, which he rubbed absently with tiny hands, and he looked at her through eyes squinted shut with fat, seething, when Taurus said to her, "In the boat." And to me,

"Cast off." She did, I did, Londie jumped in as light and precise as a fawn, and we motored out of the club.

That was about the biggest adventure of the day. It got a little rough, but nobody puked. We kept our stomachs full with cold Coca-Cola and nice big chunks of ice. Coke can taste very good in salty conditions, I've noticed.

We went to Fig Island, which is one island too small for the Arabs to bother to take. It was nice. We played in the water. Londie and I worked on our kissing nerve by trying to swim at each other underwater and embrace and then kiss, but each time one or both of us burst out laughing in embarrassment before we got our lips situated, big blasts of bubble obliterating the target and the moment, and we'd have to surface for air and laugh and laugh more to conceal how scared we were to actually do it. And then I saw something that really took the wind out of my sails.

There was Taurus and his girl about a hundred yards away in chest-deep water, and she had her arms at full length draped on his shoulders, and maybe it was a trick of light and water or something but I swear I saw large pale surfaces between them and I thought it was her tits floating. It destroyed our game, made it so silly. I don't even know if it was her tits, if boobs even float like that, if it wasn't a fish belly. But the idea was enough. Me and old A'londine was way down in the minors, so I suggested we walk the island.

It had a shell ring. That's a ring of oystershells piled about head-high in a circle about fifty yards across. Indians made them, they say for ceremonies and whatnot, and of course even live sacrifices get bandied about, but my information is that they don't really know. The rock hounds and anthropods come out and remove chunks of the rings like bites out of a doughnut, but I don't think they ever find anything but oystershells. The digs are all old-looking. My guess is it's where the Indians had their oyster roasts, and a fine way to use the shells too, because it cuts out the wind for 360 degrees.

Anyway, we thought about the ghosts of Indians and rumrunners and all those old things that took place on a coast, and we didn't really square off for the kissing like we wanted to. Just became regular jake friends while Taurus, etc. I felt little.

But at least he went to bat for me, and if I whiffed, it wasn't his fault, maybe not my fault, certainly not button-nosed Altalondine Jenkins's fault, and most certainly not that big wobbly blessing's fault, for if ever there was a walking incitement to riot she was it. Call her my first love, fine with me.

I think that was his plan, really, to show me not cutiecakes but what you can find if you look for genteel Diane Parkers—big, wonderful, warm girls who are just a hint upset about things. A smudge of abandon. Maybe that's my motto. Me and old Mike can team up. He can worry about being an ignoramus and I can worry about the round, wonderful girls with their edges ruined by life's little disasters, who remain solid and tough in their drive to feel good—to themselves and to you—and offer a vision of snug harbor.

from *Rich in Love*

JOSEPHINE HUMPHREYS (1945–)

Josephine Humphreys grew up in Charleston, where she attended Ashley Hall School. She studied with novelist Reynolds Price at Duke University, from which she graduated, and attended the University of Texas and Yale University. She has written four novels, all but one based in the Charleston area: *Dreams of Sleep* (1985), for which she received the Ernest Hemingway Foundation Award for first fiction; *Rich in Love* (1987), from which the excerpt below is taken and which became a motion picture filmed in Mt. Pleasant and Charleston; *The Fireman's Fair* (1991); and *Nowhere Else on Earth* (2000), a Civil War tale that takes place in North Carolina, and which won the Southern Book Award. Humphreys's books present evocative landscapes and strong, iconoclastic characters addressing—or trying to avoid—the kinds of issues that change people's lives.

Humphreys continues to live in the Charleston area, an active participant in the life of the region. A personal essay, accompanied by family photographs of the author and her sisters, appears in *A World Unsuspected: Portraits of Southern Childhood* (1987), edited by Alex Harris, which also contains an essay by Padgett Powell. She has received fellowships from the Woodrow Wilson, Danforth, and Guggenheim foundations, and was inducted into the South Carolina Academy of Authors in 1994.

In old cities there are always statues. Charleston had John C. Calhoun, Henry Timrod (Poet of the Confederacy), and a toga-clad woman who was meant to be Confederate Motherhood, sending her naked son into battle with the Yankees.

But my favorite was Osceola, the Seminole chief. Down the road from our house was Fort Moultrie, where his statue rose from the top of a hill, looking seaward. I imagined his view, over the brick fort and the housetops of red and silver, the dark cumulus trees, to the slice of white dunes, blue water, Fort Sumter, and finally in the distance a black, jagged, double line of rocks, jetties that held the channel for incoming ships. From his perch he watched for whatever would be coming over the horizon—freighters, shrimpboats, seabirds, the sun and moon.

Bees lived in him. They appeared to get in through a hole in his neck, which made me wonder if he was hollow. And if hollow, was he filled with honey? He never flinched, in that wild swarm. I had grown up under his watch, and he had come to be a landmark and something of a hero to me, my idea of what a man should be. A warrior, secretly filled with sweetness.

In life Osceola had been betrayed in Florida, captured under a flag of truce, and sent here as a prisoner, where he died under what I considered suspicious circumstances. Caught a cold and died, they said. Well—perhaps. But in the fort was a portrait that the government was careful to get painted of him just weeks before he caught the fatal cold. He knew something was afoot, you can tell from the portrait. The eyes have the gentle serenity of a man who sees fools and traitors all around him. When he died, the attending physician sawed off his head and took it home to Savannah, where he pickled it and hung it on his son's bedpost whenever the child misbehaved. I swear this is true. The headless body was buried at the fort. A ten-foot cypress representation of the head in profile can now be seen marking the entrance to Osceola Pointe, a bankrupt development on the bypass.

You won't find the whole Osceola story in the history books, of course. I discovered these facts in the South Carolina Room at the library, where I worked on Friday afternoons. The room was kept locked—they said, to keep out winos and children. But I made some discoveries in that room, and I think I know the real reason they locked it. There was a lot of history in there that they didn't want to let out. . . .

We drove across the bridge and into the city, down to the Carolina Yacht Club. In the parking lot Wayne pulled right up to the steps and parked next to two Jaguars with cellular phones. "They're married," he said, standing between the cars and laying each hand on a Jaguar fender. "Guy practices with my father. He drives the car a year, then gives it to his wife. His is always a year newer than hers."

Dr. Frobiness was waiting in the lounge. He was puzzled to see me, and only vaguely remembered meeting me before, but it did not seem to bother him that I had come along. We went through the buffet line in the dining room. I helped myself to crab casserole, fried flounder, shrimp pie, rice, civvy beans and yellow squash. Wayne stared at my plate. His own contained a slice of watermelon, which he had sawed off the centerpiece, a watermelon cut in the shape of a basket and filled with fruit-balls.

I shrugged. I couldn't help loading up, the food was so pretty, and my stomach was hurting. There was the long table and its thick dusky rose cloth, warm lights bathing the dishes in gold. I was adding a crab cleverly deviled in its own shell, when I saw that behind the buffet table was an eight-foot aquarium in which large gray bulldog-faced fish swam slowly from one end to another and around to the start again. I could not tell how it was that they achieved forward motion; they seemed never to flutter their tails or twist their thick bodies, but steadily drifted forward, making the circuit of the tank.

Ordinarily I loved the Yacht Club. From its porch you could see across the harbor to Mt. Pleasant, the very reverse of the view I had seen that morning. You could sit in the dark, cool dining room and eat old-fashioned food and look out into the dazzling sun where young Townsends and Pringles in sailing attire skippered their Sunfish back and forth, barely missing the dock. People eating there were always quiet and well-behaved. There was a high turnover in waiters, but often one of them was a Wando High black guy who would bring me double portions of the charlotte russe. But today I didn't feel right in there. The aquarium was a new addition. It is hard to eat seafood while seafood swims in a tank before your eyes, especially when it swims glumly, the corners of its mouth downturned.

Dr. Frobiness started right in on Wayne once we were seated and had been served our iced tea. Wayne was ready to bolt. He had never liked the Yacht Club. I watched him squirm. Everything his father said or did annoyed him, down to the way Dr. Frobiness pronounced words and blinked his eyes. You know a relationship has deteriorated past the point of salvage when one person detests another's gestures.

"I understand your interest in the downtrodden," Dr. Frobiness said. "I like to think that as a young man I was drawn to medicine for similar humanitarian reasons. But look at yourself, son. Look at yourself. What's happening to you? Don't allow yourself to be pulled into their world. That's the danger. You've got to stay within your own world and help from there, not leap in with these people." He blotted his lips with the dusky rose napkin. Wayne's eyes were glued to the napkin: up to the mouth, blot, blot, down to the lap. Wayne coughed.

"Now, I have a proposal to make." Dr. Frobiness paused for Wayne to respond, but Wayne was staring at something in the vicinity of his father's hand. "What I propose is this," his father said. "You take the remainder of the summer and do with it what you will. Continue at the Center if you like. Then in September you enroll at the College of Charleston. I know it's not Sewanee, but at this point I'll settle for any four-year accredited institution. I'll pick up the tab for tuition and rent. You get some sort of job, a *paying* job, to cover food and transportation. I'll expect you to maintain a decent average, but nothing spectacular. Just stay in, that's all I hope for. I've lowered my sights considerably." He smiled at me. "What do you think, Lucille? A new bachelor apartment? Maybe you can help me get this young man on the right track."

"What is that on your finger?" Wayne said.

Dr. Frobiness looked at his hand. "It's a ring," he said.

Wayne was aghast. "What for?"

"Why, for nothing. A ring to wear."

"That's diamond in it."

"Just a small one. It was a good investment. It's called a Man's Diamond. It was advertised in the *New Yorker*. A little less than two carats, but high quality. But, ah, look, son, if you don't mind, don't mention this to your mother. It might upset her."

"Dad, she said you were in debt because of setting up the new office and all the expenses to build up the practice."

"I am, I am. She's absolutely correct. My God, the cost of secretarial equipment alone was over fifteen thousand, and I want you to guess how much I have to pay for liability insurance. Guess."

"I couldn't begin to."

"No, just take a wild guess. What do you think I have to cough up?"

"I don't know." Wayne was stubborn. I knew he wouldn't guess.

"Take a guess, son," Dr. Frobiness insisted.

"A million dollars," I said.

"Heh, no, little lady, not quite that much. No, I'm ponying up *twenty-one thousand* dollars a year for insurance." He pronounced the first syllable of "thousand" with a wide open mouth, and made his eyes big.

"Holy smoke," I said, to be polite. In truth, I thought this was a pretty good bargain. Suppose he botched a liposuction or misaligned an implant? If I were the insurance company, I would not have insured Dr. Frobiness for any amount.

He went on to say that some fathers, himself and Ronald Reagan included, had a lot at stake in the careers of their sons. It wasn't as if the sons of such fathers were free agents. "My heart aches for the President," he said.

"Excuse me," I said. I wanted seconds before they wheeled the roast beef away. It was already three o'clock, and the steamboat round was carved down like a saddle. The waiter in charge of slicing meat was standing over by the aquarium with two other waiters. I waited politely by the meat, plate in hand, but they were engaged in an argument, and a partially melted seahorse made of ice stood between me and them. They didn't notice me. One said, "Maître d' said, get that mother *out*." Another said, "Get him out how?" "I don't know, but get him out." "Shit, man, I ain't reaching my hand in there. It's crabs in there." "He ain't dead yet anyhow." "Sure he is." "Naw, he ain't. His gills is opening and closing, that's his breathing." "Any fish that is upside down is dead in my book." "Said get him out fast before a member sees him." "Get him out, James." "Go for it, James." "All *right, James.*"

From behind the ice sculpture I watched as James took the roast beef fork and speared the ailing bulldog-fish. It was an expert move—not a splash, not a sound. The fish was spirited into the kitchen. James returned to the roast beef table where he carved me a slice of well-done gray beef. I thought I recognized him from school, maybe the basketball team; but I couldn't be sure, he was dressed in a waiter's black pants and coat, and he didn't let on that he saw anything recognizable in me. He only looked at the meat and sawed; he used a regular fork to hold it down, I was glad to see.

When I got back to my seat, I looked at my roast beef and realized I could not eat it. I put my napkin casually across the plate. Probably there was not a good filter system in the tank, not enough oxygen. The fish got sluggish, going round; lost whatever dim sort of consciousness fish possess; and bellied up.

"Wayne," I started to say, but he was gazing at his father, who was writing his club number on the check.

"We are all going to have to tighten our belts," Dr. Frobiness said. "For the time being. I can manage the college tuition and an apartment for you, but that's about it. Your mother's going to have to find an apartment as well as some kind of job. Has she discussed this with you?"

Wayne said nothing.

Dr. Frobiness said, "I spoke with a radiologist whose wife runs a dress shop. She has several gals helping her out part-time, and she needs somebody else in the afternoons."

"Lucille," Wayne said sharply to me. "Do you feel sick?"

"Mmmm."

"Lucille throws up at the drop of a hat," Wayne said.

Dr. Frobiness looked alarmed. He glanced around at the few remaining diners.

"Now?" Wayne said. I nodded. "Excuse us, Dad. We'll talk later." He ushered me out the door and onto the porch, down the steps and into the Ram Charger.

"Fantastic," Wayne said. "What a girl."

"I need air."

"Me, too. Me, too. God*damn*. I'm sorry you had to witness that."

"I need to get some fresh air or I'm going to be sick."

"Sick? I thought you were faking. I thought you were doing it to get me out of there."

"No. The fish in the aquarium made me dizzy."

"You look awful. Your skin is clammy. Here, let's get out and walk down the dock." He ran around to my side, opened the door, and gave me a hand down. My knees wobbled.

"I never thought your father was the type for a diamond ring," I said.

"He's converting to tangibles. Hidable tangibles. Come the day of reckoning, he turns over his financial records for a settlement, and there won't be as much on paper as she thought."

"I see."

A red Sunfish hit a green Sunfish, and the young sailors hollered blame at each other. They appeared to be no older than nine or ten. Rich people are careless with their children, I observed. A chill ran down my spine to think of letting a child go alone into the harbor on a small plank with a tiny sail. There were tankers and freighters out there. But the children seemed perfectly at ease, even when they wrecked or capsized, and they would be back at it again tomorrow.

"Lucille, give me another chance." He spoke without looking at me. He leaned on the railing and watched the children. "I'm desperate," he said.

Well, that broke me because I knew it was the truth. His bow tie was too small for his neck and had lost its grip on one side. His pain was bright, shining in his eyes and skin and shoulders. I made a mistake that girls commonly make. Out of a sense of honor (he was a good boy who deserved something from a good girl) I said yes. It was the generous and friendly thing to do, but it was a mistake. We agreed to meet the next night on the dock in front of my house. He looked happy.

"Longitude Lane"

AUGUST KLEINZAHLER (1949–)

August Kleinzahler, who has Charleston cousins, was born in Jersey City and educated at the Horace Mann School, alma mater of William Carlos Williams and Jack Kerouac. He attended the University of Wisconsin and the University of Victoria (British Columbia). The former poet laureate of Fort Lee, New Jersey, he has published several volumes of poetry, including *Earthquake Weather* (1989), which was nominated for the National Book Critics Circle Award; *Green Sees Things in Waves: Poems* (1999), where the poem below was first published; and *The Strange Hours Travelers Keep* (2004), winner of the International Griffin Poetry Prize. He has been the recipient of a Guggenheim Fellowship in poetry, the Lila Acheson Wallace Reader's Digest Award for Poetry, an Academy Award in Literature from the American Academy of Arts and Letters, and a Berlin Prize Fellowship. Allen Ginsberg has written, "August Kleinzahler's verse line is always precise, concrete, intelligent and rare—that quality of 'chiseled' verse memorable in Basil Bunting's and Ezra Pound's work. A loner, a genius." Kleinzahler resides in San Francisco.

The oleander on Longitude Lane
flares among the langours and fevers of June
below the south-facing piazzas
the sea breezes find
or don't quite find
along the corridors of ivy-colored brick
Carolina gray brick and wrought iron
that wind away inland from the Battery

History just sits out there, a kind of weather
in the harbor and beyond
on the plantations and through the low country

with its bogs and herons
its skirmishes never forgotten

And the manners in town so antique, so elegant
an underwater Kabuki in summer dress
The old families and Huguenot names

The long siege and storied cannondes

Turkey buzzards over the market
water rats under the pantry

The precious settee and the wild, wild daughters

from *Prince of Tides*

PAT CONROY (1945–   )

Pat Conroy, a native of Atlanta, grew up in a military family in Beaufort, South Carolina, and graduated from The Citadel. He lived for a time in Atlanta and California and now resides on Fripp Island, near Beaufort. He is one of the most widely read living American novelists, his books regularly appearing on best-seller lists. His novels include *The Great Santini* (1976), *The Lords of Discipline* (1980), *The Prince of Tides* (1986), *Beach Music* (1995) and *South of Broad* (2009). Many of them have been made into successful movies.

Much of Conroy's body of work is lightly fictionalized autobiography, including his earliest books *The Boo* (1970), whose main character is based on Lt. Col. Thomas Nugent Courvoisie, assistant commandant of cadets at The Citadel when Conroy attended the school, and *The Water Is Wide* (1972), about Conroy's experiences teaching on Daufuskie Island, South Carolina. In 2002 he published a nonfiction account of his Citadel basketball team's 1966–67 season, *My Losing Season*.

The Prince of Tides includes beautiful descriptions of the Lowcountry's tidal marshlands. The passage chosen for this volume, the story of an albino porpoise, is firmly based in fact: an albino bottlenose dolphin named Carolina Snowball was frequently sighted in the waters of St. Helena Sound in the late 1950s and early '60s. The porpoise was eventually captured by officials from the Miami Seaquarium, against the wishes of the local populace, and died shortly afterward in captivity.

In 1999 Conroy received the inaugural Stanley W. Lindberg Award for significant contributions to the literary heritage of Georgia. He was inducted into the South Carolina Academy of Authors in 1988.

My wound is geography. It is also my anchorage, my port of call.

I grew up slowly beside the tides and marshes of Colleton; my arms were tawny and strong from working long days on the shrimp boat in the blazing South Carolina heat. Because I was a Wingo, I worked as soon as I could walk; I could pick a blue crab clean when I was five. I had killed my first deer by the age of seven, and at nine was regularly putting meat on my family's table. I was born and raised on a Carolina sea island and I carried the sunshine of the low-country, inked in dark gold, on my back and shoulders. As a boy I was happy above the channels, navigating a small boat between the sandbars with their quiet nation of oysters exposed on the brown flats at the low watermark. I knew every shrimper by name, and they knew me and sounded their horns when they passed me fishing in the river.

My family lived in splendid isolation on Melrose Island in a small white house my grandfather had helped build. The house faced the inland waterway, and the town of Colleton could be seen down the river, its white mansions set like chess pieces above the marsh. Melrose Island was a lozenge-shaped piece of land of twelve hundred acres surrounded on four sides by salt rivers and creeks. The island country where I grew up was a fertile, semitropical archipelago that gradually softened up the ocean for the grand surprise of the continent that followed. Melrose was only one of sixty sea islands in Colleton County. At the eastern edge of the county lay six barrier islands shaped by their daily encounters with the Atlantic. The other sea islands, like Melrose, enscarved by vast expanses of marshland, were the green sanctuaries where brown and white shrimp came to spawn in their given seasons. When they came, my father and other men like him were waiting in their fine and lovely boats.

To describe our growing up in the lowcountry of South Carolina, I would have to take you to the marsh on a spring day, flush the great blue heron from its silent occupation, scatter marsh hens as we sink to our knees in mud, open you an oyster with a pocketknife and feed it to you from the shell and say, "There. That taste. That's the taste of my childhood." I would say, "Breathe deeply," and you would breathe and remember that smell for the rest of your life, the bold, fecund aroma of the tidal marsh, exquisite and sensual, the smell of the South in heat, a smell like new milk, semen, and spilled wine, all perfumed with seawater. My soul grazes like a lamb on the beauty of indrawn tides.

I am a patriot of a singular geography of the planet; I speak of my country religiously; I am proud of its landscape. I walk through the traffic of cities cautiously, always nimble and on the alert, because my heart belongs in the marshlands. The boy in me still carries the memories of those days when I lifted crab pots out of the Colleton River before dawn, when I was shaped by life on the river, part child, part sacristan of tides.

I was ten when I first saw the white porpoise known as Carolina Snow following our shrimp boat as we returned to the dock after a day dragging the beaches along Spaulding Point. It was the only white porpoise ever sighted along the Atlantic seaboard in the memories of the shrimping brotherhood, and some said the only white porpoise ever to inhabit the earth. Throughout Colleton County, with its endless miles of salt rivers and tidal creeks, the sighting of the Snow was always cause for wonder. She was never seen with other porpoises, and some shrimpers, like my father, surmised that porpoises, like humans, were not kind to their freaks and that the Snow was sentenced by her remarkable whiteness to wander the green waters of Colleton, exiled and solitary. That first day, she followed us almost all the way to the bridge before she turned back toward the sea. Snow lent to the county a sense of specialness, and all who saw her remembered the first moment for the rest of their lives. It was like being touched by a recognition that the sea would never forfeit its power to create and astonish.

Through the years, the Snow had become a symbol of luck in our town. Colleton would prosper and flourish as long as the Snow honored these waters with her visitations. There are times when she disappeared for long periods and then suddenly would return to the waters of the Carolina sea islands. Even the paper noticed her comings and goings. Her entrance into the main channel and her slow, sensual passage through the town would bring the entire citizenry to the river's banks. Commerce would cease and collectively the people of the town would stop what they were doing to acknowledge her return. She visited the main river rarely, and because of its rarity, her appearance was a precious town-stopping thing. She approached us always as a symbol, monarch, and gift; she approached us always alone, banished, and the people on the shore, calling her by name, shouting out in greeting, acknowledging her divine white passage, formed the only family she would ever know.

Grandpa started the motor and headed the small boat out toward the channel. The Snow rose out of the river ahead of us, her back lilying in the dimming light.

"She's going our way," Grandpa said, steering the boat toward her. "Now if that ain't proof of a living God then nothing is. You'd think he'd be satisfied with just a plain porpoise. That's as beautiful as any creature on earth. But no, he's still up there dreaming up things even more beautiful to please man's eye."

"I've never seen her this close," Savannah said. "She's pure white, like a tablecloth."

But it was not a pure white we were seeing when she surfaced twenty yards from us. Faint ores of colors shimmered across her back as she cut through the water, a brief silvering of her fins, evanescent color that could not be sustained. You knew she could never be the same color twice.

We watched her as she circled the boat, saw her beneath us, and she flowed like milk through water. Rising, she hung suspended, concolorous with peaches and high-risen moons, then down as milk again.

These are the quicksilver moments of my childhood I cannot recapture entirely. Irresistible and emblematic, I can recall them only in fragments and shivers of the heart. There is a river, the town, my grandfather steering a boat through the channel, my sister fixed in that suspended rapture she would later translate into her strongest poems, the metallic perfume of harvested oysters, the belling voices of children on the shore. . . When the white porpoise comes there is all this and transfiguration too. In dreams, the porpoise remains in memory's waters, a pale divinity who nourishes the fire and deepest cold of all the black waters of my history. There were many things wrong with my childhood but the river was not one of them, nor can the inestimable riches it imparted be traded or sold.

As we passed under the bridge I looked back and saw the shadows of people who had gathered to watch the Snow's passage. Their heads appeared in clusters above the bridge's cement railing, at intervals, like the beads of a damaged rosary. I heard the voice of a small girl begging the Snow to return beneath the bridge. Men and women began assembling on the floating docks, which bobbed in the moving tide; they were all pointing toward the last spot the porpoise had surfaced.

When the white porpoise came, it was for my grandfather like seeing the white smile of God coming up at him from below.

"Thank you, God," my grandfather said behind us in one of the unrehearsed prayers that burst naturally from him when he was deeply moved by the external world. "Thank you so much for this."

I turned. My sister turned. And that good man smiled at us.

Later, long after my grandfather was dead, I would regret that I could never be the kind of man that he was. Though I adored him as a child and found myself attracted to the safe protectorate of his soft, uncritical maleness, I never wholly appreciated him. I did not know how to cherish sanctity; I had no way of honoring, of giving small voice to the praise of such natural innocence, such generous simplicity. Now I know that a part of me would like to have traveled the world as he traveled it, a jester of burning faith, a fool and a forest prince brimming with the love of God. I would like to have walked his southern world, thanking God for oysters and porpoises, praising God for birdsong and sheet lightning, and seeing God reflected in pools of creek water and the eyes of stray cats. I would like to have talked to yard dogs and tanagers as if they were my friends and fellow travelers along the sun-tortured highways, intoxicated with a love of God, swollen with charity like a rainbow, in the thoughtless mingling of its hues, connecting two distant fields in its glorious arc. I would like to have seen the world with eyes incapable of anything but wonder, and with a tongue fluent only in praise.

It was almost summer when the strangers arrived by boat in Colleton and began their long, inexorable pursuit of the white porpoise. My mother was baking bread and the suffusion of that exquisite fragrance of the loaves and roses turned our house into a vial of the most harmonious seasonal incense. She took the bread fresh from the oven, then slathered it with butter and honey. We took it steaming in our hands down to the dock to eat, the buttery honey running through our fingers. We attracted the ornery attention of every yellow jacket in our yard, and it took nerve to let them walk on our hands, gorging themselves on the drippings from our bread. They turned our hands into gardens and orchards and hives. My mother brought the lid of a mayonnaise jar full of sugar water down to the dock to appease the yellow jackets and let us eat in peace.

We had almost finished the bread when we saw the boat, *The Amberjack*, bearing Florida registry, move through the channels of Colleton River. No gulls followed the boat, so we were certain it was not a fishing vessel. It lacked the clean, luxurious lines of a yacht, yet there was a visible crew of six men whose sun-stained burnt-amber color announced them as veteran mariners. We would learn the same day that it was the first boat ever to enter South Carolina waters whose function was to keep fish alive.

The crew of the *Amberjack* were not secretive about their mission and their business in these waters was known all over Colleton late that afternoon. Captain Otto Blair told a reporter from the *Gazette* that the Miami Seaquarium had received a letter from a Colleton citizen, who wished to remain anonymous, that an albino porpoise frequented the waters around Colleton.

Captain Blair and his crew planned to capture the porpoise, then transport it back to Miami, where it would be both a tourist attraction and a subject for scientific inquiry. The crew of the *Amberjack* had come to Colleton in the interest of science, as marine biologists, inspired by a report that the rarest creature in the seven seas was a daily sight to the people of the lowcountry.

They may have known all there was to know about porpoises and their habits, but they had badly misjudged the character of the people they would find in the lower part of South Carolina. The citizens of Colleton were about to give them lessons free of charge. A collective shiver of rage passed invisibly through Colleton; the town was watchful and alarmed. The plot to steal Carolina Snow was an aberrant, unspeakable act to us. By accident, they had brought the rare savor of solidarity to our shores. They would feel the full weight of our dissent.

To them the white porpoise was a curiosity of science; to us she was the disclosure of the unutterable beauty and generosity of God among us, the proof of magic, and the ecstasy of art.

The white porpoise was something worthy to fight for.

The *Amberjack*, mimicking the habits of the shrimpers, moved out early the next morning, but it did not sight the porpoise that day and it set no nets. The men returned to the shrimp dock grim-lipped and eager for rumors about recent sightings of the Snow. They were met with silence.

After the third day, Luke and I met their boat and listened to the crew talk about the long fruitless days on the river, trying to sight the white porpoise. Already, they were feeling the eloquent heft of the town's censure and they seemed eager to talk to Luke and me, to extract any information about the porpoise they could from us.

Captain Blair brought Luke and me on board the *Amberjack* and showed us the holding tank on the main deck where specimens were kept alive until they could reach the aquariums in Miami. He showed us the half mile of nets that they would use to encircle the porpoise. A man's hand could pass easily through the meshing of their nets. The captain was a cordial middle-aged man and the sun had burned deep lines in his face, like tread marks. In a soft, barely discernible voice he told us how they trained a porpoise to eat dead fish after a capture. A porpoise would fast for two weeks or more before it would deign to feed on prey it would ignore in the wild. The greatest danger in the capture of a porpoise was that the animal would become entangled in the nets and drown. Hunting porpoises required a swift and skilled crew to ensure that drowning did not occur. He then showed us the foam rubber mattresses they laid the porpoises on once they got them on board.

"Why don't you just throw them in the pool, Captain?" I asked.

"We do, usually, but sometimes we've got sharks in the pool and sometimes a porpoise will hurt himself thrashing around in a pool that small. Often it's better to just lie 'em down on these mattresses and keep splashing 'em with seawater so their skin won't dry out. We move 'em from side to side to keep their circulation right and that's about all there is to it."

"How long can they live out of the water?" Luke asked.

"I don't rightly know, son," the captain answered. "The longest I ever kept one out of the water was five days, but he made it back to Miami just fine. They're hardy creatures. When's the last time you boys spotted Moby in these waters?"

"Moby?" Luke said. "Her name is Snow. Carolina Snow."

"That's what they've named her down at Miami, boys. Moby Porpoise. Some guy in the publicity department came up with that one."

"That's the dumbest name I've ever heard," Luke said.

"It'll bring the tourists running, son," Captain Blair answered.

"Speaking of tourists, a whole boatful spotted the Snow yesterday morning in Charleston Harbor as they were heading out for Fort Sumter," said Luke.

"Are you sure, son?" the captain asked, and one of the crewmen leapt to his feet to hear the rest of the conversation.

"I didn't see it," Luke said, "but I heard it on the radio."

The *Amberjack* left for Charleston harbor the next day, cruising the Ashley and the Cooper Rivers looking for signs of the white porpoise. For three days they searched the waters around Wappoo Creek and the Elliott Cut before they realized that my brother Luke was a liar. They had also taught my brother how to keep a porpoise alive if the need ever arose.

The call to arms between the *Amberjack* crew and the town did not begin in earnest until the evening in June when the crew tried to capture the white porpoise in full view of the town. They had sighted the Snow in Colleton Sound, in water much too deep to set their nets for a successful capture. All day, they had followed the porpoise, remaining a discreet distance behind her, stalking her with infinite patience until she began moving into the shallower rivers and creeks.

Just as the crew tracked the porpoise, the shrimpers of the town kept issuing reports on the position of the *Amberjack* on their shortwave radios. Whenever the boat changed course, the eyes of the shrimp fleet noted and remarked upon the shift of position, and the airwaves filled up with the voice of the shrimpers passing messages from boat to boat, from boat to town. The shrimpers' wives, monitoring their own radios, then got on the telephone to spread the news. The *Amberjack* could not move through county waters without its exact bearing being reported to a regiment of secret listeners.

"*Amberjack* turning into Yemassee Creek," we heard one day through the static of the radio my mother kept above the kitchen sink. "Don't look like they found any Snow today."

"Miami Beach just left Yemassee Creek and appears to be settin' to poke around the Harper Dogleg up by Goat Island."

The town carefully listened to these frequent intelligence reports of the shrimpers. For a week the white porpoise did not appear, and when she did it was one of the shrimpers who alerted the town.

"This is Captain Willard Plunkett and Miami Beach has got the Snow in sight. They are pursuing her up the Colleton River and the crew is preparing the nets on deck. It looks like Snow is heading for a visit to town."

Word passed through the town in the old quicksilvering of rumor, and the prefigured power of that rumor lured the whole town to the river's edge. People kept their eyes on the river and talked quietly. The sheriff pulled into the parking lot behind the bank and monitored the shrimpers' reports. The eyes of the town were fixed on the bend in the Colleton Rivers where the *Amberjack* would make its appearance. That bend was a mile from the point where the river joined three of its sister rivers and bloomed into a sound.

For twenty minutes we waited for the *Amberjack* to make the turn, and when it did a collective groan rose up in the throats of us all. The boat was riding high above the marsh on an incoming tide. One of the crewmen stood on the foredeck with a pair of binoculars trained on the water in front of the boat. He stood perfectly still, rapt and statuesque, his complete immersion a testament to the passion he brought to the task.

Luke, Savannah, and I watched from the bridge, along with several hundred of our neighbors who had gathered to witness the moment of capture of the town's living symbol of good luck. The town was only curious until we saw Carolina Snow make her own luxurious appearance as she rounded the last curve of the river and began her silken, fabulous promenade through the town. She silvered as the sunlight caught her pale fin buttering through the crest of a small wave. In her movement through town she achieved a fragile sublimity, so unaware was she of her vulnerability. Burnished by perfect light, she dazzled us again with her complete and ambient beauty. Her dorsal fin broke the surface like a white chevron a hundred yards nearer the bridge, and to our surprise, the town cheered spontaneously and the apotheosis of the white porpoise was fully achieved. The ensign of Colleton's wrath unfurled in the secret winds and our status as passive observers changed imperceptibly as a battle cry, unknown to any of us, formed on our lips. All the mottoes and passwords of engagement appeared like fiery graffiti on the armorial bearings of the town's unconscious. The porpoise disappeared again, then rose up, arcing toward the applause that greeted her sounding. She was mysterious and lunar. Her color was a delicate alchemy of lily and mother-of-pearl. The porpoise passed argentine beneath the sun-struck waters. Then we looked up and saw the *Amberjack* gaining ground on the Snow and the crew getting the nets into a small boat they were going to lower into the water.

The town needed a warrior and I was surprised to find him standing beside me.

Traffic jammed the bridge as drivers simply parked their cars and went to the bridge's railing to watch the capture of the porpoise. A truck loaded down with tomatoes from one of Reese Newbury's farms was stuck on the bridge and the driver was leaning on his horn in vain, trying to get the other drivers back into their cars.

I heard Luke whisper to himself, "No. It just ain't right," and he left my side and mounted the back of the truck and began to toss crates of tomatoes down among the crowd. I thought Luke had gone crazy. But suddenly I understood, and Savannah and I bashed a crate of tomatoes open and began to pass them along the railing. The driver got out and screamed for Luke to stop, but Luke ignored him and continued passing the wooden crates down to the outstretched arms of his friends and neighbors. The driver's voice grew more and more frantic as people began taking tire tools from their trunks and splitting the crates wide open. The sheriff's car moved out of the parking lot and headed toward the Charleston highway on the opposite side of town.

When the *Amberjack* neared the bridge, two hundred tomatoes hit the deck in a green fusillade that put the man with the binoculars to his knees. The tomatoes were hard and green and one of the crewmen working on the nets near the aft of the boat was holding his nose, blood leaking through his fingers. The second salvo of tomatoes followed soon afterward and the crew scrambled, dazed and insensible, toward the safety of the hold and cabin. A tire tool cracked against a lifeboat and the crowd roared its approval. Boxes of tomatoes were passed down the line, the driver still screaming and not a single soul listening to his pleadings.

The *Amberjack* disappeared beneath the bridge and two hundred people crossed to the other side in a delirious, headlong rush. When the boat reappeared we showered it with tomatoes again, like archers on high ground pouring arrows on an ill-deployed infantry. Savannah was throwing hard and with accuracy, finding her own good rhythm, her own style. She was screaming with pure pleasure. Luke threw a whole crate of tomatoes and it smashed on the rear deck, sending ruined tomatoes skittering like marbles toward the battened-down hold.

The *Amberjack* pulled out of range of all but the strongest arms when the porpoise, in a thoughtless gesture of self-preservation, reversed her course and turned back toward the town, passing the boat trailing her on its starboard side. She returned to our applause and our advocacy. We watched her move beneath the waters below the bridge, grizzling the bright waves like some abstract dream of ivory. When the boat made its long, hesitant turn in the river, even more crates of tomatoes were passed through the mob. By this time, even the truck driver had surrendered to whatever mass hysteria had possessed the rest of us and he stood with his arm cocked, holding a tomato, anticipating with the rest of us the *Amberjack*'s imminent return. The boat started back for the bridge, then turned abruptly away from us and moved north on the Colleton River as Carolina Snow, the only white porpoise on our planet, moved back toward the Atlantic.

The next day the town council passed a resolution enfranchising Carolina Snow as a citizen of Colleton County and making it a felony for anyone to remove her from county waters. At the same time, the South Carolina state legislature passed a similar law rendering it a felony for anyone to remove genus *Phocaena* or genus *Tursiops* from the waters of Colleton County. In less than twenty-four hours, Colleton County became the only place in the world where it was a crime to capture a porpoise.

Captain Blair went straight to the sheriff's office when he reached the shrimp dock that night and demanded that Sheriff Lucas arrest everyone who had thrown a tomato at the *Amberjack*. Unfortunately, Captain Blair could not provide the sheriff with a single name of even one of the miscreants, and the sheriff, after making several phone calls, could produce four witnesses who would swear in a court of law that no one had been on the bridge when the *Amberjack* passed beneath it.

"Then how did I get a hundred pounds of tomatoes on the deck of my boat?" the captain had asked.

And in a laconic reply that was well received in each Colleton household, the sheriff had answered, "It's tomato season, Captain. Those damn things will grow anywhere."

But the men from Miami quickly recovered their will and developed a new plan for the capture of the porpoise. They kept out of sight of the town and did not enter the main channel of the Colleton River again. They began to hunt the outer territorial limits of the county, waiting for that perfect moment when the Snow would wander out of county waters and beyond the protection of those newly contracted laws. But the *Amberjack* was shadowed by boats from the South Carolina Game and Fish Commission and by a small flotilla of recreational boats commanded by the women and children of the town. Whenever the *Amberjack* picked up the trail of the porpoise, the small crafts would maneuver themselves between the porpoise and the pursuing vessel and slow their motors. The *Amberjack* would try to weave between the boats, but these women and children of Colleton had handled small boats all their lives. They would interfere with the Florida boat's progress until the white porpoise slipped away in the enfolding tides of Colleton Sound.

Each day Luke, Savannah, and I would take our boat and ride up the inland waterway to join the flotilla of resistance. Luke would move the boat in front of the *Amberjack*'s bow, ignoring the warning horn, and slow the whaler by imperceptible degrees. No matter how skillfully Captain Blair maneuvered his boat, he could not pass Luke. Savannah and I had our fishing gear rigged and we trolled for Spanish mackerel as Luke navigated between

The *Amberjack* and the white porpoise. Often, the crew would come out to the bow of the ship to threaten and taunt us.

"Hey, kids, get out of our goddamn way before we get pissed off," one crewman yelled.

"Just fishing, mister," Luke would shoot back.

"What're you fishing for?" The man sneered in exasperation.

"We hear there's a white porpoise in these waters," said Luke, slowing the motor with a delicate movement of his wrist.

"Is that right, smartass? Well, you're not doing such a good job catching it."

"We're doing as good as you are, mister," Luke answered pleasantly.

"If this were Florida, we'd run right over you."

"It ain't Florida, mister. Or haven't you noticed?" Luke said.

"Hicks," the man screamed.

Luke pulled back the throttle and we slowed almost to a crawl. We could hear the big engines of *The Amberjack* throttling down behind us as the bow of the boat loomed over us.

"He called us hicks," Luke said.

"Me, a hick?" Savannah said.

"That hurts my feelings," I said.

Up ahead, the white porpoise turned into Langford Creek, the alabaster shine in her fin disappearing behind a green flange of marsh. There were three boats waiting at the mouth of the creek ready to intercept the *Amberjack* if it managed to get past Luke.

After thirty days of delay and obstruction, the *Amberjack* left the southern boundaries of Colleton waters and returned to its home base of Miami without the white porpoise. Captain Blair gave a final embittered interview to the *Gazette*, listing the many obstacles the citizens of Colleton had erected to disrupt the mission of the *Amberjack*. Such deterrence, he said, could not be allowed to frustrate the integrity of scientific investigation. But on their last day, he and his crew had taken sniper fire from Freeman's Island and he, as captain, had made the irrevocable decision to discontinue the hunt. The shrimp fleet observed the *Amberjack* as it passed the last barrier islands, maneuvered through the breakers, then turned south, angling toward the open seas.

But the *Amberjack* did not go to Miami. It traveled south for forty miles, then turned into the mouth of the Savannah River, putting in to the shrimp dock at Thunderbolt. There it remained for a week to resupply and to let the passions in Colleton County cool, still monitoring the shortwave radio, following the travels of the white porpoise by listening to the Colleton shrimpers give accurate reports of her soundings. After a week the *Amberjack* left the harbor in Savannah in the middle of the night and turned north out beyond the three-mile limit. They cruised confidently out of sight of the shore-bound shrimp trawlers. They were waiting for one signal to come over the radio.

They had been offshore for three days when they heard the words they had been waiting for.

"There's a submerged log I just netted in Zajac Creek, shrimpers. You boys be careful if you're over this way. Out."

"There's no shrimp in Zajac Creek anyhow, Captain," a voice of another shrimp boat captain answered. "You a long way from home, ain't you, Captain Henry? Out."

"I'll catch the shrimp wherever I can find them, Captain. Out," my father answered, watching the Carolina Snow moving a school of fish toward a sandbar.

Zajac Creek was not in Colleton County and the *Amberjack* turned west and came at full throttle toward the creek, the crew preparing the nets as the shoreline of South Carolina filled the eyes of Captain Blair for the last time. A shrimper from Charleston witnessed the capture of the white porpoise at 1130 hours that morning, saw Carolina Snow panic and charge the encircling nets, saw when she entangled herself, and admired the swiftness and skill of the crew as they got their ropes around her, held her head above the water to keep her from drowning, and maneuvered her into one of the motorboats.

By the time the word reached Colleton, the *Amberjack* was well outside the three-mile limit again, set on a southerly course that would take them into Miami in fifty-eight hours. The bells of the church were rung in protest, an articulation of our impotence and fury. It was as if the river had been deconsecrated, purged of all the entitlements of magic.

"Submerged log" was the code phrase my father had worked out with Captain Blair and the crew of the *Amberjack*. He had agreed to fish the boundary waters at the edge of the county until he sighted the white porpoise moving into the territorial waters of Gibbes County to the north. My father was the anonymous Colletonian who had written the Miami Seaquarium informing them of the presence of an albino porpoise in our county. Two weeks after the abduction of Snow and a week after her picture appeared in the *Colleton Gazette* being lowered into her aquarium tank in her new Miami home, my father received a letter of gratitude from Captain Blair and a check for a thousand dollars as a reward for his assistance.

"I'm ashamed of what you did, Henry," my mother said, barely able to control her temper as my father waved the check in front of us.

"I earned a thousand big ones, Lila, and it was the easiest money I ever made in my life. I wish every porpoise I passed was an albino so I could spend all my time eating chocolate and buying banks."

"If anybody in this town had any guts, they'd go to Miami and set that animal free. You'd better not let anyone in town hear that you're responsible, Henry. Folks are still steaming mad about that porpoise."

"How could you sell our porpoise, Daddy?" Savannah asked.

"Look, sweetie, that porpoise is gonna be in fat city, chowing down on gourmet mackerel and jumping through hoops to make kids happy. Snow doesn't have to worry about a shark the rest of her life. She's retired in Miami. You got to look at it in a positive light."

"I think you've committed a sin that not even God can forgive, Daddy," Luke said darkly.

"You do?" My father sneered. "Hey, I never saw 'Property of Colleton' tattooed on her back. I just wrote the Seaquarium that Colleton had a natural phenomenon that could lure in the crowds and they rewarded me for being on my toes."

"They couldn't have found him if you hadn't radioed every time you spotted him in the river," I said.

"I was their liaison officer in the area. Look, it's not that great a shrimping season. This thousand bucks is going to put food on the table and clothes on your back. This could pay for a whole year of college for one of you kids."

"I wouldn't eat a bit of food you bought with that money," Luke said. "And I wouldn't wear a pair of Jockey shorts you bought with it either."

"I've been watching the Snow for more than five years now," my mother said. "You once punished Tom for killing a bald eagle, Henry. There's a lot more eagles in the world than white porpoises."

"I didn't kill the porpoise, Lila. I delivered it to a safe harbor where it will be free of all fear. I look upon myself as the hero of this affair."

"You sold Snow into captivity," my mother said.

"They're going to make her a circus porpoise," Savannah added.

"You betrayed yourself and your sources," Luke said. "If it was a businessman, I could understand. Some low-life creepy Jaycee with shiny hair. But a shrimper, Dad. A shrimper selling Snow for money."

"I sell shrimp for money, Luke," my father shouted.

"Not the same," Luke said. "You don't sell what you can't replace."

"I saw twenty porpoises in the river today."

"And I promise you, Daddy, not one of them was white. None of them was special," Luke said.

"Our family is the reason they captured the Snow," said Savannah. "It's like being the daughter of Judas Iscariot, only I bet I'd have liked Judas a lot better."

"You shouldn't have done what you did, Henry," my mother said. "It'll bring bad luck."

"I couldn't have had any worse luck than I've had," my father answered. "Anyway, it's done. There's nothing anyone can do about it now."

"I can do something about it," Luke said.

Three weeks later, in the languorous starry dark, when my parents were asleep and we could hear the soft chaos of my father's snoring, Luke whispered a plan to us. It should not have surprised us, but years later, Savannah and I would talk and wonder about the exact hour when our older brother turned from a passionate, idealistic boy into a man of action. Both of us were terrified and exhilarated by the boldness of his proposal, but neither of us wanted any part of it. But Luke continued to urge us quietly until we found ourselves imprisoned by the magnetic originality of his gentle eloquence. His decision was already made and he spent half the night enlisting us as recruits in his first real dance on the wild side. Ever since the night we watched him facing the tiger alone in the barn, we had known Luke was brave, but now we were faced with the probability that Luke was also reckless.

Three mornings later, after Luke had made exhaustive preparations, we were on Highway 17, thundering south, with Luke stepping hard on the accelerator, and the radio turned up high. Ray Charles was singing "Hit the Road, Jack" and we were singing it along with him. We were drinking beer iced down in a cooler and had the radio tuned to the Big Ape in Jacksonville as we shot across the Eugene Talmadge Memorial Bridge in Savannah. We slowed up at a toll gate and Luke handed the old man doling out tickets a dollar for a round tripper.

"You gonna do a little shopping in Savannah, kids?" the old man asked. "No, sir," Luke replied, "we're on our way to Florida to steal us a porpoise."

from *The Mermaid Chair*

SUE MONK KIDD (1948–)

Sue Monk Kidd was raised in the rural Georgia town of Sylvester. She credits her father's storytelling abilities, as well as early encounters with Thoreau's *Walden* and Kate Chopin's *The Awakening*, as significant influences in her desire to become a writer. She graduated from Texas Christian University with a degree in nursing in 1970. She worked as a registered nurse for a decade, married, and had two children before moving to South Carolina, where her career as a writer began. Influenced by C. G. Jung and Thomas Merton, she wrote many nonfictional, spiritual, and inspirational pieces for various publications and journals, culminating in her first books *God's Joyful Surprise* (1988) and *When the Heart Waits* (1990). A new interest in feminist theology resulted in the publication of *The Dance of the Dissident Daughter* (1996). She turned to fiction and studied creative writing at Emory and Sewanee, and at Breadloaf and other writer's conferences. After she moved to the Charleston area, *The Secret Life of Bees* was published in 2002 and occupied the *New York Times* best-seller list for two years. It was made into a motion picture in 2008. The following excerpt is from *The Mermaid Chair* (2005), set on a lowcountry barrier island. On the island is a monastery modeled loosely on Mepkin Abbey, near Charleston.

I hesitated as I stepped onto the ferry, one foot on the floating dock and one on the boat, caught momentarily by the rush of light across Bull's Bay. A half-dozen great white egrets flew up from the marsh grass nearby with their low-pitched throat calls. I moved on board and watched them through the plastic windows, the familiar ribbon they made crossing the bay, how they turned in unison toward Egret Island.

The ferry was actually an old pontoon boat named *Tidal Run*. I propped my suitcase beside a dirty-white cooler, beneath two red cardboard tide clocks nailed onto the wall. I sat down on a bench. Hugh had arranged for a driver to take me from the air-port to the ferry landing in Awendaw. I'd made it just in time for the last run of the day. It was four o'clock.

There were only five other passengers, perhaps because it was winter and the tourists had not descended in full force. They usu-ally came in the spring and summer to see the marsh brimming with egrets, how they teemed into the trees along the creeks, sit-ting in heaps of brightness. A few tourists—the hard-core history crowd that trickled over from Charleston—came to take Hepzibah's Grand Gullah Tour, which included a visit to the slave cemetery. Hepzibah was the culture keeper on the island or, as she liked to say, the African griot. She knew a thousand folk-tales and could speak perfect Gullah, a language the slaves had fashioned out of English and their native African tongues.

I studied the passengers, wondering if any were islanders I might recognize. Fewer than a hundred people, besides the monks, still lived on the island, and most had been there since I was a girl. I decided that everyone on the boat was a tourist.

One wore a Hard Rock Cafe T-shirt from Cancún and a red bandanna tied around his head. I imagined he must be freezing. He saw me looking at him and asked, "Have you ever stayed at the Island Dog?"

"No, but it's nice. You'll like it," I said, having to raise my voice over the boat engine.

A two-story, pale blue house with white hurricane shutters, it was the only B&B on the island. I wondered if Bonnie Langston still owned it. She was what Hepzibah called a comya, Gullah for somebody who comes from another place. If your ancestry was on the island, then you were a binya. Comyas were rare on Egret, but they did exist. My sole purpose after the age of ten had been to leave the island. "I want to be a goya," I'd told Hepzibah once, and at first she'd laughed but then stopped and looked at me, down into the heartsick place that made me want to leave. "You can't leave home," she said with her gentlest voice. "You can go other places, all right—you can live on the other side of the world, but you can't ever leave home."

I felt now I'd proved her wrong.

"Be sure to eat at Max's Café," I told the tourist. "Order the shrimp and grits."

Actually, if he wanted to eat, the café was his only choice. Like the B&B, it'd been named for Max, the black Lab whose mind Benne could supposedly read. He met the ferry twice a day without fail and was something of a local celebrity. In warm weather, when the tables spilled out onto the sidewalk, he would trot around with an acquired sense of canine entitlement, giving mere human beings the opportunity to adore him. They would scramble for their cameras as if Lassie had come onto the set. He was famous not only for meeting the ferry with uncanny accuracy but for his immortality. Purportedly he was twenty-seven years old. Bonnie swore to it, but the truth was, the current Max was the fourth in a string of them. I'd been loving various Maxes since I was a kid.

There was a sand beach on the front of the island called Bone Yard, so named because driftwood formed huge, contorted sculptures along it. Hardly anyone ventured there, though, because the currents made it too dangerous for swimming and it was full of sand gnats. You only had to stand there to know that the ocean would take the island back one day.

Most of the tourists came for the guided tour of the monastery, St. Senara's abbey. It was named for a Celtic saint who'd been a mermaid before her conversion, and it had started as a simple outpost—or, as the monks said, "a daughter house"—of an abbey in Cornwall, England. The monks had built it themselves in the thirties on land donated by a Catholic family from Baltimore, who'd used it for a summer fishing camp. In the beginning the place was so unpopular that Egret Islanders—all of them Protestants—called it "St. Sin." Now Protestants were more or less extinct here.

The local guidebooks played up the monastery as a minor Lowcountry attraction, mostly because of the mermaid chair that sat in a side chapel in the church. A "beguiling chair," the books always said, and it was, actually. It was a replica of a very old, somewhat famous chair in the abbey's mother house. The arms had been carved into two winged mermaids painted with jeweled colors—vermilion fish tails, white wings, golden orange hair.

As children Mike and I used to slip into the church when no one was about, lured, of course, by the titillation of the nipples on the mermaids' exposed breasts, four shining inlaid garnet stones. I used to give Mike a hard time about sitting with his hands cupped around them. The memory of this caused me to laugh, and I looked up to see if the other passengers had noticed.

If the tourists were lucky and the chapel wasn't roped off, they could sit in the mermaid chair themselves and say a prayer to Senara, the mermaid saint. For some reason sitting in it was supposed to guarantee you an answer. At least that was the tradition. Mostly the whole thing came off like throwing pennies into a fountain and making wishes, but now and then you would see a real pilgrim, someone in a wheelchair rolling off the ferry, or someone with a small oxygen tank.

The ferry moved slowly through the salt creeks, past tiny marsh islands waving with yellowed spartina grass. The tide had ebbed, laying bare miles of oyster rakes. Everything looked undressed, exposed.

As the creeks widened out into the bay, we picked up speed. V's of brown pelicans flapped alongside us, outpacing the boat. I focused on them and, when they'd vanished, on the lifelines hanging in sloppy coils inside the ferry. I didn't want to think about my mother. On the plane I'd been saturated with dread, but out here that lifted some, maybe because of all the wind and freedom.

I tilted my head back against the window and breathed the marsh's sulfurous smell. The boat captain, in his faded red cap and wraparound metallic sunglasses, began to speak into a microphone. His voice coasted through the little speaker over my head in a memorized oration designed for tourists. He told them where to rent the golf carts that would take them around the island, gave them a little spiel about the egret rookery and fishing charters.

He closed with the same joke I'd heard the last time I'd come: "Folks, just remember there are alligators on the island. I doubt you'll see one this time of year, but if you do, keep in mind that you can't outrun an alligator. Just be sure you can outrun whoever you're with."

Acknowledgments

Special thanks to the following individuals and institutions for their assistance in making this edition of *Literary Charleston* possible:

Patrick Allen, Amy Boucher, the Charleston County Public Library, the Charleston Library Society, Gene Furchgott, Harlan Greene, Susan Hoffius, Jim Hutchisson, Sandy Kidd, Nick Lindsay, Rhonda McFadden, Sarah Nawrocki, Tom Payton, Lynne Ravenel, Harriet and Jim Rigney, Stephanie Robinson, Louis D. Rubin, Jr., Jeff Schwaner, Bill Starr, Bill Thompson, Jane Tyler, Jodie Underwood, the Waring Historical Library at the Medical University of South Carolina, George W. Williams, W. C. Worthington Jr., and Pete Wyrick.

I would especially like to recognize Steve Hoffius, whose contributions to this project in so many ways merit the title of coeditor; my family for their continuing patience and generosity; and of course, the writers themselves.

Any errors of omission or commission are the editor's alone.

Shelby Foote, excerpt from *The Civil War: A Narrative*. Copyright © 1963 by Shelby Foote. Used by permission of Random House, Inc.

William Price Fox, "Coley Moke" from *Southern Fried Plus Six*. Reprinted by permission of Sandlapper Publishing Inc.

George Gershwin, letter to his mother (1934). Copyright © 1934 by the George Gershwin Family Trust. Used by permission.

Albert Goldman, "Charleston! Charleston!" from *Esquire* (1977). Copyright © 1977. Reprinted with the permission of Deborah Karl.

Harlan Greene, excerpt from *Why We Never Danced the Charleston*. Copyright © 1984 by Harlan Greene. Reprinted with the permission of Raines & Raines.

DuBose Heyward, excerpt from *Porgy*. Copyright © 1985. Reprinted by permission of the DuBose and Dorothy Heyward Memorial Fund.

Josephine Humphreys, excerpt from *Rich in Love*. Copyright © 1987 by Josephine Humphreys. Used by permission of Viking, a division of Penguin Group (USA) Inc.

Sue Monk Kidd, excerpt from *The Mermaid Chair*. Copyright © 2005 by Sue Monk Kidd. Used by permission of Viking, a division of Penguin Group (USA) Inc.

August Kleinzahler, "Longitude Lane." Used by permission of the author.

Ludwig Lewisohn, excerpt from *The Case of Mr. Crump*. Copyright © 1965 by Farrar, Straus & Giroux, LLC. Reprinted by permission.

Nick Lindsay, excerpts from *An Oral History of Edisto Island: Sam Gadsden Tells the Story* and *An Oral History of Edisto Island: The Life and Times of Bubberson Brown*. Reprinted by permission of Nick Lindsay.

Robert W. Marks (John Colleton), excerpt from *The Trembling of a Leaf*. Copyright © 1971 by John Colleton. Reprinted with the permission of Simon & Schuster, Inc.

Walker Percy, excerpt from *The Last Gentleman*. Copyright © 1966 by Walker Percy. Reprinted by permission of Farrar, Straus & Giroux, LLC.

Padgett Powell, excerpt from *Edisto*. Copyright © 1983, 1984 by Padgett Powell. Reprinted by permission of Farrar, Straus & Giroux, LLC.

Louis D. Rubin, Jr., "Finisterre." Reprinted from the *Southern Review* by permission of the author.

Wendy Salinger, "Charleston, South Carolina, 7 P.M." from *Folly River*. Copyright © 1980 by Wendy Salinger. Used by permission of Viking Penguin, a division of Penguin Group (USA) Inc.

Herbert Ravenel Sass, "Carolina Marshes." Reproduced courtesy of *Country Life Magazine*, London.

Andy Warhol, "Love (Prime)" from *The Philosophy of Andy Warhol*. Copyright © 1975 by Andy Warhol. Reprinted by permission of Houghton Mifflin Harcourt Publishing Company.

ALSO AVAILABLE

Literary Nashville
edited by Patrick Allen

Literary Savannah
edited by Patrick Allen

Literary Washington, D.C.
edited by Patrick Allen